KU-518-925

MILLER'S

buying affordable
antiques

Fellows & Sons
AUCTIONEERS & VALUERS

We hold over 60 specialist auctions per year of antique and modern jewellery, furniture, porcelain, clocks, silver, watches, paintings, toys and collectors items.

Illustrated online catalogues available at: www.fellows.co.uk

Live bidding for selected auctions available through: www.ebayliveauctions.com

Tel: 0121 212 2131
Fax: 0121 212 1249

Email: info@fellows.co.uk

Fellows & Sons,
Augusta House,
19 Augusta Street,
Hockley, Birmingham B18 6JA

AUCTIONEERS & VALUERS OF ANTIQUE & LATER JEWELLERY,
SILVER, WATCHES & CLOCKS, FURNITURE & PICTURES

MILLER'S

buying affordable
antiques

Created and designed by
Miller's Publications
The Cellars, High Street
Tenterden, Kent TN30 6BN
Telephone: 01580 766411
Fax: 01580 766100

Managing Editor: Valerie Lewis
Production Co-ordinator: Kari Reeves
Editorial Co-ordinator: Deborah Wanstall
Editorial Assistants: Joanna Hill, Maureen Horner
Designer: Philip Hannath
Advertisement Designer: Simon Cook
Jacket Design: Victoria Bevan
Advertising Executive: Emma Gillingham
Advertising Co-ordinator & Administrator: Melinda Williams
Production Assistants: Gillian Charles, Helen Clarkson, Léonie Sidgwick, Ethne Tragett
Production Controller: Sarah Rogers
Additional Photography: Robin Saker
Indexer: Hilary Bird
US Advertising Representative: Katharine Buckley,
Buckley Pell Associates, Locust Grove Farm, 1851 Salt Point,
Salt Point, New York, NY 12578–2328
Tel: 845 266 4980 Fax: 845 266 4988 E-mail: buckley@moveworld.com

First published in Great Britain in 2004
by Miller's, a division of Mitchell Beazley,
imprints of Octopus Publishing Group Ltd,
2–4 Heron Quays, London E14 4JP

Reprinted in 2005 by Bounty Books,
a division of Octopus Publishing Group Ltd,
2–4 Heron Quays, London E14 4JP

© 2004 Octopus Publishing Group Ltd

A CIP catalogue record for this book is
available from the British Library

ISBN 0 7537 1177 X

ISBN13 9780753711774

All rights reserved. No part of this work may be
produced or utilized in any form or by any means, electronic
or mechanical, including photocopying, recording or by
any information storage and retrieval system, without the prior
written permission of the Publishers

While every care has been exercised in the
compilation of this guide, neither the authors
nor publishers accept any liability for any financial
or other loss incurred by reliance placed on the
information contained in
Miller's Buying Affordable Antiques Price Guide

Illustrations: 1.13, Whitstable, Kent
Printed and bound in China

Front Cover Illustrations:

Victorian nursing chair, with button back. **£170–190** / €240–260 / $280–310 SWO
Royal Worcester figural group, 'The Dancers', by Doris Lindner, 1933.
£700–900 / €970–1,250 / $1,150–1,450
Gilt- and pebble-decorated glass beaker, Bohemian, 19thC, 4½in (11.5cm) high.
£260–290 / €360–400 / $430–470 SWO

Miller's is a registered trademark of
Octopus Publishing Group Ltd

Contents

MILLER'S

Contributors

FURNITURE:

Lawrence Bright works for Sotheby's Furniture Department. He has a particular interest in good English 18th-century furniture and also Arts & Crafts furniture.

CERAMICS:

John Axford is a director of Woolley & Wallis Salisbury Salerooms. For ten years he had been head of their Ceramics, Glass and Oriental Department, which recently won the BACA award for best specialist department within a UK auction house. He regularly lectures, teaches and writes about ceramics and has been a BBC *Antiques Roadshow* expert for the past five years.

SILVER & PLATE:

Daniel Bexfield has specialized in Silver for 22 years. He regularly contributes to BBC television and radio programmes and a variety of publications on the subject, including *Miller's Silver & Plate Buyer's Guide*. He carries an extensive range of stock at his premises in Burlington Arcade, London, W1.

GLASS:

Andy McConnell was a dealer in antique glass for 25 years, becoming a full-time writer/historian on the subject six years ago. Readers wishing to contact him may do so through his website www.decanterman.com

PAPERWEIGHTS:

Anne Metcalfe deals solely in glass paperweights from Sweetbriar Gallery, Helsby, Cheshire. She is the author of *Miller's Paperweights of the 19th & 20th Centuries: A Collector's Guide*.

CLOCKS, WATCHES & BAROMETERS:

Jonathan Hills is a deputy director of Sotheby's and a senior specialist in the clock department at Sotheby's Olympia. He is the sixth generation of his family to be involved with clocks: his great, great, great, grandfather, Benjamin Hills, established a clock making business in Suffolk in the early 19th century. He has been an auctioneer for over 20 years.

ANTIQUITIES:

Chantelle Waddingham has worked at Bonhams as a specialist in the Antiquities department for over four years. She trained in general archaeology at Southampton University before completing an MA in Archaeological Heritage Management and Museum Studies at Cambridge University. While her work covers a variety of eras, her personal interest lies in the ancient cultures of Egypt and the Near East.

ARCHITECTURAL:

Rupert van der Werff is head of the Garden Statuary and Architectural section of Sotheby's Sussex, Summers Place, Billingshurst, West Sussex.

ARMS & ARMOUR:

John Spooner's interest in antique Arms and Armour was initially fired by his great grandfather's shotgun dating to the mid-19th century. He started collecting over 40 years ago and turned his hobby into a business in 1980 but still regards it as a hobby. He lectures and has broadcast on the subject and appeared on British television in *Going for a Song*.

BOXES:

Alan and Kathy Stacey are specialist dealers of the finest quality tea caddies and boxes. Their particular area of interest is in the tortoiseshell and ivory field. Together they have 35 years experience in the antiques trade. They are members of both LAPADA and BAFRA.

DOLLS, TEDDY BEARS & TOYS:

Joy and Robert Luke are owners of Joy Luke Auctioneers & Appraisers in Bloomington, Illinois, USA. Between them they have 62 years experience in the antiques business and hold many specialized sales throughout the year, including Dolls and Toys, Jewellery and Native American Artefacts.

KITCHENWARE:

Janie Smithson married into a farming family and discovered an interest in country kitchenware. Along with her husband Skip, she has been dealing in antique kitchenware since 1988, and her particular enthusiasm is for early Victorian and dairy items. They show at the NEC, Alexandra Palace and the Battersea Decorative Fairs.

LIGHTING & TEXTILES:

Joanna Proops has been trading in period textiles and lighting for the last 30 years from her shop, Antique Textiles, in Bath. In 2002 she won the BACA Specialist Dealer award for costume and textiles.

METALWARE & SCULPTURE:

James Jackson is the president and Chief Executive Officer of Jackson's International Auctioneers & Appraisers, which was founded in 1969, and holds sales of fine art and antiques throughout the year. He is also a recognized authority on Russian Icons and ecclesiastical works. The auction house is located in Iowa, in the heartland of America, and employs 24 specialists.

RUGS & CARPETS:

Desmond North has been collecting and selling Oriental rugs for 30 years. He and his wife, Amanda, sell their rugs from home and hold sale exhibitions every May and October.

SCIENTIFIC INSTRUMENTS:

Charles Tomlinson has been a specialist dealer in antique scientific instruments for the last 30 years. He has a particular interest in antique slide rules and mechanical calculators.

WOODEN ANTIQUES:

Daniel Bray MRCIS is a senior auctioneer at Bracketts, Tunbridge Wells, Kent. He has been an auctioneer for six years.

Dates	British Monarch	British Period	French Period
1558–1603	Elizabeth I	Elizabethan	Renaissance
1603–1625	James I	Jacobean	
1625–1649	Charles I	Carolean	Louis XIII (1610–1643)
1649–1660	Commonwealth	Cromwellian	Louis XIV (1643–1715)
1660–1685	Charles II	Restoration	
1685–1689	James II	Restoration	
1689–1694	William & Mary	William & Mary	
1694–1702	William III	William III	
1702–1714	Anne	Queen Anne	
1714–1727	George I	Early Georgian	Régence (1715–1723)
1727–1760	George II	Early Georgian	Louis XV (1723–1774)
1760–1811	George III	Late Georgian	Louis XVI (1774–1793) Directoire (1793–1799) Empire (1799–1815)
1812–1820	George III	Regency	Restauration Charles X (1815–1830)
1820–1830	George IV	Regency	
1830–1837	William IV	William IV	Louis Philippe (1830–1848)
1837–1901	Victoria	Victorian	2nd Empire Napoleon III (1848–1870) 3rd Republic (1871–1940)
1901–1910	Edward VII	Edwardian	

German Period	U.S. Period	Style	Woods
Renaissance	Early Colonial	Gothic	Oak Period (to c1670)
		Baroque (c1620–1700)	Walnut period (c1670–1735)
Renaissance/ Baroque (c1650–1700)			
	William & Mary		
	Dutch Colonial	Rococo (c1695–1760)	
Baroque (c1700–1730)	Queen Anne		Early mahogany period (c1735–1770)
Rococo (c1730–1760)	Chippendale (from 1750)		
Neo–classicism (c1760–1800)	Early Federal (1790–1810)	Neo–classical (c1755–1805)	Late mahogany period (c1770–1810)
Empire (c1800–1815)	American Directoire (1798–1804)	Empire (c1799–1815)	
	American Empire (1804–1815)		
Biedermeier (c1815–1848)	Late Federal (1810–1830)	Regency (c1812–1830)	
Revivale (c1830–1880)	Victorian	Eclectic (c1830–1880)	
Jugendstil (c1880–1920)		Arts & Crafts (c1880–1900)	
	Art Nouveau (c1900–1920)	Art Nouveau (c1900–1920)	

How to use this book

It is our aim to make this book easy to use. In order to find a particular item, consult the contents list on page 5 to find the main heading – for example, Silver & Plate. Having located your area of interest, you will find that sections have been sub-divided alphabetically. If you are looking for a particular factory, designer or craftsman, consult the index which starts on page 291.

Miller's compares...

A. Silver cake basket, with swing handle, pierced sides and ball feet, maker's mark 'RFM', Sheffield 1907, 11½in (29cm) wide, 13oz.
£140–155 / €195–220
$230–250 WW ⚲

B. Silver cake basket, by Elkington & Co, with handle, pierced and embossed sides and floral scroll border, Birmingham 1903, 13in (33cm) wide, 23oz.
£300–330 / €420–460
$490–540 WW ⚲

Item B is by Elkington & Co, who are renowned for the high quality of their products. It is made of thicker gauge silver than Item A and also has a thick applied rim, giving it more stability.

Find out more in

Miller's Silver & Plate Buyer's Guide, Miller's Publications, 2002

Silver sugar bowl, with a gilt interior, the part-lobed body with two applied rococo cartouches, on four scrolling paw feet, maker's mark part rubbed, London 1797, 4¼in (11cm) diam, 8oz.
£85–100 / €120–140
$140–165 SWO ⚲

What is casting?

Cast silver items are made by pouring molten silver into a cast or mould of the desired shape. When the silver has solidified the mould is broken away, leaving the casting. Complete items such as tea-spoons and candle-sticks, or parts such as spouts, handles, feet etc may be made this way.

Silver sucrier, with embossed and chased scrollwork, maker's mark 'D.S.', Sheffield 1862, 5½in (14cm) wide.
£150–165 / €210–230
$250–270 SWO ⚲

Victorian silver sugar bowl, by George Fox, with gilt interior, initialled, London 1872, 4¼in (11cm) diam, 4.75oz. The design of this bowl was influenced by Indian silversmiths.
£170–185 / €235–260
$280–300 WW ⚲

The look without the price

It was very fashionable for the Victorians to send plain pieces to the silversmith to be decorated. This does affect the price considerably.

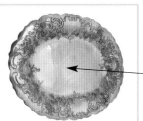

Four embossed silver-gilt dishes, reshaped and later decorated, hallmarked London 1822, 13½in (34.5cm) wide, 69oz.
£480–530 / €670–740
$780–870 WW ⚲

Find out more in directs the reader towards additional sources of information.

Miller's compares explains why two or three items which look similar have realized very different prices.

Price guide these are based on actual prices realized shown in £sterling with a €Euro and US$ conversion. Remember that Miller's is a price guide not a price list and prices are affected by many variables such as location, condition, desirability, whether it is a dealer ⊞ or auction ⚲ price (see the source code below) and so on. Don't forget that if you are selling it is quite likely you will be offered less than the price range. Price ranges for items sold at auction tend to include the buyer's premium and VAT if applicable. The exchange rate used in this edition is 1.63 for $ and 1.39 for €.

The look without the price highlights later items produced 'in the style of' earlier counter-parts. It illustrates how you don't have to spend a fortune to have the original look.

Source code refers to the Key to Illustrations on page 286 that lists the details of where the item was photo-graphed. The ⚲ icon indicates the item was sold at auction. The ⊞ icon indicates the item originated from a dealer.

Caption provides a brief description of the item. It explains, where possible, why an item is valued at a particular price.

Information box covers relevant collecting information on factories, makers, fakes and alterations, period styles and designers.

Introduction

Back in the mists of time I stumbled into an antiques world that presented itself as both mysterious and insular, populated by secretive dealers and decidedly dodgy runners. These were traders renowned for keeping their cards close to their chests and who communicated in their own peculiar jargon. Those of us new to the 'antiques game' began to wonder if those involved had endured some form of ritual initiation before being admitted into this secretive society.

Fast forward 30 years and the present day infatuation with all things antique and collectable would have you believe that all has now been revealed to the world at large. Despite far more people being aware, one misconception remains – that antique equals expensive.

I never fail to find it a sobering experience when visiting a department store to read the price tags on brand new furniture and furnishings. Now, I'm not suggesting for one moment that what's on offer might be considered vastly overpriced. It does, however, beg the question why on earth buy new when the antique might be had for a little more or, in many instances, even less money.

Admittedly, top-flight antique furniture, silver, jewellery and ceramics always command big prices and moreover tend to attract the attention of television programmes and related magazines. Consequently, viewer and reader might be forgiven for reaching the conclusion that antique does indeed equal expensive. Enter *Miller's Buying Affordable Antiques Price Guide*. Those nice people at Miller's have obviously made it their mission to boldly go out to the masses in an attempt to redress this widely held misconception. The good news is that, after browsing through almost 300 pages crammed with 1,500

colour illustrations, it soon becomes apparent that most of the objects featured are not only affordable but also represent excellent value for money. On top of all that, when purchased over a period of years the *Guide* should prove an interesting barometer reflecting the ever-changing trends and price structures.

At the end of the day, it really does not matter what you collect as long as the pursuit gives you pleasure and the price you pay doesn't break the bank. *Miller's Buying Affordable Antiques Price Guide* provides ample evidence that collecting antiques is open to those with both shallow and slightly deeper pockets.

Eric Knowles

Types of Wood

Bird's-eye maple ▶

Bird's-eye maple, or American sugar maple, describes the very attractive figuring in maple. It was popular for veneers during the Regency period, and was also used in Victorian and Edwardian bedroom suites. The wood of the maple is whitish, and responds well to polishing. Bird's-eye maple is also popular today for picture frames.

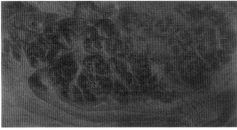

◀ Burr walnut

Burr walnut is the term used for walnut with knotty whorls in the grain where injuries occurred on the trunk or roots of the tree. It was often used in decorative veneers. Walnut is a close-grained hardwood, the colour varying between light golden brown to dark grey-brown in colour with dark streaks, often with a rich grain pattern.

Calamander ▶

Calamander is a member of the **ebony** family and derives from Ceylon. Popular in the Regency period, it is light brown in colour, striped and mottled with black, and was used for veneers and banding. Calamander was also used in the manufacture of small decorative boxes. Ebony is close-grained, black in colour, and is resistant to decay.

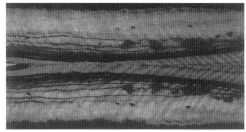

◀ Elm

The English variety of elm is hard and durable, but liable to warp, and prone to woodworm. Chairs were made from elm from the Georgian period, and the seats of Windsor chairs were elm from the 18th century. The wych elm has a particularly attractive grain and polishes well. **Burr elm** was used for veneers and cabinet-work in the early 18th century.

Kingwood ▶

Kingwood is related to rosewood, which was first imported to Britain from Brazil in the late 17th century. It is a rich brown with purplish tones, giving it an alternative name of violet wood. Also known as princewood, it was used as a veneer or for parquetry decoration, particularly in France. From c1770 it was used for crossbanding and borders.

Oak ▶

Oak is a slow-growing tree, taking between 150 and 200 years to reach maturity. The wood is hard and pale in colour, but darkens to a rich brown with age and polishing. Furniture made from oak is usually heavy and solid, and simple in design. From the middle of the 17th century oak was used mainly for the carcases of furniture and drawer linings, but became popular again in the late 19th century with the Arts and Crafts movement.

Satinwood ▶

Satinwood was used widely for veneers and inlaid decoration, the pale colour making it particularly suitable for painting. The grain varies from plain to rich figuring, the latter having a more transparent grain under polish or varnish. Cabinet-makers of the 19th century preferred the West Indian variety, which is darker than the East Indian variety, and was used as a veneer in fine furniture from c1765. It was rarely used in the solid, and not for chairs until c1800. The Eastern type, imported in the late 18th century, was pale yellow and used mainly for crossbanding.

◀ Mahogany

Mahogany is a close grained hardwood, native to northern and central South America and the West Indies. It varies in colour from dark brown to red, and sometimes has a spotted effect. Furniture made from mahogany became very popular with cabinet-makers in Britain from the mid-18th century, followed by France and the rest of Europe. African mahogany, which is lighter in weight, was used from the 1800s onwards.

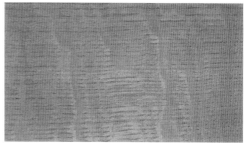

◀ Rosewood

Rosewood is a very dark brown hardwood, with an almost black wavy grain. The name comes from the scent released when the wood is cut. Rosewood was used for inlaid decoration in the 17th century, and for veneer, but was not used for making solid furniture until the early 19th century. It was also used for decorative banding and small panels from the late 18th century.

◀ Sycamore

Sycamore is a European wood related to the North American maple, and is as strong as oak. It is hard, milky-white, with a fine even grain with natural lustre. In medieval times furniture was made in solid sycamore, and from the late 17th century it was used in floral marquetry on walnut furniture. When quarter-sawn the figuring is known as **fiddleback**, as it was often used in the manufacture of violins. Sycamore treated with iron oxide or stained green or grey was known as **harewood.**

Furniture

Now in its second year, this publication provides those who are interested in antiques with a guide to finding a range of pieces at affordable prices. It may come as a surprise to anyone who hitherto regarded antiques as rather exclusive items exactly how much good quality is currently available on the market and at such a small cost. This is perhaps most applicable in the field of furniture, where a gentle downslide in the market over the last ten years has meant that prices have remained relatively static. However, this has not been the case in the market as a whole. What is happening now is a polarization between the top end, where pieces continue to reach record levels and the lower end, where the market is struggling. The reason for this is that people's tastes are changing.

A few years ago Victorian brown furniture and the more ornate Louis XV and XVI style of the 19th century were very fashionable. Nowadays, buyers are guided by a more minimalist attitude towards interior design and are therefore more selective. Such a buyer may, for example, have a comfortable modern sofa suite, hence certain pieces like the prie-dieu chair or the Victorian easy chair become surplus to requirements. Conversely, the plain panel-seated hall chair remains a popular choice, providing little comfort but whose simple clean lines are suited to the modern home.

Practical requirements of the modern age have also been a contributing factor towards the decline of certain types of furniture. The Georgian bureau or the Victorian davenport that were once the mainstay of auctions have fallen out of favour simply because neither can accommodate a computer. A good George III mahogany bureau can now be bought for under £1,000 / €1,400 / $1,650 and a Victorian davenport for much less, with only good Regency examples stubbornly holding on to their value. Conversely, the Victorian library table with its large flat surface has remained commercial for the very reason that a computer can be comfortably used on it.

So what is out and what is in? What is a good investment or what might prove to be a bad choice? The first question is easy to answer. As well as bureaux and davenports, Pembroke tables and drop-leaf cente tables are struggling at the moment. The once ubiquitous Victorian balloon-back chair has also lost its appeal and even sets of eight are not as sought-after. Instead, the sturdier late Georgian chair has become the preferred choice. An indicator of this has been the growth in demand for good-quality late 19th-century copies of the Georgian style, which can be bought at a fraction of the price of an original set.

From an investment point of view, like stocks and shares there is always a risk and the golden rule is to only buy something because you like it. In the current market the conditions are perfect for the buyer and there is now a large quantity of pieces priced at under £1,000 / €1,400 / $1,650. For this reason, do not buy the first piece you see – you can afford to be a bit selective. For instance, there are some very good examples of Regency mahogany bowfronted chests, or late Georgian examples for under £1,000 / €1,400 / $1,650. Make sure the price reflects the quality, condition and colour of the piece – an example at £900 / €1,250 / $1,450 should be better than one at £400 / €560 / $650. Taking time to go round the auction rooms, shops and markets will enable you to make more of an informed choice. Finally, the following section will show you that it is possible to buy into a 'look' without breaking the bank.

Lawrence Bright

Beds & Cradles

◀ **A brass bed,** 19thC, 56in (142cm) wide. This is missing the side rails to hold the base, hence the low price.
£150–180
€210–250
$240–290 DuM ➤

A Victorian mahogany cradle, c1860, 36in (91.5cm) long.
£150–200 / €210–280
$240–330 BWL ➤

Early Victorian mahogany-framed day bed, on square section tapering legs with brass caps and ceramic casters, 59¾in (152cm) wide. The high back on this day bed and the need for complete reupholstery have resulted in a low price at auction. However, the frame is good quality and had this piece been a chaise longue with a low back it might have fetched £600–900 / €840–1,250 / $980–1,450.
£340–380 / €470–530
$560–620 CGC ➤

Cast-iron and brass bedstead, with a blue verdigris finish, c1895, 30in (76cm) wide.
£380–430 / €530–600
$620–700 SeH ▦

Victorian iron and brass bedstead, 61½in (156cm) wide. This attractive bed frame is good value in view of its decorative qualities and turned brass elements.
£400–440 / €560–610
$650–720 B(Kn) ➤

Find out more in

Miller's Antiques Price Guide,
Miller's Publications, 2004

Cast-iron bedstead, c1875, 54in (137cm) wide.
£630–700 / €880–980
$1,050–1,150 SeH ▦

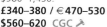

◀ **Cast-iron and brass bedstead,** the head and foot panels inset with a decorative bird plaque, c1890, 36in (91.5cm) wide.
£590–650 / €820–910
$960–1,050 SeH ▦

Cast-iron bedstead, c1885, 60in (152.5cm) wide.
£720–800 / €1,000–1,100
$1,200–1,300 SeH ▦

Benches

A pine settle, Irish, c1870, 72in (183cm) wide.
£320–400 / €450–560
$520–650 Byl ⊞

A late Victorian oak monk's bench,
43¼in (110cm) wide.
£420–525 / €580–730
$690–860 B(Ba) ⚒

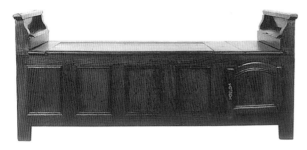

◄ **Stained oak and elm seat,** the hinged top between two armrests and candle boxes, the panelled front with an arched moulded door to the right, on square feet, 18thC, 71in (180.5cm) wide.
£550–600 / €770–840
$900–980 WL ⚒

Miller's compares...

A. George III oak settle, with five-panel back, turned arm supports and turned front legs, 72in (183cm) wide.
£300–330 / €420–460
$490–540 SWO ⚒

B. George III oak settle, with four-panel back, turned arm supports and cabriole front legs, 72½in (184cm) wide.
£620–680 / €860–950
$1,000–1,100 L ⚒

The colour of Item A is not as attractive as the deep rich tone of Item B. The elegant cabriole front legs on Item B date from c1770 and contribute to its higher value, whereas the legs on Item A may be as late as 1825.

Bookcases

Pine hanging bookcase, 1900, 41in (104cm) wide.
This was formerly the top half of a dresser.
£110–120 / € 155–165
$180–195 DFA ⊞

Bamboo bookcase, c1890, 28½in (72.5cm) wide.
£160–180 / € 220–250
$260–300 AL ⊞

Pine bookcase, c1890,
36in (91.5cm) wide.
£275–300 / € 385–420
$450–490 AL ⊞

Pine bookcase,
c1880, 43in
(109cm) wide.
£230–250
€ 320–350
$380–410 Byl ⊞

**Victorian mahogany book-
case,** damaged, 49¼in (125cm)
wide. In better condition and
with its missing corbel intact
this piece might be worth
£400 / € 560 / $650.
£280–310 / € 390–430
$460–510 B(Ba) ✐

**Art Nouveau oak
bookcase,** c1900,
24in (61cm) wide.
£310–340
€ 430–470
$510–560 NAW ⊞

ANN LINGARD

ROPE WALK ANTIQUES, RYE, SUSSEX
TEL: 01797 223486 FAX: 01797 224700
Email: ann-lingard@ropewalkantiques.freeserve.co.uk

**LARGE SELECTION OF
HAND FINISHED ENGLISH ANTIQUE
PINE FURNITURE KITCHEN SHOP
and
COMPLEMENTARY ANTIQUES**

Open Monday–Friday 9.00am–5.30pm
Saturday by chance

 LAPADA MEMBER

SHIPPERS WELCOME

 LAPADA MEMBER

▶ **Edwardian bamboo and japanned revolving bookcase,** 18¾in (47.5cm) wide. Late Victorian and Edwardian bamboo furniture was very much in demand a few years ago and if in good condition is still appreciated for its decorative qualities. Revolving bookcases of this type are uncommon.
£460–500
€640–700
$750–820 SWO ⚒

Mahogany revolving bookcase, c1900, 30in (76cm) high.
£340–380 / €470–530
$560–620 GBr ⊞

Edwardian satinwood and mahogany bookcase, with pierced brass three-quarter gallery and adjustable shelves flanked by banded panels, on square tapering legs with brackets, 35¾in (91cm) wide. Satinwood is desirable and the elegant construction of this piece, with the added feature of a brass gallery, make this a good buy.
£500–550 / €700–770
$820–900 B&L ⚒

Late George III mahogany bookcase, with two astragal-glazed doors, 45in (114.5cm) wide. This piece is the upper section to a bookcase and with a suitable base it might be worth at least £1,000 / €1,400 / $1,650.
£620–680 / €860–950
$1,000–1,100 B(Ch) ⚒

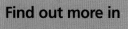

Edwardian mahogany bookcase, with astragal-glazed doors, on bracket feet, 37½in (95.5cm) wide. The bookcase is a popular piece of furniture and rarely remains unsold at auction.
£680–750 / €950–1,050
$1,100–1,200 SWO ⚒

◀ **Victorian mahogany bookcase,** with a moulded cornice above five adjustable shelves, on a plinth base, 46in (117cm) wide. This is a good size bookcase of solid construction.
£780–860 / €1,100–1,200
$1,250–1,400 SWO ⚒

Find out more in

Miller's Late Georgian to Edwardian Furniture Buyer's Guide, Miller's Publications, 2003

Canterburies

Mid-Victorian mahogany canterbury, on turned legs with brass casters, 17in (43cm) wide.
£280–310 / €390–430 $460–510 B(W) ⚖

Mahogany canterbury, on turned legs, 19thC, 20in (51cm) wide. The price of this piece is kept down by the tall legs, faded colour and possible repaired break to one of the uprights.
£500–550 / €700–770 $820–900 SWO ⚖

Victorian figured-walnut canterbury, with four turned finials, above spindle-turned supports, and a single frieze drawer above ring-turned legs with china casters, 22in (56cm) wide.
£550–610 / €770–850 $900–1,000 BR ⚖

The look without the price

This is a good quality reproduction canterbury with two drawers rather than the usual one, and is faithful to the original style. An equivalent George III example would be worth well over £1,000 / €1,400 / $1,650 at auction.

George III-style beaded mahogany canterbury, with two drawers, on four brass casters, 19in (48.5cm) wide.
£330–360 / €460–500 $540–590 NOA ⚖

Late George III mahogany canterbury, the dipped top with acorn finials, with a single drawer above turned legs with casters, 19in (48.5cm) wide. Some of the uprights are different in colour suggesting that they may be replacements.
£550–610 / €770–850 $900–1,000 G(L) ⚖

▶ **Early Victorian rosewood canterbury,** on turned legs with brass casters, 22in (56cm) wide. The brass paterae at the ends of the top-rail indicate a well-made piece and the style of the carving is reminiscent of designs by W. Smee & Sons of the 1850s, making this example good value.
£700–770 / €980–1,050 $1,150–1,250 WW ⚖

Regency rosewood canterbury, with X-form divisions, a single drawer above reel-turned legs with brass casters, some damage and losses, 19¾in (50cm) wide.
£620–680 / €860–950 $1,000–1,100 Bea(E) ⚖

Chairs

Mahogany chair, with scrolled arms and drop-in seat, on carved tapering legs, c1840. The fact that this is a single chair reflects the lower price.
£50–55 / €70–75
$80–90 BWL 🔨

George III mahogany chair, the shaped back-rail carved with pendant swags and paterae, three channelled uprights and stuff-over seat.
£30–35 / €42–48
$50–60 G(L) 🔨

Pair of Victorian armchairs. These chairs represent good value as they could have fetched £200 / €280 / $330 at auction.
£100–110 / €140–155
$165–180 B(W) 🔨

Mahogany open armchair, with a turned horizontal splat, moulded arms and turned front legs, early 19thC. If this chair had reeded rather than plain turned legs it would be worth around £250 / €350 / $410.
£150–165 / €210–230
$245–270 WW 🔨

George II provincial red walnut and beech chair, with double arched back and solid vase splat, the drop-in seat upholstered in cut velvet, on cabriole legs with pad feet.
£130–145 / €180–200
$210–235 G(L) 🔨

George I yew and other wood side chair, with later caned seat.
£140–155 / €195–215
$230–250 L 🔨

▶ **Victorian mahogany hall chair.** Hall chairs increase in value if they are pairs or larger sets. A pair of chairs such as this would be worth £600–800 / €840–1,100 / $980–1,300.
£160–175 / €220–245
$260–285 B(Ba) 🔨

Upholstery

Reupholstery is common and does not reduce the value, as original fabric rarely survives in good condition. However, old upholstery such as needlework is desirable.

▶ **Oak-framed open armchair,** reupholstered in leather, 19thC. Had the leather been in poor condition, this chair would have sold for less than £100 / €140 / $165.
£170–185 / €235–260 $280–300 SWO ⚒

William IV rosewood prie-dieu, with a gros point back and seat.
£190–210 / €265–290 $310–350 B(Ch) ⚒

What is a Prie-dieu?

A prie-dieu is a chair with a low seat and a tall back designed for prayer, usually dating from the 19th century.

Pair of George III elm elbow chairs, with arched top-rails, on pierced and waisted splats, with drop-in seats, with a pair of similar chairs. In addition to being a matched set, four chairs do not sell well as most people require six for dining rooms. These factors have had an effect on their value.
£200–220 / €280–310 $330–370 AH ⚒

◀ **Ebonized side chair,** the cane panelled back with a carved cresting rail and pierced with four eagle heads, the turned legs joined by wavy stretchers, on braganza feet, late 17thC.
£200–220 / €280–310 $330–370 B ⚒

Set of three George III mahogany dining chairs. This is a good example of how dining chairs become devalued when split. If they had sold as a set of six, each chair would be worth the price of this set of three.
£200–220 / €280–310 $330–370 L ⚒

Pair of beech-framed *fauteuils*, one arm loose, French, late 19thC. Chairs in both Louis XV, such as this, and Louis XVI styles were made in abundance in the late 19thC and can vary greatly in quality. A fall in standards came with the mass production of the early 20thC, so the carving and quality of the timber should be closely examined. These chairs are particularly affordable since they are made from beech rather than walnut.
£200–220 / €280–310
$330–370 B(Kn) ✯

Pair of mahogany dining armchairs, the backs with inset top-rails and twin reeded horizontal bars joined by bobbin-turned spindles, the open reeded arms on vase-turned uprights, with drop-in seats and turned legs, early 19thC.
£210–230 / €290–320
$350–380 PF ✯

Victorian walnut side chair, with a floral woolwork back and seat. This is a charming Victorian chair and a good buy as the fabric looks original and is in good condition.
£220–240 / €310–330
$370–390 DN ✯

South Yorkshire back stool, with two arched splats carved with foliage and acorn pendants, the scrolled finials on square-section uprights, with a panel seat and turned block legs, late 17thC and later.
£240–270 / €330–380
$390–440 AH ✯

Louis XV-style polychrome *fauteuil*, the padded back surmounted by a floral crest, the scrolling arms and cabriole legs with conforming carving, on acanthus feet, late 19thC. This would have been made as part of a salon suite with a matching chair, sofa and two or more side chairs. The whole set would make at least £2,000–3,000 / €2,800–4,200 / $3,300–4,900 at auction.
£240–270 / €330–380
$390–440 NOA ✯

Dining habits

By the second half of the 18th century the dining room had become the focal point of any great house. There the main meal of the day was taken and the long D-end dining tables which permanently graced the rooms cried out for equally 'long' sets of chairs to accommodate the diners.

Until then meals had usually been quite intimate affairs eaten in private apartments off folding tables while seated on parlour or side chairs. While breakfast and supper might still be taken in that way, by 1800 the importance of the dining room as the centre of the house was established, and so it continued through the 19th century.

Now, despite our reversion to less formal eating habits, the demand for sets of dining chairs remains strong with premiums being paid for large sets.

Victorian mahogany low armchair,
with floral inlay.
**£250–280 / €350–390
$410–460** HiA ⊞

**Pair of child's beech and
mahogany correction
chairs,** 19thC.
**£250–280 / €350–390
$410–460** HiA ⊞

**Louis XVI-style provincial
fruitwood *fauteuil*,** with
padded arms and seat, on
turned tapering legs and *toupie*
feet, late 19thC.
**£260–290 / €360–400
$430–470** NOA ⚒

**Louis XV-style provincial walnut
armchair,** the low padded back
surmounted by a floral crest, on cabriole
legs with floral carving and scrolled toes,
late 19thC.
**£260–290 / €360–400
$430–470** NOA ⚒

**Victorian walnut nursing
chair,** with buttoned back,
on carved cabriole legs.
**£260–290 / €360–400
$430–470** AMB ⚒

◀ **Harlequin set of seven
oak dining chairs,** the backs
with wide top-rails and single
horizontal bars, on tapering
legs, Welsh, mid-19thC. The
value of these chairs is low
owing to the fact that they are
matched but not all identical,
making them very affordable.
**£260–290 / €360–400
$430–470** PF ⚒

**Set of four inlaid
mahogany chairs,** 1900.
**£260–290 / €360–400
$430–470** PaA ⊞

What is a harlequin set?

The term harlequin is
used to denote that a
group of chairs did not
originate as a set but
has been assembled
as a group of near-
matching items.

Late Victorian oak swivel office open armchair, the wrap-around back on a pierced splat and scroll support, with scroll legs on copper casters.
£260–290 / €360–400
$430–470 WW ⚹

The look without the price

Mahogany-framed bergère, with arched top-rail, caned back, scrolling drop-in seat, on turned baluster legs with brass caps and casters, 19thC.
£270–300 / €380–420
$440–490 CGC ⚹

These chairs have become very popular in the last few years. This example is affordable because it is quite late in date, and not the best quality. However, its basic shape, with the scrolled armrests, is similar to earlier, more valuable ones. The turned legs and curved back are unmistakably Victorian.

Walnut side chair, the burr-walnut-veneered pierced and shaped splat with crossbanding and inlaid stringing, with a drop-in seat and cabriole front legs, early 18thC.
£280–310 / €390–430
$460–510 WW ⚹

Prie-dieu, the twist-turned uprights with carved leaf cappings, upholstered back and seat, on bobbin-turned front legs, 19thC.
£280–310 / €390–430
$460–510 SWO ⚹

◀ **Set of four early Victorian rosewood side chairs,** the curved and flared top-rail above a carved splat, with drop-in seats, moulded front rails, on turned and ribbed tapering legs.
£280–310 / €390–430
$460–510 WW ⚹

What are bergères?

As with many furniture terms, bergère is used not altogether correctly. Often used to describe a particular type of armchair and settee with caned sides and back, a bergère was originally any armchair with upholstered sides.

This particular form of seating first appeared in France c1725 and gradually spread in popularity to other European countries displacing chairs with open arms.

The name is now most frequently applied to a style of chair which was popular during the Regency period: often of square form but sometimes with a curved back and having caned sides, back and seat (usually fitted with a squab cushion).

◀ **Pair of Regency mahogany open armchairs,** on sabre legs. These are high quality chairs and represent good value.
£280–310 / €390–430
$460–510 B(Kn) ⚲

George II fruitwood dining chair, with cabriole front legs.
£300–330 / €420–460
$490–540 L ⚲

Miller's compares...

A. Beech and elm Windsor open armchair, with pierced splat, the solid seat on crinoline stretchered leg supports, late 19thC. This model is based on an 18thC example and would have made £500–800 / €700–1,100 / $820–1,300 if it had been original.
£300–330 / €420–460
$490–540 AMB ⚲

B. Yew-wood Windsor open armchair, the pierced splat carved with a roundel, the elm seat on turned legs and stretchers, early 19thC.
£400–440 / €560–610
$650–720 E ⚲

Item B is made of yew-wood which is more desirable than the beech in Item A, it also has a richer and more attractive colour.

Victorian mahogany tub desk chair, with open back and scroll-carved splat, on a swivel base with four outswept legs, upholstered in leather, alterations.
£300–330 / €420–460
$490–540 B(W) ⚲

◀ **Mid-Victorian rosewood-framed nursing chair,** with upholstered button back, on turned legs with brass casters.
£300–330 / €420–460
$490–540 B(W) ⚲

▶ **Oak hall chair,** in the style of Bridgens, 19thC. Richard Bridgens worked in the mid-19thC and many of his designs were in the Jacobean style.
£320–350 / €450–490
$520–570 WAW ▦

The look without the price

This affordable library chair is of average quality and condition. A good quality example from this period might cost £600–800 / €840–1,100 / $980–1,300. The metamorphic library chair has its origins in the Regency period and was developed by Morgan & Saunders. Good mahogany examples from this earlier period are extremely sought-after and have been known to fetch over £10,000 / €14,000 / $16,000 at auction.

Oak metamorphic library step chair, c1870.
£320–350 / €450–490
$520–570 S(O) ✗

Louis XV-style carved beechwood upholstered *bergère-en-cabriolet*, with floral-carved serpentine crest-rail, on conforming cabriole legs, French, c1900.
£330–370 / €460–520
$540–610 NOA ✗

Mahogany side chair, in the style of Thomas Sheraton, the pierced urn splat centred by an inlaid swag, the padded seat on moulded and bead-carved square legs, c1900. The crisp carving to the splat and the central satinwood tablet is an indication of a good maker, possibly Edwards & Roberts.
£330–370 / €460–520
$540–610 NOA ✗

Colonial hardwood music chair, the back pierced and carved overall, the padded seat on outswept legs, 19thC.
£350–390 / €490–540
$570–640 DN ✗

Georgian-style carved mahogany corner chair, the central cabriole leg with a claw-and-ball foot, with drop-in seat, 1825–50.
£360–400 / €500–560
$590–650 NOA ✗

Corner chairs

Corner chairs are usually found singly rather than in pairs or sets as pairs are hard to find. Good quality examples are found in rosewood, mahogany and walnut. More basic corner chairs are in oak and other country woods, such as elm, and have straight legs and no carving.

Miller's compares...

A. Set of four rosewood balloon-back chairs, c1860.
£350–390 / €490–540
$570–640 S(O) ⚒

B. Set of four mahogany balloon-back chairs, c1860.
£530–590 / €740–820
$870–960 S(O) ⚒

Although the chairs in Item A are of rosewood, which is generally more popular than mahogany, it is the cabriole legs of the chairs in Item B that make them more desirable. The upholstery of Item B is also in better condition than that of Item A and the additional cost of reupholstering must be taken into account.

Balloon-back chairs

This style of chair was made between c1850 and c1890, and was inspired by Continental designs. They were originally intended for the salon, rather than as dining chairs, so carvers are extremely rare. The finer examples have cabriole front legs and are usually in walnut, but there are also many less attractive examples. Fakes are unlikely as they have always been in plentiful supply and modestly priced. However, copies have been known to have been imported from the Far East and are heavier than the Victorian originals.

Regency mahogany-framed armchair, with button-upholstered back and padded scrolling arms, the stuff-over seat above turned legs with brass caps and casters. If the legs of this chair had been reeded rather than turned it would have fetched a higher price at auction. The now unfashionable Dralon fabric also affected the price adversely.
£380–420 / €530–590
$620–690 CGC ⚒

Pair of mahogany side chairs, each with a drop-in seat, and acanthus-carved cabriole legs with hairy paw feet, mid-18thC. Had this set of chairs been made of walnut they would have fetched £700 / €980 / $1,150. The low price also suggests that the carving on the legs may be of only average quality.
£400–440 / €560–610
$650–720 NOA ⚒

Mahogany elbow chair, with anthemion-incised top-rail, pierced and carved mid-rail and scroll arms, the cane seat on incised sabre legs, c1815.
£430–480 / €600–670
$700–780 PSA ⊞

Chests & Coffers

Pine, leather and brass-bound travelling trunk, the domed cover with brass title 'Guellagu', 19thC, 37¾in (96cm) wide. In better condition this trunk could have made £400 / €560 / $650.
£105–115 / €150–160
$170–190 S(O) ↗

Oak chest, the hinged cover with three panels, over carved front and sides, restored, 18thC, 55¼in (140.5cm) wide. The reasonable price of this chest reflects the restoration and possibly later carving.
£200–220 / €280–310
$330–370 WW ↗

Brass- and iron-mounted chest, with an overall pattern of raised rondels, each end with two wrought-iron handles, 1850–75, 33in (84cm) wide.
£290–320 / €400–450
$470–520 NOA ↗

How to identify types of wood

Different woods and the quality of the timber used to make furniture result in a variation of colour (see pages 12–13). Good quality walnut was imported from France during the early 18th century and is highly prized for its good figuring and attractive mellow colour – pieces with exceptional colour and patina can achieve six-figure sums. Early walnut furniture can, however, still be found for under £1,000 / €1,400 / $1,650. After the early 18th century, walnut was not commonly used, but became fashionable again in the mid-19th century. At this time the walnut was sometimes imported from America but the timber was, on the whole, of inferior quality.

Oak becomes darker with age and early oak furniture from the 16th century is much sought-after. This tends to be very dark in colour whereas 18th-century oak is often quite red in tone. Mahogany also varies according to age and can range from a dark red-brown dating from c1750 to a more orange-red colour that is found on much of the furniture made in the 19th century.

Oak coffer, top damaged, 17thC, 49in (124.5cm) wide. With better colour and condition and without the damage this coffer could have made £600 / €840 / $980.
£300–330 / €420–460
$490–540 L ↗

▶ **Oak mule chest,** with a cupboard at each end, 17thC, 49½in (125.5cm) wide. The later feet and side cupboards have reduced the value of this piece.
£300–330
€420–460
$490–540 L ↗

Oak coffer, with carved front panels, restored, later carving, late 17thC, 56in (142cm) wide. Carving was often added to coffers in the Victorian era to make them more ornate. Similar motifs and repeat patterns were often used, making it hard to distinguish the additional carving from any original decoration.
£350–390 / €490–540
$570–640 B(Kn) ✗

Identifying origins by the type of timber

Oak was mainly used for chests in northern Europe, while walnut was used further south. Pine was probably used much more than surviving examples would suggest; being subject to woodworm and rot, pre-19th-century pine chests are rare. Aromatic cypress and cedarwood are repellent to moths and other insects, and were therefore used in chests intended for clothes and textiles, particularly in northern Italy and the southern alpine regions. Ash and lime were used, notably in southern Germany and Switzerland; chestnut and walnut in southern France. Sometimes more than one type of timber was employed in a single piece.

Oak coffer, the panelled front carved with a meandering vine and stylized tulips, the stile feet with later applied facings, mid-17thC, 41in (104cm) wide. Always check the wear on the feet of coffers. This piece dates from the 1600s and as expected the wear to the feet is considerable, hence the application of later facings to strengthen them.
£400–440 / €560–610
$650–720 Bea ✗

▶ **Plank coffer,** with a hinged lid, the sides extending to feet, 17thC, 30¾in (78cm) wide.
£460–510 / €640–710
$750–830 AH ✗

Oak coffer, the front with a moulded diamond pattern and a carved frieze, on block feet, late 17thC, 56½in (143.5cm) wide.
£430–480 / €600–670
$700–780 NOA ✗

Find out more in

Miller's Pine & Country Furniture Buyer's Guide, Miller's Publications, 2001

◀ **Colonial brass-mounted blanket chest,** with a studded top and internal candle box, 19thC, 50¾in (129cm) wide.
£480–540
€670–750
$780–880 SWO ✗

Oak coffer, the moulded top above a moulded frieze and front, on stile feet, stamped 'WW', 17thC, 54¾in (139cm) wide.
£550–600 / €770–840
$900–980 CGC ✗

Chests of Drawers & Commodes

Mahogany chest of drawers, with four long graduated drawers, on spade bracket feet, distressed veneer, replacement handles and escutcheons, 19thC, 39in (99cm) wide. In better condition and with original handles and escutcheons this chest would be worth over £400 / €560 / $650.
**£100–110 / €140–155
$165–180 B(Kn) ↗**

Mahogany commode, the hinged front modelled as two dummy drawers, 19thC, 25¼in (64cm) wide. The commode no longer has a function in the modern home and can be bought as a novelty item at a reasonable price.
**£160–175 / €220–245
$260–285 B(Ba) ↗**

What is a commode?

A commode is a Continental chest of drawers or side cabinet. English versions of these, in the French taste, were fashionable from the mid-18th century, but they were not made in great quantities due to the expense of producing the elaborate shapes and decoration. In Victorian times this name was given to any piece of furniture that concealed a chamber pot.

▶ **Mahogany chest of drawers,** the two short and four long graduated drawers with ebonized cockbeading and turned wooden knob handles, on turned feet, early 19thC, 42in (106.5cm) wide. This is an attractive chest with unusual ebonized cockbeading, but the colour is rather orange which may account for the low price.
**£200–220 / €280–310
$330–370 PF ↗**

George II chest of drawers, 39¾in (101cm) wide. This piece was originally the upper section of a chest-on-chest. These can be recognized by examining the top which will not have been veneered as it would have been too tall to be visible. A later veneer will be of a different colour and grain to the rest of the chest. The feet will be of a later date, and there are likely to be three short drawers at the top – original low chests were generally made with two.
**£300–330 / €420–460
$490–540 B(Ba) ↗**

◀ **Mahogany chest of drawers,** the three long drawers fitted with replacement brass plate handles, on bracket feet, 19thC, 36¼ (91cm) wide.
**£300–330
€420–460
$490–540 WW ↗**

To find out more about antique furniture see the full range of Miller's books at
www.millers.uk.com

◄ **Mahogany bowfronted chest of drawers,**
early 19thC, 40in (101.5cm) wide.
£320–350 / €450–490
$520–570 L ✦

George III mahogany chest of drawers, 43½in
(110.5cm) wide. Although the wood is attractive,
this piece is inexpensive because it is very low and
wide and the proportions are clumsy.
£360–400 / €500–560
$590–650 L ✦

Mahogany chest of drawers, the top with
reeded edge above four long graduated drawers with
later brass handles, early 19thC, 42½in (108cm) wide.
£380–420 / €530–590
$620–690 WW ✦

**Victorian mahogany chest of
drawers,** the top with a moulded
edge, the two short and three
long graduated drawers with
original handles, the brass locks
stamped 'VR Crowned Patent',
with applied base moulding,
on flattened bun feet, 48½in
(122.5cm) wide. This chest of
drawers has some attractive
features such as the moulded top
and handles, the ivory escutcheons
and cockbeading to the drawers.
As there are many chests of
drawers of this style to be found
at auction, these features make
it more desirable.
£400–440 / €560–610
$650–720 WW ✦

The look without the price

**18thC-style walnut and
crossbanded *bombé*
commode,** German, c1900,
43¼in (110cm) wide.
£380–420 / €530–590
$620–690 B(Ba) ✦

If this piece had been
from the mid-18th
century it would
cost £1,500–2,500 /
€2,100–3,500 /
$2,500–4,200.

▶ **Satinwood and chequer-strung music chest,** the four drawers with drop fronts, on square tapering legs, 1875–1925, 21in (53.5cm) wide. Although satinwood is very desirable, this piece is affordable as music chests have little use in the home today. It would have been worth a great deal more if it had been a chest of drawers.
£400–440 / €560–610
$650–720 DN ✕

◀ **George III mahogany bowfronted chest of drawers,** the two short and three long graduated drawers with replacement handles, on splayed bracket feet, 41in (104cm) wide.
£480–530 / €670–740
$780–870 B(Kn) ✕

Mahogany bowfronted chest of drawers, in two stages, the upper section with two short and one long drawer, the base with two short and four long cockbeaded drawers, all with brass repoussé handles, with a shaped apron on splayed feet, early 19thC, 45in (114.5cm) wide.
£420–460 / €590–640
$690–750 PF ✕

Mahogany chest of drawers, with brushing slide and four long drawers, early 19thC, 37in (94cm) wide.
£500–550 / €700–770
$820–900 B(Kn) ✕

Mahogany chest of drawers, with ebony banding, the three long drawers with ebony handles, top possibly later, mid-19thC, 24in (61cm) wide.
£540–600 / €750–840
$880–980 HiA ⊞

◀ **George IV mahogany bowfronted chest of drawers,** the two short and three long graduated drawers with cockbeading and turned wooden handles, on bracket feet, 41in (104cm) wide.
£590–650 / €820–900
$960–1,100 JAd ✕

William IV mahogany chest of drawers, with central hat drawer, c1835, 47¾in (121.5cm) wide.
£610–670 / €850–930
$1,000–1,100 S(O)

Chippendale-style mahogany chest of drawers, the top with a foliate-carved edge, two short over three long drawers, on later carved ogee bracket feet, mid-18thC, 38¼in (97cm) wide. If the carving and the feet had been original this chest of drawers would have been worth £1,000–1,500 / €1,400–2,100 / $1,650–2,500.
£680–750 / €950–1,050
$1,100–1,200 Bea

William IV mahogany chest of drawers, with protruding black slate top and plain frieze on turned columns, the three small drawers over three long drawers with turned ebonized handles and stringing, on turned feet, 53½in (136cm) wide. The influence of early 19thC French Empire can be clearly seen on this chest of drawers and the unusual ebony stringing is a desirable feature.
£620–680 / €860–950
$1,000–1,100 AH

Figured-mahogany bowfronted chest of drawers, early 19thC, 41in (104cm) wide.
£680–750 / €950–1,050
$1,100–1,200 S(O)

Mahogany bowfronted chest of drawers, with two short over three long crossbanded drawers, on splayed feet, early 19thC, 40¾in (103.5cm) wide.
£820–900 / €1,150–1,250
$1,350–1,450 HOLL

George III mahogany and crossbanded chest of drawers, the back with Royal inscription 'G R, Pavillion, V R, 1872, room 12', 37¾in (96cm) wide.
£820–900 / €1,150–1,250
$1,350–1,450 S(O)

Looking at drawers to date a piece

The drawer linings of the best quality pieces of furniture are almost always oak. A general guide, though not a foolproof one, for dating a piece is to look at the bottom of each drawer. If the grain runs front to back it will probably be pre-1750, if it runs from side to side it is likely to be later.

Cupboards

Victorian mahogany hanging cabinet, alterations, 18½in (47cm) wide.
£60–65 / €85–90
$100–105 B(Ba) 🔨

Oak display cabinet, with a bowed glass front, American, c1900, 42½in (108cm) wide. The value of this piece has been reduced by the fact that it is not in perfect condition.
£125–140 / €175–195
$195–230 DuM 🔨

George III mahogany night commode, with tray top, two doors and chamfered legs, 18in (45.5cm) wide. Pairs of night commodes are scarce and, although this is quite a provincial piece, a pair could have made as much as £800–1,200 / €1,100–1,600 / $1,300–2,000.
£130–145 / €180–200
$210–235 G(L) 🔨

Display cabinets

Designs for 'china cases' appeared in the middle of the 18th century. Intended for drawing rooms, dressing rooms and boudoirs, these glazed cabinets were used for the display of fine pieces of Oriental porcelain.

By the beginning of the 20th century the display cabinet was an important piece of furniture in any middle-class home, although styles had reverted to those of the late 18th century.

Table cabinet, painted with gilt flower-filled urns, decorated with mother-of-pearl, the two doors enclosing an arrangement of small drawers, Italian, 18thC, 18in (45.5cm) wide.
£200–220 / €280–310
$330–370 L 🔨

Painted pine hanging corner cupboard, formerly with a lower section, c1800, 36¾in (93.5cm) wide.
£210–230 / €290–320
$350–380 S(O) 🔨

Gothic revival oak buffet, each graduating section with blind and pierced tracery, two cupboards above a frieze drawer, the potboard back with linen-fold panels, 19thC, 34in (86.5cm) wide. This piece was inexpensive as it would have little practical use today.
£240–270 / € 330–380
$390–440 SWO 🔨

George III mahogany hanging cupboard, with dentil-moulded cornice and two panelled doors above a long drawer, on bracket feet, 48in (122cm) wide.
£340–380 / € 470–530
$560–620 G(L) 🔨

Edwardian mahogany and satinwood-banded display cabinet, 19in (48.5cm) wide.
£240–270 / € 330–380
$390–440 B(Ba) 🔨

Buffets

From the Middle Ages, social status was reflected by the lavish display of both the delicacies and the plate that were arranged on the buffet or sideboard in the principal eating room. Although the dresser, with its tiered superstructure, sufficed during the medieval period, during the 16th century it was superseded in the most sophisticated households by the court cupboard, which was an early type of sideboard.

Walnut pot cupboard, c1890, 30in (76cm) high.
£340–380 / € 470–530
$560–620 PGO ⊞

George III mahogany corner cupboard, the astragal-glazed door enclosing shelves, 31in (78.5cm) wide. This piece would make an attractive display cabinet.
£360–400 / € 500–560
$590–650 L 🔨

► **Georgian mahogany bed-side cabinet,** with a folding top, 14in (35.5cm) wide.
£380–420
€ 530–590
$620–690 SAW ⊞

Oak display cabinet, with a bowed glass front, American, c1900, 43in (109cm) wide.
£380–420 / €530–590
$620–690 DuM ⚘

Oak corner cabinet, with canted corners and blind fretwork, 19thC, 41in (104cm) high. Attractive colour and interesting features such as the door moulding and blind fretwork make this piece good value for money.
£380–420 / €530–590
$620–690 SWO ⚘

Edwardian bowfronted painted display cabinet, inlaid with stringing, the glazed door with lead glazing bars and coloured glass motifs, on square tapering legs, 24in (61cm) wide. The coloured glass motifs are reminiscent of Scottish Art Nouveau furniture of this date. They add some appeal to this type of cabinet which has experienced a recent decline in popularity and consequently price.
£380–420 / €530–590
$620–690 PF ⚘

◀ **Mahogany hanging corner cabinet,** c1910, 17in (43cm) wide.
£450–500 / €630–700
$730–820 S(O) ⚘

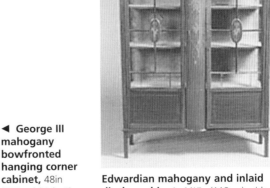

◀ **George III mahogany bowfronted hanging corner cabinet,** 48in (122cm) high. The value of this piece has been reduced by the fact that it is not in perfect condition.
£450–500
€630–700
$730–820 SWO ⚘

Edwardian mahogany and inlaid display cabinet, 44½in (113cm) wide. Apart from those of exceptional quality by recognized makers such as Edwards & Roberts, display cabinets have come down in value – now might be a good time to invest in such pieces of furniture.
£480–530 / €670–740
$780–870 B(Ba) ⚘

Oak hanging corner cupboard, the dentil-moulded cornice above a crossbanded door enclosing shelves, flanked by fluted pilasters, 18thC, 42in (106.5cm) high.
£500–550 / €700–770
$820–900 BWL 🔨

Victorian mahogany chiffonier, 37in (94cm) wide. Victorian chiffoniers have fallen in value over the last few years.
£540–600 / €750–840
$880–980 HiA ⊞

Dressers

Most dressers were made from oak, but fine examples in elm, ash, fruitwood, yew, chestnut and walnut exist. Pine dressers were made in Scotland, Ireland and south west England, and many of them were painted.

The look without the price

This piece is a rather late example. A George III linen press of comparable quality might have made up to £1,500 / €2,100 / $2,500. Linen presses are often bought for the American market and the trays removed to accomodate a television.

Mahogany linen press, the top with sliding trays, possibly Irish, c1835, 52½in (133.5cm) wide.
£530–590 / €740–820
$870–960 S(O) 🔨

◄ **Early Victorian mahogany cupboard,** the panelled doors enclosing sliding trays, on turned feet, 50in (127cm) wide. Although this was originally a piece of bedroom furniture, it could be useful as a dining room side cabinet.
£550–600
€770–840
$900–980 DN 🔨

▶ **Victorian satinwood dresser,** with two glazed doors, 51in (129.5cm) wide.
£800–900
€1,150–1,250
$1,300–1,500
P&T ⊞

Desks & Writing Tables

Edwardian pine clerk's desk, the hinged writing slope enclosing a void interior, above two apron drawers, c1910, 47½in (120.5cm) wide. The use of pine for this desk is reflected in the price. Victorian mahogany examples can make over £1,000 / €1,400 / $1,650.
£175–190 / €250–270
$290–310 S(O) ↗

Victorian oak desk companion, the fall-front carved with Ionic fluted pillars operating a sprung fully-fitted pigeonhole and drawer interior with folding leather-lined writing surface, 18in (45.5cm) wide. Condition is very important with small travelling desk companions and often they are not in a good state. If this piece had been made of mahogany rather than oak it could have fetched £400 / €560 / $650.
£250–280 / €350–390
$410–460 EH ↗

The look without the price

George III-style mahogany bureau, 1901–10, 36¼in (92cm) wide.
£120–130 / €165–180
$195–210 B(Ba) ↗

If this piece had been an original George III bureau it could have made over £500 / €700 / $820.

What is patina?

The patination on a piece of antique furniture can greatly influence its value. Patina is built up through years of polishing and waxing until the surface of the piece acquires a deep, soft, smooth sheen that is particularly pleasing to the eye and to the touch. The effect is difficult to acquire on reproduction pieces, even though it is often attempted. As a guideline to the collector, a good patina is, in fact, of more importance than signs of wear which can add to the character of the piece.

Late Victorian oak pedestal desk, 19thC, 44in (112cm) wide.
£290–320 / €400–450
$470–520 SWO ↗

Miller's compares...

A. Victorian mahogany pedestal desk, with later *faux* leather top, 48in (122cm) wide.
£360–390 / €500–540
$590–640 B(Kn) ✎

B. Victorian carved mahogany pedestal desk, the inverted breakfront moulded top inset with a leather writing surface, alterations, 19thC, 54in (137cm) wide.
£800–880 / €1,100–1,250
$1,300–1,450 G(B) ✎

Item A is a typical Victorian pedestal desk of c1870, at an affordable price, although the timber is not of exceptional quality. Such desks have often been converted from dressing tables and this is suggested here by the replacement *faux* leather top. Item B is slightly later in date, c1890, but has a very Regency shape, with tapering sarcophagus pedestals that allow more leg room. The inverted breakfront also makes the piece more desirable and contributes to the price difference.

Late George III inlaid mahogany writing table, on tapering legs with brass casters, 16¾in (42.5cm) wide. This was an excellent buy which went for well below its reserve price and should have made over £1,000 / €1,400 / $1,650.
£480–530 / €670–740
$780–870 Bea ✎

Victorian inlaid figured-walnut davenport, the top with inset leather writing surface, the base with four real and four opposing dummy drawers with wooden knob handles, on turned feet with casters, 22in (56cm) wide. Davenports have fallen in value over the past ten years and are less practical in the modern home than the bureau.
£520–570 / €720–790
$850–930 PF ✎

Edwardian Sheraton revival lady's desk, with a long frieze drawer above two drawers with central kneehole, crossbanded and with painted decoration, on square tapering legs with spade feet, 24½in (62cm) wide. Sheraton revival furniture in satinwood is still doing well in the market and is popular for its highly-decorative nature.
£620–680 / €860–950
$1,000–1,100 L&E ✎

Dumb Waiters

Mahogany lazy Susan, 1875–1925, 21in (53.5cm) diam.
£200–220 / €280–310
$330–370 SWO ⚒

▶ **Kingwood and parquetry dumb waiter,** with pierced brass galleries, 32½in (100.5cm) high.
£400–440
€560–610
$650–720 G(B) ⚒

▶ **Late Regency mahogany dumb waiter,** the two tiers with moulded edges, on turned and ribbed supports and moulded splay legs, with applied side rondels to the toes with brass casters, 26in (66cm) diam. The top tier is slightly warped, hence the low price of this piece.
£480–530 / €670–740
$780–870 WW ⚒

Miller's compares...

A. Mahogany dumb waiter, the moulded scroll legs with brass casters, 19thC, 37in (94cm) high.
£580–640 / €810–890
$950–1,050 WW ⚒

B. Mahogany dumb waiter, 19thC, 24½in (62cm) diam.
£820–910 / €1,150–1,300
$1,350–1,500 B(Kn) ⚒

Item A has rather plain, simple turned columns and the wood used is not of good quality and some warping has occurred. However, although Item B is 19th century, it is a copy of a 1760s model and has a spiral-carved knop which makes the piece more attractive. It is also made of superior wood and is generally in better condition than Item A, all of which contribute to its higher value.

Mahogany dumb waiter, in the Chippendale style, c1920, 32in (81.5cm) high. If this dumb waiter, with the gallery to each tier and the carved legs, had been an 18thC Chippendale piece the value would increase to £6,000–8,000 / €8,300–11,000 / $9,800–13,000.
£710–780 / €990–1,100
$1,150–1,300 Che ⊞

Mirrors & Frames

George III mahogany toilet mirror, with cheval stand, 22in (56cm) high. The very low price reflects the simplicity of this mirror.
£30–35 / €42–48
$50–60 G(L) 🔎

George III mahogany toilet mirror, the bowfronted plinth crossbanded and fitted with three short drawers, on ogee bracket feet, 21¾in (55.5cm) wide. This piece would have been more expensive if it had a serpentine shape rather than the simple bowfront.
£80–90 / €110–125
$130–150 L 🔎

◀ **Giltwood mirror,** the moulded frame surmounted by a palmette, late 19thC, 17½in (44.5cm) high.
£130–145 / €180–200
$210–230 NOA 🔎

▶ **Fruitwood mirror,** with a canted and gilt slip-moulded frame, mid-19thC, 40¼in (102cm) wide.
£140–155 / €195–210
$230–250 S(O) 🔎

Carved giltwood mirror, the cresting modelled as a bow, French, late 19thC, 20in (51cm) high.
£110–120 / €155–165
$180–195 NOA 🔎

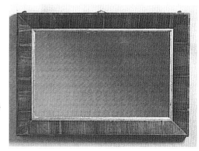

How to care for antique mirrors

If the silver backing of an antique mirror has badly deteriorated, repair should not be attempted as any restoration will always substantially devalue the piece.

There are three traditional methods used to clean the fronts of mirrors. The first is to wipe the glass with a lint-free linen cloth moistened with methylated spirits. The second is to wipe the glass with a lint-free cloth which has been wrung out in lukewarm water to which a few drops of ammonia have been added. The third is to lightly moisten a lint-free cloth with paraffin and wipe the glass. This last method works well, but leaves a smell of paraffin in the air for some time.

Whichever method is chosen, it is essential to avoid any moisture getting behind the glass, as this will cause further deterioration of the silvering.

George IV mahogany toilet mirror, 21½in (54.5cm) wide.
£140–155 / €195–215
$230–250 L 🔎

William and Mary-style walnut-veneered mirror, late 19thC, 17¼in (44cm) wide. This mirror is based on a late 17thC design, and would have made nearer £1,000 / €1,400 / $1,650 had it been original and in good condition.
£180–200 / €250–280 $300–330 NOA

The look without the price

Sheraton revival mahogany and marquetry cheval mirror, with boxwood and ebony stringing, the supports with urn finials, on splayed legs with brass terminals and casters, late 19thC, 65½in (166.6cm) high.
£260–290 / €360–400 $430–470 DN

If this mirror had been an original late 18thC Sheraton piece, the value would be around £700 / €980 / $1,150.

Pier mirror, the moulded inverted breakfront cornice above a foliate baton, the later plate flanked by reeded Egyptian head pilasters, later gilding and restoration, c1825, 32in (81.5cm) wide. The style is George IV but the later gilding and restoration has brought the price of this mirror down from around £700–1,000 / €980–1,400 / $1,150–1,650.
£200–220 / €280–310 $330–370 WW

Victorian rosewood wall mirror, fitted with three shaped mirrors and open shelves, with all-over floral inlay, 21in (53.5cm) wide.
£220–240 / €280–330 $370–390 AMB

Gilt gesso frame, with engraved brass presentation plaque, in a rosewood surround, c1870, 22¼in (56.6cm) high.
£300–330 / €420–460 $490–540 S(O)

What is gilding?

There are two types of gilding: water gilding, which has a yellow tone, and oil gilding with its distinctive deeper orange tone. Most English 18th- and 19th-century furniture was water gilded. Layers of gesso were applied to the carved wood base, then recut to define the decoration. A liquid clay base, or bole, was applied, and the gold leaf laid upon it before being burnished to achieve the final tone.

Oil gilding was less common and involved the application of an oil size to which the gold leaf was then stuck.

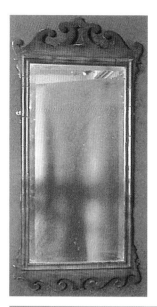

► **Early George III mahogany toilet mirror,** 16¼in (41.5cm) wide.
£300–330 / €420–460
$490–540 L 🔨

◄ **Walnut pier glass,** with later bevelled plate, the moulded frame with fret-cut cresting and base, damaged, mid-18thC, 49in (124.5cm) high. The later plate and missing fret carving have kept down the price of this mirror. Had the plate been original it would have cost almost twice as much.
£300–330 / €420–460
$490–540 PF 🔨

Buyer beware!

Be suspicious of any mirror in perfect condition. All old mirrors will have deteriorated to some extent, and will have non-reflective spots. Resilvering reduces the value, particularly that of cheval and dressing table mirrors. Mirror glass can be replaced, but the original glass should be retained and stored carefully.

◄ **Late Georgian mahogany dressing mirror,** the serpentine front with three drawers, on bun feet, 19in (48.5cm) wide.
£320–350
€450–490
$520–570 BWL 🔨

Giltwood and gesso mirror, carved with foliage, rockwork and a diaper border, French, 19thC, 25in (63.5cm) high. This mirror has a very unusual shape.
£360–400 / €500–560
$590–650 WW 🔨

► **Silver strut mirror,** within a panelled and mirrored border surmounted by a shell and scrolling foliate crest, London 1905, 18½in (47cm) high.
£440–490
€610–680
$720–800 AH 🔨

George III giltwood and gesso picture frame, 37¾in (96cm) high.
£520–570 / €720–790
$850–930 SWO ✒

▶ **Regency mahogany cheval mirror,** with associated Victorian plate, 62½in (159cm) high. This cheval mirror is rather plain for a Regency example and would have been worth more had the plate been original.
£590–650 / €820–910
$960–1,100 S(O) ✒

Great care must be taken with gilt furniture. Never apply water as the gold will wash off; instead, seek the advice of a specialist gilder. Likewise, avoid hanging mirrors in bathrooms or other rooms with high humidity.

Giltwood mirror, the beaded and moulded frame with incised Greek key pattern, 1850–75, 50in (127cm) high.
£620–680 / €860–950
$1,000–1,100 NOA ✒

◀ **Early Georgian giltwood mirror,** the scroll cresting centred by a cartouche, the shaped apron centred by a shell, 30in (76cm) high. The small plate has had a detrimental effect on the price of this mirror. Larger early Georgian mirrors start at £2,000 / €2,800 / $3,300 and can make much more.
£700–770 / €980–1,100
$1,150–1,300 G(L) ✒

Regency giltwood and gesso convex wall mirror, with ring and acanthus quarter collets, and scrolling gilt and gesso metal candle sconces with applied leafwork, 21¾in (55.5cm) diam.
£800–880 / €1,100–1,250
$1,300–1,450 NES ✒

Screens

Giltwood *faux* bamboo fire screen, the screen now behind glass, surmounted by an asymmetrical crest, the end supports with splayed bamboo legs, late 19thC, 42in (106.5cm) high. The gilding on this fire screen is in very good condition, making it excellent value.
£110–120 / €155–165 $180–195 NOA

Victorian walnut fire screen, the floral needlework panel beneath pierced cresting, on spiral-turned supports and stretcher, with moulded scroll legs, 32¾in (83cm) wide. The ornate and delicate fret-carved cresting is echoed in the scroll decoration of the needlework. This is a very attractive piece and a good buy.
£180–200 / €250–280 $300–330 WW

Victorian oak pole screen, the turned stem with quatreform base, 53in (134.5cm) high. The low value of this pole screen is due to the fact that it is made of oak and the design is fairly simple. If it had been a William IV rosewood example it would be worth around £200–300 / €280–420 / $320–490.
£140–155 / €195–210 $230–250 WW

Ebonized and gilt fire screen, with a woolwork and beaded picture of a saint, 19thC, 43¾in (111cm) high. The ebonizing and Gothic influences are typical of Aesthetic Movement furniture of the 1870s.
£180–200 / €250–280 $300–330 SWO

Victorian mahogany fire screen, with two pull-out screens and glass panel, on plain side supports. Although this screen is rather plain the pull-out screens are not common and therefore add to the interest.
£240–265 / €330–370 $390–430 JAd

◀ **KPM porcelain lithophane,** in a black-patinated Prussian cast-iron foliate frame, the shaft fitted with an adjustable candle holder, German, 19thC, 23½in (59.5cm) high.
£620–680 / €860–950 $1,000–1,100 NOA

Shelves

Miller's compares...

A. Set of mahogany open hanging shelves, 19thC, 27in (68.5cm) wide. A comparable set of shelves from the Georgian period would make over £700 / €980 / $1,150, and pairs are particularly desirable.
£110–120 / €155–165
$180–195 WW ✣

B. Set of walnut open hanging shelves, with adjustable central tier, 19thC, 34¾in (88.5cm) wide.
£200–220 / €280–310
$330–370 WW ✣

Item A, a Victorian hanging shelf, is very plain. Item B, however, is of a more interesting 'waterfall' design, where the shelves cascade from a narrower top to a deeper lower shelf. It is also made of walnut which is not as common as mahogany.

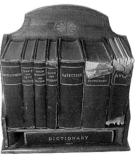

Edwardian inlaid mahogany book shelf, containing an Asprey reference library of eight books, label, books damaged, 8½in (21.5cm) deep.
£90–100 / €125–140
$150–165 TMA ✣

Pair of Louis XVI-style carved and stained limewood bracket shelves, 1875–1900, 16in (40.5cm) wide. Limewood is often used for carving and these shelves are very good value.
£190–210 / €265–290
$310–350 NOA ✣

Set of mahogany hanging shelves, with turned supports, c1820, 18in (45.5cm) wide.
£300–330 / €420–460
$490–540 F&F ✣

The look without the price

Regency-style mahogany and brass shelves, the top shelf with a three-quarter pierced brass gallery, the reeded brass supports with vertical X-form stretchers, on toupie feet, c1900, 32in (81.5cm) high.
£360–400 / €500–560
$590–650 NOA ✣

These shelves are very decorative, but the low price reflects the late date. A set of original Regency shelves would make £2,000–3,000 / €2,800–4,200 / $3,300–4,900 at auction.

Sofas

Edwardian mahogany two-seater settee, the part-open back with two pierced vertical splats, on two stylized cabriole front legs and curved back legs, 42in (106.5cm) wide. Edwardian settees do not generally fetch high prices. This piece is particularly appealing – its fluid lines reflect a strong French Art Nouveau influence.
£200–220 / €280–310
$330–370 FHF ⚖

Edwardian mahogany-framed two-seater settee, with shaped top-rail, scrolled arms, and tapering legs with spade feet, 41½in (105.5cm) wide. The shape of the back of this settee is typical of the Victorian era, and the legs are 18thC in style – however, this does not detract from the overall look of the piece.
£320–350 / €450–490
$520–570 FHF ⚖

▶ **Victorian mahogany-framed settee,** with stuff-over arms and serpentine front, on foliate-carved bun front legs, 80in (203cm) wide.
£300–330
€420–460
$490–540 PFK ⚖

Settee or sofa?

The word 'settee' was used throughout the 18th century to describe any appropriate piece of seat furniture, whether it had a carved or upholstered back, while the term 'sofa' came to be applied just to more heavily upholstered examples. Now the words are almost interchangeable.

Most settees of the 18th century, whether upholstered or carved, formed parts of suites and as such their designs matched those of the chairs in the suites. Also, since they were made to stand against walls, their backs were plain and unadorned.

The elegant, French-influenced designs of the late 18th century gave way to far heavier and extravagantly shaped pieces during the period of the Regency of the reigns of George IV and William IV. By 1860, the French taste had once again brought a lighter touch to the form of Victorian furniture, and the settee and the chaise longue had taken on new curvaceous, organic lines. During the last quarter of the century the sumptuously upholstered and buttoned Chesterfield gained a level of popularity which it has never really relinquished.

◀ **Louis XV-style giltwood seven-piece salon suite,** comprising a canapé, two *fauteuils* and four salon chairs, restored, late 19thC. An unrestored example, even if not of very good quality, could achieve £1,000–1,500 / €1,400–2,100 / $1,650–2,450.
£400–440 / €560–610
$650–720 B(Ch) ⚖

Gilt canapé, 19thC, 43¾in (111cm) wide.
£410–450 / €570–630
$670–730 B(Kn) ⚖

Stands

The look without the price

Mahogany torchère, on three scroll legs, top chipped, c1910, 42in (106.5cm) high.
£60–65 / €85–90
$100–110 WW ✗

The price of this torchère reflects the fact that it is a reproduction. It is based on an early 19thC version and would have made at least £800 / €1,100 / $1,300 if it was original.

► **Mahogany washstand,** with a frieze drawer, 19thC, 13in (33cm) wide.
£140–155
€195–210
$230–250 B(Kn) ✗

Victorian brass rotating magazine stand, by W. T. & S., the tubular divides with lozenge decoration, the moulded oak base rotating on a brass tripod stand, 14¼in (36cm) wide.
£220–240 / €310–330
$370–390 B(W) ✗

George III mahogany washstand, with two tiers and a raised back, the lower tier with a central drawer flanked by dummy drawers, on square tapering legs joined by pierced and shaped stretchers with a jug stand, 21¾in (55.5cm) wide.
£280–310 / €390–430
$460–510 L&E ✗

Late Victorian mahogany and line-inlaid torchère, 40in (101.5cm) high. The general design of this piece is influenced by Sheraton. It would have been worth a great deal more if it had been late 18thC.
£180–200 / €250–280
$300–330 WW ✗

What is a stand?

The term 'stand' is used in a wide-ranging sense and implies any kind of support. Stands were specifically designed to be both highly practical and easily portable. Although they were often embellished with the fashionable decorative qualities of the day, the common feature of these pieces is that function always prevailed over style.

▶ **George III mahogany bowfronted washstand,** with raised gallery back, the lower tier with a central drawer flanked by dummy drawers, on square legs with outward-curving ends, 24in (61cm) wide.
£360–400
€500–560
$590–650 L&E ⚶

Faux **bamboo stick stand,** c1910, 28in (71cm) wide.
£390–430 / €540–590
$640–700 PICA ⊞

Naval washstand, with three tiers, two with fitted brass galleries, on brass spindle supports, 19thC, 27in (68.5cm) wide.
£390–430 / €540–600
$640–700 BWL ⚶

George III mahogany basin stand, 11in (28cm) diam. Basin stands are also known as wig stands – the basin would be used to hold the wig powder which was then applied to the wig. The value of Georgian basin stands is relatively low, since they no longer have a function and are bought nowadays as stands.
£420–460 / €590–640
$690–750 L ⚶

Victorian walnut and burr-walnut-veneered teapoy, the interior later lined with fabric, the turned stem on four carved cabriole legs, repairs to legs, 17in (43cm) wide. If this item had been Regency and made of rosewood rather than walnut it could have fetched over £1,000 / €1,400 / $1,650.
£520–570 / €720–790
$850–930 WW ⚶

◀ **Mahogany washstand,** with scrolling gallery over a King of Prussia marble top, above cyma-moulded frieze drawers and cupboard doors flanked by classical pilasters and scroll feet, American, 1825–50, 40½in (103cm) wide.
£730–800 / €1,000–1,100
$1,200–1,300 NOA ⚶

Steps & Stools

◄ **Beech or sycamore cheese stool,** c1900, 14in (35.5cm) high.
£30–35 / €42–48
$50–60 SDA ⊞

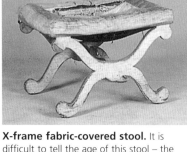

X-frame fabric-covered stool. It is difficult to tell the age of this stool – the form is typically Regency and this piece probably dates from that period. The poor condition is reflected in its low value and if the condition of the upholstery and the timber had been better it could have made £400 / €560 / $650.
£35–40 / €48–55
$60–65 SDA ⊞

Oak saddle seat stool, 1880, 18in (45.5cm) wide.
£70–80 / €95–110
$115–130 DFA ⊞

Ash and elm stool, with four turned legs, c1850, 21in (53.5cm) high.
£60–65 / €85–90
$100–105 F&F ⋩

► **Beech stool,** with four legs, Welsh, 1880, 12in (30.5cm) high.
£70–80 / €95–110
$115–130 COF ⊞

► **Edwardian spindle-turned mahogany stool,** 17in (43cm) high. This is a good quality stool and well worth the money.
£140–155
€195–210
$230–250 RPh ⊞

Ash and elm miniature country stool, c1800, 7½in (19cm) high.
£90–100 / €125–140
$150–165 SDA ⊞

Fruitwood stool, c1780, 18in (45.5cm) high.
£150–165 / €210–230 $245–270 F&F ⚘

Victorian upholstered rosewood piano stool, the iron mechanism stamped 'Marsden's Patent', 19¼in (49cm) high.
£155–170 / €210–230 $250–280 B(Kn) ⚘

Upholstered mahogany stool, the padded top above a concave base, on a further carved base with bun feet, 1850–75, 19in (48.5cm) high.
£165–180 / €230–250 $270–295 NOA ⚘

The look without the price

The design of this piano stool is based on a model by Gillows of Lancaster. The value depends on the quality of the timber and the crispness of the carving. This example is a good buy as similar examples can make over £600 / €840 / $980.

William IV mahogany revolving piano stool, with a leather seat.
£190–210 / €265–290 $310–350 BWL ⚘

Georgian upholstered mahogany footstool, in the Chippendale style, on square-section legs with fretted spandrels and H-form stretcher, 12½in (32cm) high.
£220–240 / €310–330 $370–390 NOA ⚘

◄ **Restauration-style provincial fruitwood stool,** the saddle seat centred with a rush panel, French, 1850–75, 17in (43cm) high.
£270–300 €380–420 $440–490 NOA ⚘

Walnut footstool, with upholstered seat, c1900, 19in (48.5cm) high.
£390–430 / €540–600 $640–700 RPh ⊞

Tables

Oak dining table, American, late 19thC, 42½in (108cm) diam.
£110–120 / €155–165
$180–195 DuM ↗

◄ **Oak folding occasional table,** on an X-frame support, late 19thC, 17in (43cm) wide.
£95–105 / €130–150
$155–170 S(O) ↗

Edwardian mahogany occasional table, with crossbanded top and undertier, on slender cabriole legs, 23¾in (60.5cm) wide. There are many late Georgian-revival tables such as this piece on the market, and they can be bought for less than £100 / €140 / $165. However, this example has the added features of crossbanding and an undertier, and is in good condition.
£180–200 / €250–280
$295–330 SWO ↗

◄ **Arts and Crafts oak writing table,** c1900, 41in (104cm) wide.
£200–220 / €280–310
$330–370 SWO ↗

Writing tables

The writing table was an important item of furniture in any late 18th-century library. Also sometimes known as library tables, they were major decorative items which were intended to reflect both the wealth and the refined taste of the owner. Some were of adjustable form (now referred to as architects' tables), and by 1800 compact, highly decorative examples had become fashionable for use in the parlour or boudoir. As the 19th century wore on designs became heavier again although with the advent of the Edwardian era (1901–10) and the 'Sheraton Revival' there was a return to finer lines and lighter proportions.

Victorian mahogany Sutherland table,
43in (109cm) wide.
£210–230 / €290–320
$350–380 B(Kn) ↗

George III mahogany and boxwood-strung fold-over tea table, on square tapering legs, 35¾in (91cm) wide. The price of tea tables has remained relatively static over the last ten years and many are still very affordable. This example is particularly so as the legs do not have the spade feet that were typical of the period, and it is made of mahogany rather than the preferred satinwood which often featured decorative inlay.
£210–230 / €290–320
$350–380 B(Kn) 🔨

Victorian walnut work table, 18in (45.5cm) diam.
£220–240 / €310–330
$370–390 L 🔨

Mahogany reading table, the top with moulded edge, curved corners and easel section, on a tapering column and quatreform base with squat turned feet, 19thC, 36in (91.5cm) wide.
£220–240 / €310–330
$370–390 TRM 🔨

◄ **Rosewood card table,** on a quatreform base, with scroll feet, 19thC, 35¾in (91cm) wide. The slightly warped top and poor colour contribute to the low price of this table.
£220–240 / €310–330
$370–390 SWO 🔨

Card tables

By the middle of the 18th century the mania for gambling which had originally been confined to Court had swept through most levels of society and, as a consequence, the demand for card or gaming tables grew. Designed with folding tops enabling them to be placed at the side of the room when not required, some had two or three hinged leaves so that they could be used for tea and chess as well as cards.

Figured walnut and satinwood were fashionable, as well as mahogany.

Andrew
Hartley
F I N E   A R T S

Independent Furniture and Fine Arts Auctioneers for three generations. Now fully extended and computerised premises with two salerooms and carefully graded general and specialist sales every week.

VICTORIA HALL SALEROOMS
LITTLE LANE, ILKLEY
WEST YORKSHIRE LS29 8EA
TEL: 01943 816363 FAX: 01943 817610
E-Mail: info@andrewhartleyfinearts.co.uk
Website: www.andrewhartleyfinearts.co.uk

◄ **Rosewood centre table,** with spiral-turned supports and stretcher, the turned feet with casters, mid-19thC, 38in (96.5cm) wide.
£220–240
€310–330
$370–390 PF ⚒

George III mahogany tea table, inlaid with stringing, the demi-lune top enclosing a polished interior, with a cockbeaded apron, on square tapering legs, 35in (89cm) wide.
£240–270 / €330–380
$390–440 PF ⚒

Edwardian mahogany wine table, with three outswept supports to a trefoil base with turned feet, 15½in (39.5cm) diam.
£240–270 / €330–380
$390–440 B(W) ⚒

George III oak tilt-top wine table, 15¾in (40cm) diam.
£250–280 / €350–390
$410–460 B(Kn) ⚒

◄ **Mahogany tilt-top table,** on a ring- and baluster-turned stem, with downswept legs and ball feet, early 19thC, 24¼in (61.5cm) wide.
£260–290 / €360–400
$430–470 AH ⚒

Victorian oak table, the top in the shape of a clover leaf, on Gothic-style legs, 23in (58.5cm) wide.
£250–280 / €350–390
$410–460 HiA ▦

Tilt-top tables

Tilt-top tables are characterized by hinged tops which enable them to be stored away when not in use.

Initially introduced for small centre and tripod tables during the 17th century, but increasingly used for larger breakfast and dining tables of the late 18th and the 19th century, tilt-tops are invariably supported on parallel lopers or bearers, which are hinged to the top of the pedestal support by wooden or, on later pieces, brass pegs or pins.

The tops were designed to be removeable. Some tables have a bird-cage attached to the top, consisting of two parallel platforms joined by columns, through which the top of the shaft or column could be inserted and then fixed by a wedge to the neck.

Satinwood sewing table, the top with rosewood cross-banding, 19thC, 12¼in (31cm) wide. Sewing tables are not very popular at present and good quality examples can be found for considerably less than £1,000 / €1,400 / $1,650. The sewing bag on this table is in poor condition which has lowered its value.
£280–310
€390–430
$460–510 CGC 🔨

Tripod table, with a carved gallery and rope-twist edge, over a ring-turned column with splayed tripod legs, 19thC, 15½in (39.5cm) wide.
£280–310 / €390–430
$460–510 SWO 🔨

Giltwood occasional table, the marble top with foliate edge banding, on serpentine tapering legs with floret capitals and foliate moulding, the caned undertier with concave moulded edging, French, 19thC, 15½in (39.5cm) diam.
£280–310 / €390–430
$460–510 TRM 🔨

Find out more in

Miller's Antiques Encyclopedia, Miller's Publications, 2003

Art Nouveau fruitwood four-tier table, with pokerwork decoration and maker's monogram 'MB', 29in (73.5cm) wide.
£290–320 / €400–450
$470–520 SAT ▦

THE BRACKLEY ANTIQUE CELLAR

Come and visit the largest purpose built centre in the Midlands!

30,000 sqft of antiques and collectables

100 independent antique dealers

• Always new stock arriving daily   • Ample free parking
• Broomfield's Tea rooms   • Disabled access and parking
• 8 miles from M40 Junction 10   • 20 miles from M1 Junction 15a

Drayman's Walk, Brackley, Northants Tel: 01280 841841
(situated under the Co-op supermarket)

Open 7 days a week 10–5pm

The look without the price

Regency mahogany side table, the reeded-edge top with rounded front corners above an ebony-strung frieze, on ring-turned and ribbed legs, 54½in (138.5cm) wide.
£300–330 / €420–460
$490–540 WW ↗

This table was originally one end of a dining table and has been made into a side table. The wood is of high quality and if it had been an original side table with smaller proportions it would have been worth at least £1,500 / €2,100 / $2,500.

Mahogany work table, the moulded top with curved angles, above two long drawers, the upper divided into compartments, the tapered well beneath with a wavy base, on baluster-turned legs, with scroll feet and casters, mid-19thC, 30in (76cm) wide.
£300–330 / €420–460
$490–540 PF ↗

▶ **Rosewood occasional table,** the inlaid top with a marble inset, on a triangular column support with gnarled decoration, on a trefoil base, 19¼in (49cm) diam.
£320–350
€450–490
$520–570 AMB ↗

William IV mahogany tea table, the fold-over top with canted corners, the quatreform moulded-edge base with carved claw feet and casters, 36in (91.5cm) wide.
£320–350 / €450–490
$520–570 TRM ↗

Tea tables

Tea was first imported into Europe by the Dutch East India Company in the early 17th century, but it was not until the late 17th century that tables specifically designed for supporting the cups, saucers and kettles required for drinking tea and coffee were introduced.

William IV rosewood games/ work table, the folding top with a chequer board, the frieze drawer with fittings above a sliding wool bag, on tapering supports with leaf-carved capitals, on turned feet, top split, 22in (56cm) wide. This table has good proportions and colour, with well-carved columns. The fact that it is also a games table makes it much more desirable.
£350–390 / €490–540 $570–640 DN ⚲

There is a huge difference between the value of low- and top-quality pieces of Georgian furniture. Colour and patination are the by-words for the avid collector, and with pedestal tables, the carving on the column and legs is also important.

Mahogany drop-leaf table, c1780, 38¼in (98cm) wide.
£410–450 / €570–630 $670–730 S(O) ⚲

The look without the price

Régence-style walnut side table, on carved shell-capped cabriole legs and hoof feet, Continental, 19thC, 28¼in (72cm) wide.
£360–400 / €500–560 $590–650 WW ⚲

If this table had been an original piece from about 1720 it could have made £2,000–3,000 / €2,800–4,200 / $3,300–4,900.

▶ **Provincial cherrywood side table,** with a single frieze drawer, on tapering legs, French, late 19thC, 31½in (80cm) wide.
£400–440 €560–610 $650–720 NOA ⚲

Drop-leaf tables

Drop-leaf tables, a type of flap table with a pivoting leg to support the extended leaf, became fashionable from c1720. By 1714 tables were usually made with cabriole legs and without understretchers. The underframing of the table was confined to the underside of the top, and the moving supports, which consisted of legs joined at right angles to sturdy rails, pivoted outward on wooden knuckle hinges set into the central underframe. The flaps wre generally secured to the central section of the top with brass rule hinges, countersunk into the underside.

Drop-leaf tables were made of oak or walnut, but mahogany was the choice for most after c1730. They continued to be widely made and can be found in other woods such as fruitwood, ash, elm and yew. Copies from the 1920s and '30s tend to have barley-twist legs.

The look without the price

This tripod table contains early elements, such as the top, but as with many tilt-top tables on the market the top and base are a marriage. Had this piece not been associated it would be worth at least £4,000 / €5,600 / $6,500.

George III-style mahogany tripod table, the tilt-top with a pie-crust edge, on a later turned pillar, restored, 18thC, 31½in (80cm) diam.
**£410–450 / €570–630
$670–730 S(O)**

William IV mahogany card table, 35¾in (91cm) wide.
**£430–470 / €600–650
$700–770 S(O)**

Mahogany-veneered tea table, with boxwood stringing, the folding top above a frieze drawer, with burr-yew tablet, on tapering legs with applied ankles, early 19thC, 36¾in (93.5cm) wide.
**£440–480 / €610–670
$720–780 WW**

Mahogany fold-over card table, on paw feet, 19thC, 36¼in (92cm) wide.
**£440–480 / €610–670
$720–780 SWO**

◄ **Early Victorian rosewood work table,** the drop-leaf top over an end drawer and a work basket, the tripod base with brass paw casters, restored, 27½in (70cm) wide.
**£460–510 / €640–710
$750–830 B(W)**

► **George III mahogany breakfast table,** the top with satinwood crossbanding, 75in (145cm) diam.
**£460–510 / €640–710
$750–830 L**

Breakfast tables

The use of burr-walnut veneers and marquetry make breakfast tables very sought-after today. They are sometimes known as loo tables, named after the Dutch card game lanterloo.

The look without the price

Wake tables were used to hold coffins, hence the unusual shape consisting of a very narrow central piece and large drop-leaf sections. An original Georgian wake table in mahogany would be highly sought-after and could make in excess of £10,000 / €14,000 / $16,500 at auction.

George III-style pine wake table, on pad feet, 19thC, 90in (228.5cm) wide.
£470–520 / €650–720
$770–850 S(O) ✕

Victorian walnut card table, with a burr-walnut-veneered serpentine fold-over top, on foliate-carved splayed scroll supports with casters, 37in (94cm) wide.
£480–530 / €670–740
$780–870 Bea ✕

George III mahogany Pembroke table, with ebony and boxwood stringing, the serpentine top with a moulded edge, the frieze drawer with a brass drop handle, each tapering leg headed by a shell patera, on brass toes and casters, 32½in (82.5cm) wide. This table is a very good buy. The wood is very fine quality and the proportions are elegant, with delicate use of inlaid decoration. The ebony-strung edges are a further sign of quality.
£500–550 / €700–770
$820–900 AH ✕

◀ **Late George III mahogany Pembroke table,** the top with a moulded edge, the frieze drawers with later brass knob handles, the tapering legs with later socket feet, damaged and repaired, 21in (53.5cm) wide. Be wary when buying Pembroke tables as the inlaid decoration is often of a later date. Smaller examples such as this are more desirable.
£500–550 / €700–770
$820–900 WW ✕

Oak side table, the moulded top above a frieze drawer, on turned legs with squared stretchers, 18thC, 35in (89cm) wide.
£550–600 / €770–840
$900–980 BWL ⚒

George III mahogany Pembroke table, with satinwood crossbanding and stringing, the top with banded edge, the frieze drawer with brass ring handles, each tapering leg headed by an inlaid panel, on brass toes and casters, 30in (76cm) wide.
£540–600 / €750–840
$880–980 AH ⚒

Find out more in

Miller's Pine & Country Furniture Buyer's Guide, Miller's Publications, 2001

Late George III rosewood side table, with boxwood stringing and chequer banding, 22in (56cm) wide.
£550–600 / €770–840
$900–980 B ⚒

Regency mahogany games table, with ebony stringing, the reeded-edge top with two hinged flaps and reversible centre section inlaid with chess board and cribbage markers over a recessed backgammon board, the frieze drawer with turned wood handles, the turned legs with brass toes and casters, 19¾in (50cm) wide.
£580–640 / €810–890
$950–1,050 AH ⚒

► **Empire-style mahogany** *guéridon*, French, c1890, 17in (43cm) diam.
£590–650
€820–910
$960–1,050 S(O) ✗

Oak side table, the moulded top over a frieze drawer with brass drop handles, on cup- and baluster-turned legs with bun feet, 17thC and later, 29in (73.5cm) wide. The price of this table reflects the fact that only parts of it are original. The legs are more recent than the top. If it were all original it would be worth at least £1,000 / €1,400 / $1,650.
£580–640 / €810–890
$950–1,050 AH ✗

Guéridons

Predominantly circular in form, they were usually inlaid with segments or geometrical patterns of specimen marbles, often on white marble or black slate grounds. Initially these featured Siena (yellow/red), rosso antico (deep red) and Sicilian Jasper (green-flecked browny/orange) marbles, as well as alabaster and various precious and semi-precious stones such as lapis lazuli and Egyptian porphyry. From 1830 Russian malachite, imported from mines in the Urals, was much used. Such specimen marble *guéridons* became fashionable throughout Europe, and although Italian quarries satisfied much of the demand, northern Europe, especially Russia which had huge mineral reserves, and Britain, produced their own specimen tops. However, the availability of Italian marbles and hardstones was restricted, and they were often prohibitively expensive, so from the mid-19th century, polished slate and granite were used as inexpensive substitutes.

George III mahogany breakfast table, with brass casters, 55in (139.5cm) wide. The price reflects the fact that this table has a plain top. A table with a crossbanded top would have fetched more.
£600–660 / €840–920
$980–1,100 G(L) ✗

► **Victorian inlaid walnut needlework table,** on carved and turned end supports joined by a turned stretcher, 24½in (62cm) wide.
£600–660 / €840–920
$980–1,100 AMB ✗

◀ **Provincial oak farmhouse table,** with a planked top above a plain frieze, on square tapering legs, French, 90in (228.5cm) long. This is a good price for this table as it could have made £1,000 / €1,400 / $1,650.
£660–720 / €920–1,000 $1,100–1,200 NOA ⚹

▶ **Rosewood work table,** with two drop leaves, a drawer and a sliding bag, the tapering column with gadrooned borders, on a quadruped base with octagonal feet, 19thC, 21in (53.5cm) wide.
£700–770 €980–1,100 $1,150–1,300 E ⚹

Empire-style mahogany *guéridon*, the marble top on three columnar supports with ormolu capitals and bases, on bun feet, c1900, 16in (40.5cm) diam.
£690–760 / €960–1,050 $1,150–1,250 NOA ⚹

Locate the source

The source of each illustration in Miller's can be found by checking the code letters below each caption with the Key to Illustrations, pages 286–290.

George III mahogany tea table, the carved-edge serpentine top opening to reveal a serving space, on moulded square legs, 1775–1800, 36in (91.5cm) wide.
£750–830 / €1,050–1,150 $1,220–1,400 NOA ⚹

Provincial fruitwood farmhouse dining table, with a dough slide to one end, the opposing end with a flatware drawer, on tapering legs, French, 1825–50, 58½in (148.5cm) long.
£870–960 / €1,200–1,300 $1,400–1,550 NOA ⚹

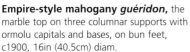

Whatnots & Trays

The look without the price

This tray is modelled on a George III example which would be worth £400–600 / €560–830 / $650–980.

Edwardian mahogany drinks tray, with a wavy edge and open brass side handles, inlaid with stringing, 24in (61cm) wide.
£160–175 / €220–250 $260–290 WW

Tôle peinte **tray,** some repainting and wear, early 19thC, 26in (66cm) wide. Toleware pieces are still very desirable. If this tray had been in good condition it could have made up to £1,000 / €1,400 / $1,650.
£280–310 / €390–430 $460–510 DN

◄ **Butler's tray,** on a folding stand, 19thC, 18½in (47cm) wide.
£300–330 / €420–460 $490–540 S(O)

► **Mid-Victorian burr-walnut and inlaid canterbury whatnot,** alterations, 28in (71cm) wide. This is quite an unusual and good quality whatnot.
£720–790 / €1,000–1,100 $1,200–1,300 B(Ch)

Miller's compares...

A. Georgian-style brass-mounted mahogany butler's tray, on a later folding stand, 1875–1900, 34in (86.5cm) wide.
£330–360 / €460–500 $540–590 NOA

B. Mahogany butler's tray, on an associated stand, early 19thC, 34¼in (87cm) wide.
£850–930 / €1,200–1,300 $1,400–1,500 S(O)

Item B is more expensive because it is earlier in date and therefore more sought-after than Item A. Both of these trays have associated stands, and this is quite typical. It is sometimes difficult to be sure whether a stand is original – it should be fairly high and the wood of the top and base should match each other. If these trays had had original bases their values would be almost double.

Victorian figured-walnut and inlaid canterbury whatnot, with pierced three-quarter gallery, on turned pillars with slatted foliate compartments enclosed within fret-pierced sides above a single drawer, the turned feet with casters, 30in (76cm) wide.
£800–880 / €1,100–1,200 $1,300–1,400 TEN

Ceramics

Whether your interest leads you to heraldry and armorials, to the Chinese export trade with Europe and America, to political satire pottery or even moustache cups, pottery and porcelain offer a world of possibilities to new collectors. The following pages show the wealth of variety from Tang Dynasty China, the famous Ming Dynasty and the prolific Qing reigns of Emperors Kangxi, Yongzheng and Qianlong to the 18th-century age of elegance represented by the great European factories of Meissen, Sèvres, Chelsea and Worcester. Mechanized industry in the 19th century brought about huge changes in ceramic production, and gave us bone china, pearlware, ironstone, parian, majolica and all manner of revived styles and patents. Huge quantities of wares were produced, particularly in Staffordshire, some of great quality, others more prosaic.

It is noticeable how many of the pieces here would not qualify as 'under £1,000 / € 1,400 / $1,650' without some degree of damage. It is vital for collectors to know how to spot clever restoration, repainting, regilding or where a vase has been cut down and thus 'losing' the damage to the neck or foot of a vase. Knowing to what extent damage matters is important, some areas of collecting, particularly pottery such as delftware or majolica, a degree of damage is acceptable, but damage to porcelain is often extremely detrimental to the value.

Knowing where to look is often an important first step for collectors. The past few years have seen a number of notable auction sales that highlight the fact there is wide interest in ceramics. The most exciting sale of 18th-century English porcelain, at least since the fabulous two sales of the Rous Lench Collection in 1986 and 1990, was the famous sale of Dr Bernard Watney's Collection by Phillips. The sale was held in three parts and focused on rarities, particularly blue and white wares from Worcester, Longton Hall, Limehouse and the Liverpool factories. Although some pieces did fetch five-figure sums, many could easily have found themselves illustrated in the pages of this book.

All manner of ceramics sales are held both in London and around the country. Some will be only for the super-rich such as the biannual London sales of fine Chinese ceramics, where rarities from the Song and Ming Dynasties can fetch six- or seven-figure sums. For the rest of us, there are sales dedicated to Clarice Cliff, Royal Worcester, Doulton, Royal commemoratives, as well as many others. Complementing the auctions, there are many antiques fairs, some of the biggest in the UK are London's Olympia, the Birmingham NEC, Newark and Ardingly, and in the US the New York International Fine Art Fair and a number of good fairs at Palm Beach, Florida.

The most important advice for the new collector is to know your subject. Find out what books are available and where to get them. It is now possible to view online many dealers' stock and auction catalogues and there are specialist auction search services which ensure that collectors never miss the chance to buy rarities, be they Lowestoft, Susie Cooper or ceramics relating to Admiral Lord Nelson.

Check a copy of the trade newspaper which advertises fairs and auctions, compare prices and don't be afraid to ask questions. Good dealers and auctioneers will be able to point you in the right direction and give advice on damage, any literature available and, of course, prices.

John Axford

Baskets & Boxes

▶ **Victorian Staffordshire pottery money box,** modelled as a cottage, 4¾in (12cm) high. Money boxes are an affordable collecting area, particularly late examples such as this.
£60–65 / €85–90
$100–105 PFK ➶

W. H. Goss bass basket, decorated with the crest of Llanberis, 1890–1910, 2¼in (5.5cm) high. With a few exceptions such as Wyckamist (those relating to Winchester College) and some WWI commemoratives, crested china is inexpensive and an easily accessible collecting area.
£18–20 / €25–30
$27–30 G&CC ⊞

Spode Pearlware basket and stand, decorated with Group pattern, unmarked, 1800–20, 9½in (24cm) wide. Group pattern is a known and listed Spode design and the shape of the piece is also indicative of the maker.
£140–155 / €195–215
$230–250 SWO ➶

Paris porcelain dressing table box, decorated with floral sprays and raised gilt scrolls, mark for Eugene Clauss, some wear, 19thC, 6¼in (16cm) diam.
£190–210 / €265–290
$310–350 SWO ➶

Miller's compares...

A. Pearlware basket, probably by Herculaneum, decorated with Net pattern, with reticulated sides, 1815–20, 8¼in (21cm) wide.
£85–95 / €120–140
$140–155 SWO ➶

B. Pair of Pearlware baskets, transfer-printed with Net pattern, with reticulated sides and twig handles, one basket damaged, 1800–25, 8in (20.5cm) wide.
£280–310 / €390–430
$460–510 TMA ➶

Although Item A is in perfect condition, the value of a pair can be four times that of a single piece. Item B, therefore, commands a much higher price, even though one of the baskets is damaged.

Locate the source

The source of each illustration in Miller's can be found by checking the code letters below each caption with the Key to Illustrations, pages 286–290.

Belleek Shamrock basket, small chips, impressed mark, 1865–89, 5in (12.5cm) wide. Although chips can be restored, the repair would be expensive and would not make this item more valuable.
£260–285 / €360–395
$430–465 S(O) 🔨

Basket checklist

Baskets are very prone to damage which will, of course, reduce the price. It is also worth noting that any regilding will greatly reduce value. When buying, check for the following:
• cracks across the rims
• chips to applied decoration, such as flowers
• cracks to the links of trelliswork
• damage to the handle
• wear to the interior and gilding

▶ **Derby porcelain basket,** with reticulated sides, painted with fruit and insects, damaged, c1765, 8in (20.5cm) diam.
£280–310 / €390–430
$460–510 WW 🔨

Caughley porcelain chestnut basket, cover and stand, transfer-printed with the Pine Cone Group pattern, the branch handles with applied flower and leaf terminals, basket repaired, minor chips, blue-printed mark, c1775, 11in (28cm) wide.
£575–630 / €800–880
$940–1,050 S(O) 🔨

◀ **Worcester porcelain basket,** with pierced trellis sides and a lobed rim, painted with flower sprays, mid-18thC, 7in (18cm) diam.
£480–530
€670–740
$780–870 AH 🔨

Belleek porcelain basket and cover, chips, impressed 'Belleek Co, Fermanagh', 1865–89, 6in (15cm) wide. The flowers and foliage on these baskets are susceptible to damage, but it is a question of degree – the fewer the chips, the higher the price.
£660–730 / €920–1,000
$1,100–1,200 S(O) 🔨

Pair of reticulated porcelain *corbeilles*, in the Paris style, with gilt decorator's mark of a windmill and initials 'D.R.', probably Dutch, 1800–25, 8½in (21.5cm) high.
£800–880 / €1,100–1,250
$1,300–1,450 NOA 🔨

Candlesticks

Pair of Clarice Cliff Bizarre candlesticks, decorated with Crocus pattern, transfer-printed factory mark, facsimile signature and 'Crocus' painted in green, 1930s, 3¼in (8.5cm) high.
£240–265 / €330–370
$390–440 PF ⚲

For more examples
of Candlesticks see Silver & Plate (pages 132–165)

◀ **Japanese-style porcelain and ormolu candle holder,** French, c1890, 7½in (19cm) high. This item would be popular with collectors of the Aesthetic Movement.
£280–310 / €390–430
$460–510 DAN ⊞

Popular figures

Items featuring shepherds and shepherdesses were very popular and made in large quantities. As a result, they have not changed in value for some time and appear to be becoming less fashionable.

The look without the price

Pair of Derby candlestick figures, on scrolling rococo bases, minor damage and restoration, 18thC, 9¾in (25cm) high.
£300–330 / €420–460
$490–540 B&L ⚲

If this pair of candlestick figures was in perfect condition it would be worth more than double this amount.

Pair of Derby porcelain candle brackets, in the form of a shepherd and shepherdess with a lamb and dog, backed by elaborate bocage, on rococo bases, c1770, 8¼in (21cm) high.
£410–450 / €570–630
$670–730 L&E ⚲

▶ **Bow candlestick group,** emblematic of Africa and Europe, modelled as women standing beneath a flowering tree, on a scroll-moulded base, some damage and restoration, c1762, 7½in (19cm) high. A perfect example of this candlestick group could fetch three times this value.
£450–500 / €630–700
$730–820 S(O) ⚲

Miller's compares...

A. Pair of Derby figural candlesticks, in the form of fruit sellers, c1770, 10in (25.5cm) high.
£450–500 / €630–700
$730–820 SWO ➤

B. Pair of Minton figural candlesticks, each holding flowers, on gilded, flower-encrusted scrolling bases, minor repairs, c1835, 9in (23cm) high.
£780–860 / €1,100–1,200
$1,270–1,400 WW ➤

Although Item B is 60 years later than Item A, the Minton examples are rarer and of much better quality.

Pair of Bow figural candlesticks, on pierced scrolling foliate bases, restored, candle nozzles damaged, c1770, 7¾in (19.5cm) high. Had these candlesticks been perfect they could have fetched up to £900 / €1,250 / $1,450.
£520–570 / €720–790
$850–930 B&L ➤

Sets/pairs

Unless otherwise stated, any description which refers to 'a set' or 'a pair' includes a guide price for the entire set or the pair, even though the illustration may show only a single item.

▶ **Pair of Meissen candlesticks,** decorated with panels of flowers on the front and reverse, crossed swords mark in blue on undersides, German, c1870, 5½in (14cm) high.
£720–790
€1,000–1,100
$1,200–1,300
DAV ⊞

Porcelain candlestick, in the form of an elephant, with a *famille rose* caparison set with a candlestick, Cantonese, 19thC, 7in (18cm) high.
£900–1,000 / €1,250–1,400
$1,450–1,650 L ➤

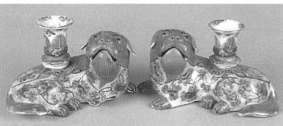

Pair of porcelain candlesticks, in the form of Buddhist lions, each with a *famille rose* jacket, 19thC, 6½in (16.5cm) wide.
£950–1,050 / €1,300–1,450
$1,550–1,700 L ➤

Find out more in

Miller's Collecting Pottery & Porcelain: The Facts At Your Fingertips, Miller's Publications, 2001

Cups, Mugs & Tea Bowls

Miller's compares...

A. Lustre tea cup and saucer, 1820–30, saucer
5½in (14cm) diam.
£25–27 / €35–40
$40–47 PSA ⊞

B. Staffordshire lustre tea cup and saucer,
c1830, saucer 5¾in (14.5cm) diam.
£70–80 / €95–110
$115–130 RdV ⊞

Item A is of inferior quality and of a simple design, whereas Item B is more finely painted
and with a typical naïve decoration. The fact that the makers of both items are unknown
has helped to keep both the values down.

◄ **Moore & Co cup and saucer,**
decorated with Polka pattern, c1840, cup
4in (10cm) diam. Although mid-19thC blue
printing is often poor quality, it is the fact
that this item is rather late that makes it
inexpensive. The best quality work was
produced around 1820, notably by Spode,
Wedgwood, Rogers and Clews.
£40–45 / €55–60
$65–75 CHAC ⊞

Flow blue mug, c1850,
2¾in (7cm) high.
£40–45 / €55–60
$65–75 CHAC ⊞

The look without the price

**Jasperware coffee
mug,** by John Dudson,
c1850, 2½in (6.5cm) high.
£45–50 / €60–70
$75–80 JAY ⊞

Jasperware from the 18th century can be very
expensive and pieces from the early 19th century
command good prices. Although this item is late
and from a less sought-after factory it is still an
attractive piece.

Grainger, Lee & Co, Worcester, Royal Flute coffee can, decorated with Pagoda pattern, c1815, 2¼in (5.5cm) high.
£45–50 / €60–70
$75–80 JAY ⊞

Tea bowl, decorated with quartered arms, a motto and a diaper border, cracked, Chinese, Qianlong period, c1790, 4½in (11.5cm) diam.
£55–60 / €70–85
$90–100 G(L) ⚒

Derby moulded tea bowl, c1790, 3¼in (8.5cm) diam.
£55–60 / €70–85
$90–100 JAY ⊞

New Hall Bute coffee can, c1812, 2½in (6.5cm) high.
£55–60 / €70–85
$90–100 JAY ⊞

Minton coffee can, c1810, 2½in (6.5cm) high.
£60–70 / €85–95
$100–115 JAY ⊞

Spode bat-printed coffee can, c1801, 2½in (6.5cm) high.
£60–70 / €85–95
$100–115 JAY ⊞

Barr Worcester coffee can, c1810,
2⅛in (6.5cm) high.
£60–70 / €85–95
$100–115 JAY ⊞

***Tek Sing* Cargo tea bowl and saucer,** Chinese, c1822, saucer
4½in (11.5cm) diam. The provenance of cargo pieces adds considerably
to the value. Without this provenance this item would only be
worth £20 / €25 / $30 at the most.
£70–80 / €95–110
$115–130 McP ⊞

Worcester tea bowl, decorated with Mansfield
pattern, c1770, 3¼in (8.5cm) diam.
£80–90 / €100–125
$130–150 JAY ⊞

**Staffordshire pink lustre
coffee can,** c1830,
2⅛in (6.5cm) high.
£85–95 / €120–130
$140–155 RdV ⊞

◄ **Chinese export
coffee cup,** with
a griffin head crest
and gilt shield-
shaped arms with
a later diaper
border, Qianlong
period, 1736–95. An
armorial can have a
huge effect on the
value of these items.
Many of those from
the late 17thC and
first 40 or so years
of the 18thC are
very desirable. This
cup is late (c1780)
and rather plain.
£90–100
€125–140
$150–165 G(L) ⚲

**Swansea porcelain cup
and saucer,** and a similar cup
with a London-shaped handle,
printed retailers marks, c1820,
cup 4in (10cm) diam.
£100–110 / €140–155
$165–180 WW ⚲

◄ **Worcester tea bowl,** decorated with Mother and Child pattern, c1780, 3¼in (8.5cm) diam.
£100–110
€ **140–155**
$165–180 JAY ⊞

Meissen chocolate cup and saucer, painted with moths, butterflies and insects and applied with roses, the cup with a wishbone handle, minor chips, underglaze blue cross swords mark with a dot to the cup, German, Academic period, 1763–74, saucer 5½in (14cm) diam.
£110–120 / € 155–165
$180–195 BR ⚲

Meissen marks

Almost every piece of Meissen is marked with the famous crossed swords.

- In the 18th century, each sword was painted in a straight line.
- During the Academic period (1763–74) a dot was painted between the sword hilts.
- During the Marcolini period (1774–1813) a star or asterisk was placed above the hilts.
- After that the swords were less neatly painted until the early 20th century, when they were gently curved and a pommel was placed at the tip of each hilt.
- From 1926–39 a dot was placed between the blades, and post-WWII pieces have thin, curved swords and no dot or pommels.

Some copied Meissen is difficult to distinguish from the real thing – the marks were fairly accurately copied in France. Recognition of the body of the piece, the way the glaze is finished – particularly on the reverse – and the quality of the painting will help to differentiate between real Meissen and a copy.

◄ **Porcelain tea bowl and saucer,** Chinese, c1785, saucer 5in (12.5cm) diam.
£115–125 / € 160–175
$190–205 DAN ⊞

◄ **Philip Christian & Co, Liverpool, tea bowl,** with floral decoration and 'crushed ice' border, c1770, 3¼in (9.5cm) diam.
£115–125
€ **160–175**
$190–210 JAY ⊞

Moustache cup and saucer, Continental, c1900, cup 3in (7.5cm) high.
£115–125 / € 160–175
$190–210 MLa ⊞

***Famille rose* lotus leaf tea bowl and saucer,** depicting a man herding a goat, the wavy rims decorated with gilt shell scrolls, each standing on a relief-moulded lotus stem, Chinese, Qianlong period, 1736–95, saucer 4½in (11.5cm) diam. If this item had been in perfect condition it could be worth £300 / € 420 / $490.
£120–130 / € 165–180
$195–210 G(L) 🪓

Chinese export coffee cup, with a goat crest and boar's-head arms, possibly French of Frenchlands or Lunsford of Sussex, with a Fitzhugh border, Qianlong period, c1770.
£130–145 / € 180–200
$210–240 G(L) 🪓

◀ **Derby Neptune mug,** with a scroll handle, red factory mark, early 19thC, 4in (10cm) high. This mug appears to have some staining which can be professionally removed, but this method does not always work. If this item had been in perfect condition it could have fetched £350 / € 490 / $570.
£130–145 / € 180–200
$210–240 WW 🪓

Wellington moustache cup and saucer, c1900, cup 3in (7.5cm) high.
£130–145 / € 180–200
$210–240 MLa ⊞

Chinese export coffee cup, decorated with the Wilson arms, Chinese, Qianlong period, c1765.
£130–145 / € 180–200
$210–240 G(L) 🪓

▶ **Chinese export coffee cup,** with the arms and motto, Qianlong period, c1760.
£140–155
€ 195–220
$230–250 G(L) 🪓

Vung Tau Cargo tea bowl, 1690–1700, 4½in (11.5cm) diam.
£145–160 / €200–220
$240–260 McP ⊞

Coffee cup, with a griffin head crest with
arms impaled, Qianlong period, c1760.
£140–155 / €195–220
$230–250 G(L) ↗

Six Spode cups and saucers, early 19thC, saucers
5in (12.5cm) diam.
£155–170 / €220–240
$250–280 SWO ↗

Westerwald tankard, chipped and cracked, with
moulded seal mark 'G.R.' between a relief-moulded
basket and a winged face mask, 18thC, 6¾in (17cm)
high. Had this tankard been undamaged it could have
achieved more than twice this amount.
£150–165 / €210–230
$250–270 SWO ↗

▶ **Chinese export *famille rose* coffee cup,** with
painted decoration of a European subject within a leafy
border, chips and damage to foot rim, Qianlong period,
1735–95.
£160–175 / €200–250
$260–290 G(L) ↗

Chamberlain's Worcester coffee can, c1810, 2¾in (7cm) high.
£160–175 / €200–250
$260–290 CoS ⊞

► **Chamberlain's Worcester mug,** with script mark beneath three feathers, 1800–50, 3½in (9cm) high.
£170–185
€240–260
$280–300 WW ⚒

Chamberlain's Worcester

Chamberlain's made many fine pieces of Regency porcelain, including the famous Nelson service which is worth many thousands of pounds. Generally, Chamberlain's is less sought-after than the Fight, Barr & Barr Worcester equivalent. The range of shapes and styles is very similar to their contemporaries at Coalport, Flight, Barr & Barr and, to some extent, Derby.

Belleek cup and saucer, First Period, 1863–90, 2½in (6.5cm) high. First Period Belleek is the most valuable of the nine periods of production.
£180–200 / €250–280
$300–330 MLa ⊞

► **Chinese export *famille rose* coffee cup,** decorated with the arms of Robinson, Bishop of Bristol and London or Robinson of Kentwell Hall, Suffolk, Qianlong period, c1765.
£190–210 / €270–290
$310–350 G(L) ⚒

◄ **Tea bowl and saucer,** decorated with a hunting scene, Chinese, Kangxi period, 1662–1722, saucer 3½in (9cm) diam. Scenes with figures and animals are generally worth more than landscapes. The hunting scene is a fairly good subject, but there are rarer and more valuable ones such as armorials, early commemoratives, European and erotic subjects.
£220–240 / €300–330
$360–390 McP ⊞

Worcester tea bowl and saucer, with blue underglaze, transfer-printed with Mother and Child pattern, hatched crescent mark, c1785, saucer 5in (12.5cm) diam.
£220–240 / €300–330
$360–390 McP ⊞

Derby coffee can, decorated in the Imari palette, c1825, 2¾in (7cm) high.
£220–250 / €310–340
$370–400 CoS ⊞

◀ *Famille rose* **tea bowl and saucer,** decorated with peonies and chrysanthemums, minor damage, Chinese, Qianlong period, 1736–95, saucer 5in (12.5cm) diam.
£230–250 / €320–350
$380–410 G&G ⊞

18th century Chinese palettes

Famille verte was popular in the Kangxi period (1662–1722) and is more sought-after than *famille rose*, which was popular from c1720 onwards. Both are generally more collectable than Chinese Imari, but there will be exceptions depending on the subject matter, date, shape, provenance or rarity of the item.

Worcester *famille verte* coffee cup, painter's mark in red, haircrack and chips, c1753. In perfect condition this item could fetch five times this amount.
£250–280 / €350–390
$410–450 S(O) ⚒

◀ **New Hall trio,** c1820, saucer 6in (15cm) diam.
£260–290
€360–380
$430–470 CoS ⊞

Tea bowl and saucer, Chinese, Kangxi period, 1662–1722, bowl 3in (7.5cm) high. The pattern on this tea bowl and saucer is a common one. A rarer pattern could multiply the price many times over.
£270–300 / €380–420
$440–490 G&G ⊞

Famille rose **cup,** painted with a boy with chickens among enamelled open rockwork and flowers, a poem to one side, Chinese, Qianlong seal mark, 19thC, 3in (7.5cm) high.
£320–350 / €450–490
$520–570 G(L) ✒

Blanc-de-chine

Blanc-de-chine is the ivory-white porcelain from the Dehua kilns in Fujian Province, and not the white undecorated porcelain from the rest of China.

▶ *Blanc-de-chine* **libation cup,** moulded with deer, cranes and a mythical fish beast, on a carved wooden stand, Chinese, 17thC, 3¼in (8.5cm) high.
£320–350
€450–490
$520–570 G&G ⊞

Derby coffee can, 1810–20, 2½in (6.5cm) high.
£330–370 / €460–520
$540–610 CoS ⊞

◀ *Famille rose* **cup and saucer,** depicting a young boy speaking to a girl at a window, the saucer with the pair watching Mandarin ducks, Chinese, Qianlong period, 1736–95, saucer 4½in (11.5cm) diam.
£340–380
€470–530
$560–620 G(L) ✒

Paris porcelain cabinet cup and saucer, by the studio of Le Petit Carousel, with *grisaille* decoration depicting children holding a rooster, the saucer with a seated maiden, restoration to handle, red printed marks, 1775–1800, cup 4in (10cm) high.
£360–400 / €500–560
$590–650 NOA ⊞

Tea bowl and saucer, Chinese, Kangxi period, 1662–1722, saucer 5¼in (13.5cm) diam.
£360–400 / €500–560
$590–650 G&G ⊞

Chinese export coffee cup, painted with nude female bathers on a *bianco-sopra-bianco* ground, Chinese, Qianlong period, 1736–95.
£360–400 / €500–560
$590–650 G(L) ⚒

Pair of Staffordshire porcelain loving cups, printed and enamelled with the Farmers Arms, the reverse with a pointer and dead partridge in a landscape, the pointer's collar marked 'T. Lowe', c1870, 5in (12.5cm) high.
£360–400 / €500–560
$590–650 WL ⚒

Porcelain mug, possibly New Hall, painted with goats and sheep and monogrammed in gilt above a sailing ship, handle missing, c1800, 3¼in (8.5cm) high.
£380–420 / €530–590
$620–690 WW ⚒

◀ **Worcester Scratch Cross-type coffee cup,** with a grooved strap handle, enamel-painted with Staghunt pattern, a border of *ruyi* heads below interior rim, chipped, incised cross on base, 1754–55, 2½in (6.5cm) high.
£400–440
€560–610
$650–720 B ⚒

Meissen custard cup, with a hand-painted floral design, German, c1780, 3½in (9cm) high.
£400–440 / €560–610
$650–720 US ⊞

Worcester fluted coffee cup, with a moulded scroll handle, painted with flowering branches beneath a scrolling leafy border, rim chips, c1753, 2in (5cm) high.
£450–500 / €630–700
$730–820 WW 🔨

Worcester tea bowl and saucer, decorated with Waiting Chinaman pattern, crescent marks, c1770, saucer 4¼in (10.5cm) diam.
£450–500 / €630–700
$730–820 B 🔨

Pair of porcelain tea bowls and saucers, possibly Liverpool, 18thC.
£460–510 / €640–710
$750–830 AH 🔨

Worcester coffee cup, cup and saucer, decorated with flower sprigs and gilt monogram 'GW', minor rubbing, crescent marks, c1780.
£540–600 / €750–840
$880–980 B 🔨

◀ **Derby coffee cup,** painted in the Trembley Rose style, with a wishbone handle, 1756–58, 2½in (6.5cm) high.
£620–680 / €860–950
$1,000–1,300 S(O) 🔨

▶ **Spode bute-shaped porcelain cup and saucer,** pattern No. 2478, painted with floral bouquets against wrythen gilding, painted mark, c1815.
£650–720 / €910–1,100
$1,050–1,200 G(L) 🔨

Dishes & Bowls

Copeland bowl, transfer-printed with Blue Italian pattern, c1885, 9½in (24cm) diam.
£23–25 / €32–35
$35–40 CHAC ⊞

Bowl, damaged, Chinese, 1675–1725, 5¾in (14.5cm) diam.
£25–28 / €35–40
$40–48 McP ⊞

Dish, decorated with Old Abbey pattern, c1880, 7¼in (18.5cm) wide.
£25–28 / €35–40
$40–48 CHAC ⊞

Miller's compares...

A. Pearlware pickle dish, modelled as a leaf, the interior moulded with leaf veins, small chip, late 19thC, 5½in (15cm) wide.
£25–28 / €35–40
$40–48 PFK ⚲

B. Lowestoft pickle dish, modelled as a vine leaf, late 18thC, 4in (10cm) wide.
£360–400 / €500–560
$590–650 MCC ⊞

Item A is pottery, whereas Item B is porcelain. Both this, and the fact that Item B is made by Lowestoft and is older, have resulted in its greater value. Pieces made by Lowestoft can be double or even quadruple the value of similar examples by Worcester or Caughley. Lowestoft is a popular collecting area, and some damage to an item can be acceptable.

◀ **Platter,** transfer-printed with Willow pattern, c1850, 12½in (32cm) wide. Willow pattern is a common design, making it affordable and easy to collect.
£40–45 / €55–60
$65–75 CHAC ⊞

Bowl, from the *Tek Sing* cargo, Chinese, c1822, 4½in (11.5cm) diam.
£40–45 / €55–60
$65–75 McP ⊞

Longchamps comport, 1900, 6in (15cm) high. Comports are not widely collected as they are difficult to display, which helps to keep prices low.
£40–45 / €55–60
$65–75 MLL ⊞

Doulton berry dish, transfer-printed in flow blue with Watteau pattern, c1898, 5in (12.5cm) diam.
£40–45 / €55–60
$65–75 CoCo ⊞

Victorian Copeland bowl, decorated with Wild Rose pattern, 13½in (34.5cm) diam. This bowl was originally part of a toilet set.
£45–50 / €60–70
$75–80 WiB ⊞

Bowl, from the *Hoi An* cargo, Vietnamese, 1450–1500, 3¼in (8.5cm) diam. Salvaged cargo ware is not usually damaged except for the glaze, which has often been corroded by the salt water. Enamelled wares, especially from the Nanking cargo (1751), are often very badly affected by the sea.
£60–65 / €85–90
$100–105 MCP ⊞

Qingbai dish, the centre incised with a stylized flowerhead, Chinese, late Song Dynasty, 960–1279, 6in (15cm) diam. Many pieces of early Chinese pottery and stoneware have appeared on the market in the last 15 years or so and many are modern fakes. These genuine items can be bought very inexpensively – high quality pieces being the exception.
£60–65 / €85–90
$100–105 L ⚒

Spongeware bowl, Irish, c1880, 6in (15cm) diam.
£70–80 / €95–110
$115–130 Byl ⊞

Porcelain comport, with incorporated side handles, painted with flowers, 19thC, 13in (33cm) diam.
£70–80 / €95–110
$115–130 B(W) ⚒

Yorkshire Pottery vegetable tureen, decorated with Albion pattern, c1840, 11in (28cm) wide.
£70–80 / €95–110
$115–130 CoCo ⊞

Patterson & Co footed sugar bowl, decorated with Bacchanalian Cherubs pattern, with lion mask handles, rim restored, cover missing, c1837, 8½in (21.5cm) high. In perfect condition this item could be worth twice this amount.
£75–80 / €105–110
$120–130 SWO ⚒

Platter, transfer-printed with Fisherman and Castle pattern, c1810, 10in (25.5cm) wide. If this platter were by a named maker it could improve the price to £120–140 / €165–195 / $195–230.
£80–90 / €110–125
$130–150 SWO ⚒

Two ironstone bowls, with relief-moulded designs, one by St John's Stone Chinaware Co, cracked, Canadian, Quebec, printed maker's mark, 1873–96, 8¼in (21cm) diam. These items were sold in Canada and achieved a higher price than their English equivalents would have fetched in the UK.
£90–100 / €125–140
$150–165 RIT ⚒

▶ **Spongeware dish,** 19thC, 8in (20.5cm) diam.
£90–100
€125–140
$150–165 MFB ⊞

Brown, Westhead Moore & Co meat plate, decorated with Morocco pattern, 1885, 21¾in (55.5cm) wide.
£95–105 / € 130–150
$155–170 SWO ⚒

► **Platter,** decorated with Roger's Camel pattern, with reticulated border, impressed mark, c1810, 10in (25.5cm) wide.
£100–110
€ 140–155
$165–180 SWO ⚒

Spongeware bowl and mug, Irish, c1880, bowl 6in (15cm) diam. The fact that these items are identifiably Irish has increased their value.
£115–130 / € 160–180
$190–210 Byl ⊞

◄ **Fruit bowl,** decorated in flow blue with views of Naples, c1830, 10in (25.5cm) diam.
£110–120
€ 155–165
$180–195 CoCo ⊞

Majolica bread tray, c1880, 11¾in (30cm) wide.
£120–135 / € 165–190
$195–220 CHAC ⊞

Meissen covered bowl, decorated with Onion pattern, German, c1890, 3in (7.5cm) diam. The Meissen Onion pattern has been copied by dozens of other makers since the 1720s and is still used today, although Meissen examples are the most prized.
£120–135 / € 165–190
$195–220 MAA ⊞

► **Majolica game pie dish,** with liner and cover, dish and liner cracked, 19thC, 10in (25.5cm) wide. The fact that this is a common shape and mostly brown in colour has made this game pie dish affordable.
£130–145
€ 180–200
$210–230 G(L) ⚒

◄ **Platter,** transfer-printed with Wild Rose pattern, 1820–30, 15¾in (40cm) wide.
£130–145 / €180–200
$210–230 CHAC ⊞

Miller's compares...

A. Bowl, from the *Hoi An* cargo, Vietnamese, 1450–1500, 9in (23cm) diam.
£145–160 / €200–220
$240–260 McP ⊞

B. Bowl, from the *Hoi An* cargo, Vietnamese, 1450–1500, 9½in (24cm) diam.
£560–620 / €780–860
$910–1,000 McP ⊞

The cobalt blue of Item A has faded and the rim appears worn. Item B has a clearer and more interesting pattern and is in perfect condition, and is therefore of higher value.

The look without the price

Tureen, painted with riverscapes, with two hare-head handles, crack to base, rim chip, cover and stand missing, Chinese, Qianlong period, 1736–95, 12½in (32cm) high.
£145–160 / €200–220
$240–260 G(L) ✎

With the original cover and in perfect condition this tureen would be worth between £500–800 / €700–1,100 / $820–1,300.

◄ **Minton footed bowl,** decorated with Chinese Marine pattern, printed mark to base, hairline crack, c1830, 10½in (26.5cm) wide.
£150–165 / €210–230
$250–270 SWO ✎

Herculaneum dish, decorated with View of the Fort Madura pattern, c1815, 9in (23cm) wide.
£150–165 / €210–230
$250–270 SWO

Meat dish, decorated with an Oriental pattern, 19thC, 20½in (52cm) wide.
£150–165 / €210–230
$245–270 DA

Spongeware pottery soup bowl, 19thC, 10in (25.5cm) diam.
£155–170 / €220–240
$250–280 MFB

The look without the price

Chamberlain's Worcester dessert dish, the inset panel painted with 'Ludlow Castle, Worcestershire', the rim gilded with foliage, script mark in red enamel, rim riveted, 1813–40, 8in (20.5cm) wide.
£160–175 / €220–240
$260–280 G(L)

If this dish were in perfect condition it would be worth four times this amount. However, it is still an attractive piece and very affordable at the price.

Pair of Riley pickle dishes, transfer-printed with Eastern Street Scene pattern, some staining, 19thC, 8¼in (21cm) wide. The staining could be partially removed professionally. In perfect condition, these dishes would be worth £300 / €420 / $490.
£190–210 / €270–290
$310–350 SWO

Royal Worcester rose bowl, shape No. H166, hand-painted, with a pierced rim, on a quatrefoil embossed foot, dated 1912, 5in (12.5cm) high. There are many collectors of Royal Worcester and prices have remained strong for some time. It is the signed pieces and those decorated by the top artists such as George Owen, Charles Baldwyn and John Stinton that command the highest prices.
£200–220 / €280–310
$330–370 B(W)

◄ **Porcelain bowl,** Chinese, Qianlong period, late 18thC, 8in (20.5cm) diam.
£200–220
€280–310
$330–370 SWO

Sauce tureen, cover and stand, transfer-printed with figures fishing from a bridge, the cover with a lion finial, cover chipped, c1820, 7in (18cm) wide. The attractive lion finial adds to the value of this piece – a plainer, scroll finial would have reduced it to £150 / €210 / $240.
£210–230 / €290–320
$350–380 SWO 🔨

Imari bowl, the fluted sides painted with fan-shaped reserves of gardens alternating with three rosettes, Japanese, early 20thC, 12½in (32cm) diam.
£260–290 / €360–400
$430–470 CGC 🔨

Meat platter, decorated with Beehive pattern, c1820, 17in (43cm) wide.
£280–310 / €390–430
$460–510 MCC 🎫

▶ **Meissen dish,** chip to rim, crossed swords mark in underglaze blue, impressed '30', c1765, 10in (25.5cm) wide.
£280–310 / €390–430
$460–510 S(O) 🔨

Derby bone china sauce tureen and cover, painted with four panels of fruit, the ground gilded with palmettes, harebells and leaf scrolls, on claw feet, handles repaired, red mark, 1815, 7¼in (18.5cm) wide. Without the damage, this tureen could have been worth £450 / €630 / $730.
£220–240 / €310–330
$370–390 G(L) 🔨

Sunderland lustre footed bowl, the interior and exterior transfer-printed and enamelled with titled scenes including 'A West View of the Cast Iron Bridge over the River Wear' and 'A Sailor's Farewell', early 19thC, 8¾in (22cm) diam.
£260–290 / €360–400
$430–470 RTo 🔨

◄ **Goodwins & Harris pearlware platter,** transfer-printed with a View of Eton Chapel from the Metropolitan Scenery series, c1830–35, 10in (25.5cm) wide.
£310–340
€**430–470**
$510–560 DSA ⊞

Arita armorial bowl and cover, painted with dragons, clouds and Buddhist objects, the interior with two medallions containing a European coat-of-arms, marked, Japanese, 18thC, 6½in (16.5cm) diam. Japanese 18thC armorial ware is far less common than Chinese. The fact that they are armorial adds significantly to the value.
£310–340 / €**430–470**
$510–560 S(O) ⚹

Celadon bowl, with impressed designs, on a high foot, Chinese, Ming Dynasty, 1450–1500, 7in (18cm) diam. Early Chinese celadon items often range in colour, but the green glaze is more desirable. The value also depends on the crispness of the decoration and the quality of the potting.
£320–350 / €**450–490**
$520–570 S(O) ⚹

Belleek sweetmeat dish, modelled as a scallop shell surmounted by a dragon, on a shell base, chipped, black printed mark, c1900, 7in (18cm) high.
£320–350 / €**450–490**
$520–570 G(L) ⚹

Belleek marks

• First Period	1863–90
• Second Period	1891–1926
• Third Period	1926–46
• Fourth Period	1946–55
• Fifth Period	1955–65
• Sixth Period	1965–80
• Seventh Period	1980–92
• Eighth Period	1993–97
• Ninth Period	from 1997

Pair of Turner platters, transfer-printed with Elephant pattern, c1794, 14in (35.5cm) wide.
£330–360 / €**460–500**
$540–590 DAN ⊞

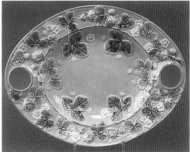

Victorian George Jones majolica strawberry dish, hairline crack and repair to the rim, impressed registration mark and painted '3217,40' to base, 14½in (36.5cm) wide.
Majolica often has damage and small amounts will only reduce the price by a small degree.
£340–380 / €**470–530**
$560–620 RTo ⚹

Kraak porselein **bowl,** painted with panels of deer beneath a barbed rim, the interior with a deer medallion surrounded by flower panels, Chinese, Wanli period, 1573–1619, 5½in (14cm) diam.
£430–470 / €600–650
$700–770 S(O) ⚒

Wood & Sons earthenware covered vegetable dish, transfer-printed with Verona pattern, 1892–1912, 8½in (21.5cm) wide.
£460–510 / €640–710
$750–830 NOA ⚒

Henan bowl, the black glaze with brown streaks on a buff pottery body, Chinese, Song Dynasty, 960–1279, 6in (15cm) diam. Henan stoneware is typically black and brown, though not always striped.
£470–520 / €650–720
$770–850 S(O) ⚒

Tazza, decorated with reserved floral and diaper panels, on a stem foot, rim crack, Chinese, Kangxi period, 1662–1722, 6¾in (17cm) diam.
£500–550 / €700–770
$820–900 G(L) ⚒

◄ **Salt-glazed stoneware punch bowl,** decorated in scratch blue, restored, c1760, 13⅜in (35cm) diam. Had this punch bowl been in perfect condition the price would have been three times this amount.
£530–590 / €740–820
$870–960 S(O) ⚒

Imari bowl, decorated with chrysanthemums, peonies and branches of cherry blossoms, the inner central roundel decorated with flying phoenixes beside a rock and foliage near a lake, Japanese, c1720, 7¼in (18.5cm) diam.
£540–600 / €750–840
$880–980 G&G ⊞

▶ **Chinese export basin,** decorated with buildings and a waterscape beneath mountains, with plug hole and stand, cracked and stapled, c1800, 26¾in (68cm) diam. Although this basin is badly damaged it made a good price, proving that it is still an attractive item.
£560–620 / €780–860
$910–1,000 B(W) ⚒

Bowl, decorated with squirrels among grapes, the sides with an everted rim, apocryphal Kangxi mark, 19thC, 8¾in (22cm) diam.
£590–650 / €820–910
$960–1,050 S(O) ✎

◀ **Chinese export tureen and cover,** decorated in the *famille rose* palette, with rabbit-head handles, 1790, 12in (30.5cm) wide.
£600–660
€840–920
$980–1,100 IM ✎

The look without the price

Famille rose **punch bowl,** Chinese, Canton, late 19thC, 11½in (29cm) diam.
£700–770 / €980–1,070
$1,140–1,260 S(O) ✎

These punch bowls were also made in very large sizes which can make six or eight times this price.

Meissen *ecuelle*, cover and stand, probably outside-decorated, with applied flowers and fruit and painted insects, some damage and repair, crossed swords in underglaze blue, 1850–1900, 9in (23cm) wide. Outside-decorated Meissen (except the early Hausmalerei wares) makes much less than the factory-decorated wares.
£600–660 / €840–920
$980–1,100 S ✎

Glazed bowl, Chinese, Liao Dynasty, 907–1125, 8in (20.5cm) diam.
£720–790 / €1,000–1,100
$1,200–1,300 GLD ⊞

Rogers meat platter, transfer-printed with the Boston State House pattern, made for the American market, impressed 'Rogers' and '18' to base, 19thC, 18¾in (47.5cm) wide.
£920–1,000 / €1,300–1,400
$1,500–1,650 TMA ✎

Figures

Smoking monkey match striker, gilt rubbed, late 19thC, 3½in (9cm) high. This was originally an inexpensive German ornament costing only a few pennies. Good quality examples are well worth collecting today.
£50–55 / €70–75
$80–90 JOA ⊞

Pair of Staffordshire models of greyhounds, damaged, 19thC, smallest 6½in (16.5cm) high. The greyhound was a common subject for models. Examples featuring more unusual animals can fetch thousands of pounds.
£80–90 / €125–140
$150–165 BWL ✦

Pair of Staffordshire pottery figures, of a fisherman and fisherwoman, each holding baskets with catch, 19thC, 13in (33cm) high.
£110–120 / €155–165
$180–195 G(L) ✦

Find out more in

Miller's Staffordshire Figures of the 19th & 20th Centuries: A Collectors Guide, Miller's Publications, 2000

Miller's compares...

◄ **A. Pair of Staffordshire models of spaniels,** with copper lustre spots, late 19thC, 9¼in (23.5cm) high.
£90–100
€125–140
$150–165
SWO ✦

► **B. Pair of Staffordshire earthenware comforter spaniels,** painted in rust enamel, 19thC, 12½in (32cm) high.
£300–330
€420–460
$490–540
G(L) ✦

Staffordshire spaniels are almost always hand-painted, but those in Item A are late and a common shape. Earlier examples, such as those of Item B with black or red brushed patches, tend to command higher prices.

Staffordshire 'Comforter' dogs

These usually resembled a spaniel, and show little variation of pose or facial expression. They were made in earthenware in five standard sizes from 18in (45.5cm) to 6in (15cm) high, although the most popular was 9in (23cm) high, and served as door porters, summer fireplace ornaments and chimney-piece ornaments. Decoration was invariably a white glaze with coloured ears and about six spots – red being the favourite and gold the least popular. They were also produced with black, brown, green grey or copper lustre ears and spots. The eyes were pencilled to resemble human eyes and they also have a small gold padlock hanging from the collar, and a gold chain falling across the chest and disappearing over the back.

Pair of Staffordshire copper lustre models of dogs, c1870, 8in (20.5cm) high.
£115–125 / €160–175
$190–210 CHAC ⊞

Tilemaker's figure of a guardian, standing on cloud scrolls, mounted as a lamp, base damaged, Chinese, Ming Dynasty, 1368–1644, 14in (35.5cm) high. This item is damaged and has been converted to a lamp, which has detracted from its value. Care should also be taken to avoid later copies. Had this figure been undamaged it could have fetched three times as much.
£115–125 / €160–175
$190–210 CHAC ⊞

◄ Staffordshire figural group, of the Princess Royal and Prince of Wales, overseen by the Angel Gabriel, c1850, 14¼in (36cm) high.
£120–130
€165–180
$195–210 BR ⚘

Pair of porcelain models of tabby cats, with gilded collars, German, late 19thC, 4in (10cm) high. Models of cats, particularly in pairs, are very popular with collectors.
£140–155 / €195–210
$230–250 PF ⚘

◀ **Porcelain planter,** encrusted with flowers and supported by three cherubs, damaged, late 19thC, 6¼in (16cm) high.
£150–165
€210–230
$250–270 SWO ⚹

Pair of Victorian models of spaniels, with painted features, collars and chains, one damaged, 10¼in (26cm) high.
£150–165 / €210–230
$250–270 PF ⚹

Pair of Staffordshire figures, entitled 'War' and 'Peace', c1850.
£220–240 / €310–330
$370–390 BR ⚹

Majolica vase, modelled as a duck, Austrian, c1880, 10in (25.5cm) wide.
£270–300 / €380–420
$440–490 MLL ⊞

Locate the source

The source of each illustration in Miller's can be found by checking the code letters below each caption with the Key to Illustrations, pages 286–290.

Meissen porcelain figure, of a female bassoon player, on a scrolling base, crossed swords mark, impressed and incised '2981', some damage, 19thC, 5½in (14cm) high.
£280–310 / €390–430
$460–510 SWO ⚹

◀ **Derby biscuit figural group,** entitled 'Two Virgins Awakening Cupid', some damage and repair, incised No. 195, c1790, 12in (30.5cm) high. This is a very low price for such a piece, indicating that the damage may be quite extensive.
£280–310
€390–430
$460–510 S(O) ✣

Pair of Staffordshire figures riding goats, on gilt-lined bases, 19thC, 12½in (32cm) high. This is a fairly unusual design, but the colours are not good. Had they been better coloured they could have fetched twice the price.
£280–310 / €390–430
$460–510 B(W) ✣

Pair of Victorian Staffordshire spill holder groups, modelled as a cow and calf standing before tree stumps, on moulded bases, horns damaged, 11¼in (28.5cm) high.
£300–330 / €420–460
$490–540 PF ✣

Sets/pairs

Unless otherwise stated, any description which refers to 'a set' or 'a pair' includes a guide price for the entire set or the pair, even though the illustration may show only a single item.

Pottery model of a recumbent lion, slight damage, possibly Scottish, c1780, 3in (7.5cm) wide.
£320–350 / €450–490
$520–570 G&G ⊞

TOP BANANA ANTIQUES MALL

Call on us.....

Because we're worth it!

1 New Church Street, Tetbury
Glos GL8 4DS
Tel: 0871 288 1102
Fax: 0871 288 1103
info@topbananaantiques.com
www.topbananaantiques.com

The look without the price

Pair of Meissen-style figural salts, modelled as a seated man and woman, on bases, restored, blue crossed swords mark, 19thC, 6in (15cm) high.
£320–350 / €450–490
$520–570 SWO ✗

If this pair of figural salts had been by Meissen they would be worth three times as much.

Pair of Derby bocage groups, modelled as a shepherd and a shepherdess, both on scrolling bases, some losses and damage, c1780, 9¼in (23.5cm) high. Chips to bocage are not too serious, but reglued heads, arms or legs can make a large difference to value.
£320–350 / €450–490
$520–570 B(W) ✗

▶ **Figure,** from the *Hoi An* cargo, Vietnamese, 1450–1500, 3½in (9cm) high.
£340–370 / €470–520
$560–610 McP ⊞

Model of an animal, from the *Hoi An* cargo, Vietnamese, 1450–1500, 2in (5cm) high.
£330–360 / €460–500
$540–590 McP ⊞

▶ **Pair of Staffordshire flatback figures,** modelled as the American evangelists Sankey and Moody, c1870, 17½in (44.5cm) high. These figures would be of particular interest to American collectors.
£340–370 / €470–520
$560–610 EH ✗

Royal Worcester figure of a Japanese gentleman, modelled by James Hadley, restored, impressed and puce marks, dated 1875, 16in (40.5cm) high. Royal Worcester figures are popular with collectors particularly those by Hadley models.
£340–370 / €470–520
$560–610 B(Kn) ✗

Pair of Staffordshire spill vase groups, of James Kent type, modelled as cows and suckling calves, on bases, c1900, 11in (28cm) high.
£340–370 / €470–520
$560–610 BR ✗

Pair of Derby smear-glazed biscuit figures, modelled as a shepherd and a shepherdess playing flutes, the bases with incised crown and crossed baton marks and numerals '369', one flute missing, late 18thC, 10in (25.5cm) high. Derby biscuit figures are usually marked, therefore unmarked examples are less valuable.
**£380–420 / €530–590
$620–690 TMA** ➹

Staffordshire pottery model of a girl riding a dog, slight losses, c1860, 8¾in (22cm) high.
**£380–420 / €530–590
$620–690 B(W)** ➹

Derby figural group, modelled as a nymph asleep among flowers, chipped, c1845, 6¾in (17cm) high.
**£400–440 / €560–610
$650–720 S(O)** ➹

Staffordshire pearlware model of a recumbent dog, chip to base, some restoration, early 19thC, 6in (15cm) wide.
**£480–530 / €670–740
$780–870 S** ➹

Staffordshire pearlware figure of an Archer, c1825, 8½in (21.5cm) high. The lady toxopholist is a common figure. This example is more expensive than most because the bocage has survived without damage.
**£450–500 / €630–700
$730–820 JRe** ⊞

Pottery model of a camel, Tang Dynasty, 618–907, 12½in (32cm) high. Most pottery animals such as this have been repaired, and there are many fakes.
**£470–520 / €650–720
$770–850 S(O)** ➹

► **Meissen porcelain figure,** modelled as a young lady spoon-feeding her lap dog, on a scrolling base, crossed swords mark, incised 'B94', late 19thC, 4¾in (12cm) high.
**£500–550 / €700–770
$820–900 SWO** ➹

Pair of Royal Dux porcelain figures, of a youth playing a mandolin and his female companion holding a basket of flowers, on rustic bases, pink triangle mark, c1900, 16½in (42cm) high.
**£500–550 / €700–770
$820–900 AH** ➹

Miller's compares...

A. Pair of Meissen-style porcelain sweetmeat figures, both with painted floral sprigs to the interior, on scroll bases, slight damage, blue crossed swords mark, incised and impressed numbers, late 19thC, 6¾in (17cm) high.
£540–600 / €750–840 $880–980 B(W) 🔨

B. Pair of Meissen porcelain sweetmeat figures, some damage and restoration, crossed swords mark in underglaze blue, incised and impressed numerals, late 19thC, 11in (28cm) wide.
£760–840 / €1,050–1,150 $1,250–1,350 S(O) 🔨

The sweetmeat figures in Item A are smaller than those of Item B and are copied in the style of Meissen. Those in Item B are clearly made by Meissen, and this provenance accounts for the price difference of over £200 / €280 / $330.

Pair of Belleek figures, modelled as Belgian Hawkers, both staves missing, impressed and black printed marks, First Period, 1863–90, 6¾in (17cm) high. Although the damage to this piece is fairly minor, it has probably made a difference of £200–300 / €280–420 / $330–490 to the price.
£600–660 / €840–920 $980–1,100 S(O) 🔨

Royal Dux porcelain group, modelled as a donkey and her foal, on a rustic base, pink triangle mark, c1900, 13in (33cm) wide.
£620–680 / €860–950 $1,000–1,100 AH 🔨

Wood-style figure of St George killing the dragon, on a plinth with a cartouche inscribed 'George & Dragon', damaged, early 19thC, 13¼in (33.5cm) high. Without damage this figure could have achieved £1,000–1,200 / €1,400–1,700 / $1,650–2,000.
£750–835 / €1,050–1,150 $1,200–1,350 SWO 🔨

Flatware

◄ **Blue and white plate,** cracked, Chinese, 1720–40, 9in (23cm) diam.
This plate would be worth three times as much if it were in perfect condition.
£25–28 / €35–38
$40–45 McP ⊞

Celadon plate, Chinese, 1800–50, 11in (28cm) diam.
£25–28 / €35–38
$40–45 McP ⊞

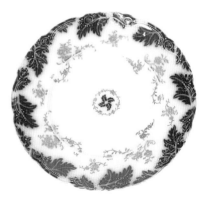

Copeland plate, transfer-printed with Blue Italian pattern, c1880, 10¾in (27.5cm) diam.
£26–29 / €35–40
$40–50 CHAC ⊞

Grindley plate, decorated in flow blue with Brazil pattern, c1900, 9¾in (25cm) diam.
£32–35 / €45–48
$55–60 CHAC ⊞

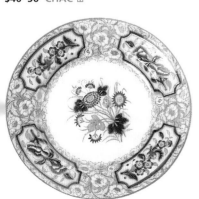

◄ **Birmingham plate,** decorated in flow blue, c1850, 10¼in (26cm) diam.
£35–40 / €48–55
$60–65 CHAC ⊞

► **Copeland soup plate,** decorated in flow blue, 1847–67, 10¼in (26cm) diam.
£35–40 / €48–55
$60–65 CHAC ⊞

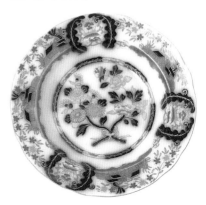

Plate, decorated in flow blue, c1845, 9½in (24cm) diam.
£40–45 / €55–60
$65–75 CHAC ⊞

Minton plate, decorated with Pinwheel pattern, c1820, 8¼in (21cm) diam.
£45–50 / €60–70
$75–80 SCO ⊞

◄ **Majolica plate,** decorated with a figure of Joan of Arc, inscribed 'Gloire Honneur, Liberté Patrie', French, 19thC, 8in (20.5cm) diam.
£45–50 / €60–70
$75–80 BWL ⚘

Ridgway stone china dinner plate, c1820, 9½in (24cm) diam.
£45–50 / €60–70
$75–80 SCO ⊞

Davenport warming plate, decorated with Rhinish Views pattern, 1825–35, 11in (28cm) diam.
£50–55 / €70–75
$80–90 MCC ⊞

Riley plate, decorated with Eastern Street Scene pattern, 1819–25, 10¼in (26cm) diam.
£55–60 / €75–85
$90–100 CHAC ⊞

Royal Worcester pottery wall dish, painted with a parakeet on a bough, impressed mark crown over 'Worcester', c1870, 12¼in (31cm) diam.
£55–60 / €75–85
$90–100 PFK ♣

Belleek plate, decorated with Limpet pattern, Second Period 1891–1926, 6in (15cm) diam.
£60–65 / €85–90
$100–105 MLa ⊞

Plate, Chinese, 18thC, 11in (28cm) diam.
£65–70 / €90–95
$105–115 McP ⊞

► **Pair of Hicks & Meigh stone china soup plates,** pattern No. 9, printed marks, c1815, 9½in (24cm) diam.
£65–70 / €90–95
$105–115 SWO ♣

NEW 3 STOREY EXTENSION AND STYLISH CAFE *Now Open*

WELCOME TO HEANOR ANTIQUES CENTRE ENTRANCE

'No Centre packs in more Dealers and gives more choice than Heanor!'

NOW 200 INDEPENDENT DEALERS
'Trade prices in a smart, warm, Dealer friendly centre'

* Over 115 - 6ft frontage units
* 150 Museum style Cabinets
* 15000 sq ft over 4 floors
* 2500 sq ft of glass shelving!
* 25 datelined Cabinets

Stylised new £60,000 cafe now serving home made steak Pie and a range of traditional food for under £4.00

Tour Organisers - contact Jane for extended opening times and other special arrangements.

Open 7 Days A week 10.30 - 4.30pm including Bank Holidays
1-3 Ilkeston Rd, Heanor, Derbyshire. Tel (01773) 531181 / 762783 Fax 01773 762759
www.heanorantiquescentre.co.uk E-mail sales@heanorantiquescentre.co.uk

H at - M1 J26 past I.K.E.A. or West Midlands Via A38

◀ **British Anchor Pottery plate,** commemorating Washington crossing the Delaware, 25th December 1776, 19thC, 10in (25.5cm) diam.
£65–70 / €90–95
$105–115 CoCo ⊞

Three Wedgwood soup plates, transfer-printed with Baskets and Flowers pattern, impressed marks, c1820, 9¾in (25cm) diam.
£65–70 / €90–95
$105–115 SWO ↗

Miller's compares...

A. Spongeware pottery bowl, c1880, 10in (25.5cm) diam.
£70–80 / €95–110
$115–130 MFB ⊞

B. Spongeware pottery bowl, 19thC, 10in (25.5cm) diam.
£150–170 / €210–240
$250–280 MFB ⊞

Item B is painted in a much stronger palette, which is more desirable than that of Item A, making it twice the value.

Plate, depicting Guys Cliff, Warwickshire, hairline crack, c1820, 9½in (24cm) diam. This plate, in perfect condition, would be worth twice this amount.
£70–75 / €95–105
$115–120 GRe ⊞

Five lustre saucers, each transfer-printed with scenes, two with cows before a house, one commemorating Princess Charlotte, one with a mother and daughter, and one with Welsh women, star crack to one base, 19thC, largest 5½in (14cm) diam.
£80–90 / €110–125
$130–50 SWO ↗

Minton plate, printed with Thatched Barn pattern from the Monk's Rock series, minor rim chips, c1800, 7¼in (18cm) diam.
**£80–90 / €110–125
$130–150 SWO** ✦

Pountney & Allies plate, decorated with a view of St Vincent's Rocks, 1825–40, 10in (25.5cm) diam.
**£90–100 / €125–140
$150–165 GRe** ⊞

Saucer dish, with a green dragon design, rim chip and crack, six character mark, Chinese, Guangxu period, 1875–1908, 7¼in (18.5cm) diam.
**£90–100 / €125–140
$150–165 G(L)** ✦

Makkum plate, decorated with Peacock pattern, marks to the underside, Dutch, 19thC, 9¼in (23.5cm) diam.
**£95–105 / €130–150
$155–170 SWO** ✦

Derby bone china dessert plate, the border gilded with serpents and palmettes, the centre painted with a pastoral scene entitled 'Near Breedon, Leicestershire', painted CBD mark in red enamel, c1820, 8¾in (22cm) diam.
**£100–110 / €140–155
$165–180 G(L)** ✦

◄ **Jones & Co plate,** transfer-printed with Landing of William of Orange pattern, from the British Series, printed mark, c1830, 8½in (21.5cm) diam. Plates printed with historical scenes are far less common than the Willow or Italian pattern, and are therefore more collectable. This example was a good buy and could have made twice the price.
**£100–110 / €140–155
$165–180 SWO** ✦

Locate the source

The source of each illustration in Miller's can be found by checking the code letters below each caption with the Key to Illustrations, pages 286–290.

Ridgway plate, transfer-printed with Christ Church, Oxford, from the Oxford & Cambridge College series, printed mark, c1820, 9¾in (25cm) diam.
£100–110 / €140–155
$165–180 SWO ⚖

Spode plate, transfer-printed with green Fox and Lion pattern, impressed Spode, c1830, 9¾in (25cm) diam. If it had been printed in blue and white, this plate could have fetched three times this price.
£110–120 / €155–165
$180–195 SWO ⚖

Delft charger, chipped, 18thC, 13¼in (33.5cm) diam. If this charger were in perfect condition the value could be as much as £150–200 / €210–280 / $245–330.
£110–120 / €155–165
$180–195 SWO ⚖

London delft plate, painted with Chinese landscapes, cracked, 18thC, 9in (23cm) diam.
£110–120 / €155–165
$180–195 G(L) ⚖

Ralph Hall plate, decorated with Sheltered Peasants pattern, restored, 1822–36, 10¼in (26cm) diam.
£110–120 / €155–165
$180–195 GRe ⊞

Plate, Chinese, Yongzheng period, 1723–35, 9in (23cm) diam.
£115–125 / €160–175
$190–220 McP ⊞

▶ **Plate,** with firing fault, Chinese, Ming Dynasty, Wanli period, 1573–1619, 8in (20.5cm) diam. Firing faults need not affect the price of an item if they are in places where they do not show. This firing crack is quite unsightly and has reduced the value of the piece.
£125–140 / €175–195
$200–230 GLD ⊞

Chinese export plate, in French pottery style, Qianlong period, c1740, 11in (28cm) diam.
£130–145 / €180–200
$210–240 McP ⊞

Qianlong period

The Chinese emperor Qianlong reigned from 1736–95. His was the last of the three great Qing Dynasty reigns of Chinese art and particularly porcelain – the others being Kangxi, (1662–1722) and Yongzheng (1723–35). Porcelain was made in huge quantities for export to Europe and also for the home market including for the Imperial household. The latter are among the finest and most costly of all Chinese porcelains.

The most familiar wares are the blue and white and *famille rose* wares made for export. These are seldom marked, whereas those made for the home market, especially the Imperial orders, usually bear a six- or four-character reign mark – a mark much copied in the 19th and 20th centuries.

Riley plate, decorated with a floral pattern, c1820, 10in (25.5cm) diam.
£135–150 / €190–210
$220–245 SCO ⊞

▶ **Soup plate,** decorated with the arms of Saunders, Chinese, Qianlong period, c1745, 6¼in (16cm) diam.
£130–145
€180–200
$210–240 G(L) ◢

Three plates, printed with The Cowman pattern, 19thC, largest 9¾in (25cm) diam.
£150–165 / €210–230
$245–270 SWO ◢

NORTHCOTE ROAD ANTIQUES MARKET

INDOOR ARCADE
OPEN 7 DAYS

30 Dealers offering a wide variety of antiques and collectables

Furniture - polished, painted, pine • China - inc. Clarice Cliff • Glass • Art Deco Flatware • Silver & plate Kitchenalia • Jewellery Lighting • Mirrors • Pictures & prints • Victoriana Collectables for everyone

Mon–Sat 10–6; Sun 12–5

ANTIQUES MARKET 020 7228 6850
155A NORTHCOTE ROAD
BATTERSEA SW11
www.spectrumsoft.net/nam

◀ **Spode plate,** decorated with a scene of Plas Newydd, Anglesey, from the Flowers and Leaves Border series, 1820–30, 8¼in (21cm) diam.
£150–165
€210–230
$250–270 GRe ⊞

Ridgway bowl, decorated with Pembroke Hall, Cambridge, damaged, 1814–30, 9¾in (25cm) diam.
£155–170 / €220–240
$250–280 GRe ⊞

The look without the price

This plate has a large amount of damage which, without it, could be worth almost £1,000 / €1,400 / $1,650. However, despite this it would still be eye-catching on display.

Kraak porselein **dish,** damaged, Chinese, c1600, 12in (30.5cm) diam.
£160–175 / €220–250
$260–290 McP ⊞

Dutch Delft earthenware plate, decorated with a bird and plants, 1750–1800, 12in (30.5cm) diam.
£160–175 / €220–250
$260–290 BERN ⚘

Worcester Flight, Barr & Barr armorial plate, with a stag's head above a motto 'A Deo Lumen', 1807–13, 9½in (24cm) diam.
£180–200 / €250–280
$300–330 G(L) ⚘

Flight, Barr & Barr porcelain

The Worcester factory was started by Dr John Wall in 1751 and soon became very successful, particularly for making blue-printed tea wares for the middle classes. Today, the very earliest pieces from the 1750s are extremely collectable and expensive. In 1783, the factory was purchased by Thomas Flight, who was joined ten years later by Martin Barr. The family partnership then ran as follows:
- Flight & Barr period 1793–1807
- Barr, Flight & Barr period 1807–13
- Flight, Barr & Barr period 1813–40

Early 19th-century porcelain can be of superb quality, finely painted and richly gilded in the most opulent Regency taste. The Worcester factory at this time produced some of the finest porcelain in Europe.

Ridgway plate, c1820, 10in (25.5cm) diam.
£180–200 / €250–280
$300–330 SCO ⊞

Enoch Wood & Sons plate, decorated with a view of Shirley House, Surrey, from the Grapevine Border series, 1820–30, 6½in (16.5cm) diam.
£195–210 / €270–310
$320–370 GRe ⊞

Pair of Derby porcelain plates, the centres painted with wild birds in wooded riverscapes within gilded acanthus panels, CBD mark in red enamel, one rim worn, c1800, 8½in (21.5cm) diam.
£200–220 / €280–310
$330–370 G(L) ✍

Plate, decorated with a view of York, from the Diorama series, 1820, 9¾in (25cm) diam.
£200–220 / €280–310
$330–370 GRe ⊞

▶ **Spode plate,** transfer-printed with Sarcophagi and Sepulchres at the Head of the Harbour at Cacamo, from the Caramanian series, impressed mark, c1810, 10in (25.5cm) diam.
£200–220
€280–310
$330–370 GRe ⊞

Plate, decorated with a landau, from the British Carriages series, c1820, 10in (25.5cm) diam.
£200–220 / €280–310
$330–370 SCO ⊞

Plate, decorated in *famille rose* palette with three maidens in a garden, cracked, Chinese, Qianlong period, 1736–95, 8½in (21.5cm) diam. In perfect condition this plate could be worth £400–500 / €560–700 / $650–820.
£200–220 / €280–310
$330–370 G&G ⊞

Riley plate, decorated with Taymoo'th Castle, Perthshire, from the Large Scroll Border series, 1820–28, 10in (25.5cm) diam.
£200–220 / €280–310
$330–370 GRe ⊞

Riley plate, decorated with Hollywell Cottage, Cavan, from the Large Scroll Border series, impressed hand mark, 1820–28, 10in (25.5cm) diam.
£200–220 / €280–310
$330–370 GRe ⊞

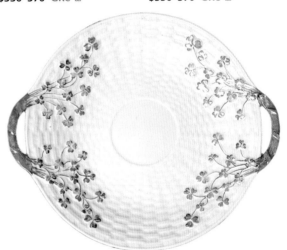

Belleek bread plate, Second Period, 1891–1926, 9in (23cm) diam.
£220–240 / €310–330
$370–390 MLa ⊞

Delft dish, with a brown rim, decorated with Peacock pattern, marked 'M 3/3', Dutch, 18thC, 10in (25.5cm) diam.
£200–220 / €280–310
$330–370 G&G ⊞

◄ Pair of Meissen plates, the pierced rims with three vignettes of flowers, the centres painted with further flowers and butterflies, crossed swords mark, impressed numerals, German, early 20thC, 8¼in (21cm) diam.
£220–240
€310–330
$370–390 B(W) ⚒

Lambeth delft plate, c1770, 9in (23cm) diam. The wide colour palette used in the design on this plate makes it particularly attractive to collectors.
£220–240 / €310–330
$370–390 JHo ⊞

Miller's compares...

A. Famille rose plate, painted with a scene from 'The Western Chamber' within a scroll, on a whorl ground, Chinese, Yongzheng period, 1723–25, 9in (23cm) diam.
£220–240 / €310–330
$370–390 G(L) ✎

B. Pair of famille rose plates, painted with a scholar pursuing a lady in a terraced garden, within a scroll, on a floral ground, Chinese, Yongzheng period, 1723–35, 8¾in (22cm) diam.
£650–720 / €910–1,000
$1,050–1,200 S(O) ✎

Item B has fetched a higher price because pairs of plates are more desirable than individual ones. The quality of the enamel in Item A may not be as good as that of Item B. Plates such as these would also fetch higher prices in a specialist Oriental sale.

Pair of Sèvres-style porcelain plates, printed marks, late 19thC, 9½in (24cm) diam. Authentic Sèvres plates would be worth several thousand pounds but these still make a good decorative item.
£230–280 / €320–360
$380–430 SWO ✎

Blue and white charger, painted with trees within a band of plantain leaves, Chinese, Kangxi period, 1662–1722, 17in (43cm) diam.
£230–260 / €320–360
$380–430 S(O) ✎

◀ **Six plates,** each painted with a floral spray and heightened in gilt, bases marked, mid-19thC, 8½in (21.5cm) diam. This set of plates represent good value as plates such as this would normally cost £600–900 / €840–1,250 / $980–1,450.
£240–270 / €330–380
$390–440 SWO ✎

Set of ten Minton plates, each painted with flowers and insects, impressed marks, 1884–85, 9½in (24cm) diam.
£260–290 / €360–400
$430–470 SWO ⚒

Famille rose **armorial saucer,** decorated with a coat-of-arms above the motto 'Ose et espère', the rim with clusters of flowers, damaged and repaired, c1765, 6¼in (16cm) diam.The chip and repair to this saucer have reduced its value by around 75 per cent.
£260–290 / €360–400
$430–470 S(O) ⚒

Kraak porselain **dish,** painted with a central panel of geese beside a pool, within eight smaller panels, cracked, Chinese, 1620–40, 14¼in (36cm) diam. Without the crack a plate such as this could be worth as much as £1,200 / €1,650 / $2,000.
£270–300 / €380–420
$440–490 WW ⚒

▶ **Enoch Wood & Sons plate,** decorated with a view of the Residence of the Marquis de la Fayette, La Grange, impressed mark, 1820–30, 10¼in (26cm) diam.
£320–350 / €450–490
$520–570 GRe ⊞

◀ **Pair of Delft plates,** decorated with Biblical scenes, restored, 18thC, 13½in (34.5cm) diam. These plates could be worth up to £700 / €980 / $1,150 in perfect condition.
£240–270 / €330–380
$390–440 BERN ⚒

English delft plate, slight glaze loss to edge, 1725–75, 14¼in (36cm) diam.
£250–280 / €350–390
$410–460 SWO ⚒

Two Dutch Delft blue and white chargers, painted with peacock patterns within yellow line rims, mid-18thC, 13¾in (35cm) diam.
£280–310 / €390–430
$460–510 CGC ⚒

Pair of Chinese Imari plates, decorated in the *famille verte* palette with bird and butterfly floral panels, Kangxi period, 1662–1722, 10in (25.5cm) diam.
£320–350 / €450–490
$520–570 G(L) ☝

Chinese Imari plate, decorated in the *famille verte* palette with a vase of flowers, Chinese, Kangxi period, 1662–1722, 8¾in (22cm) diam.
£320–350 / €450–490
$520–570 G&G ⊞

Two dishes, each painted with a jardinière of flowers within a Greek key border, floral sprays to the interior, one cracked and chipped, six character mark, Chinese, Yongzheng period, 1723–25, 3½in (9cm) diam.
£380–420 / €530–590
$620–690 G(L) ☝

Chinese export plate, decorated with the arms of the Nordic Society, London, Qianlong period, c1785, 9in (23cm) diam. The Nordic Society was founded in 1783 for Scandinavian residents and visitors to England.
£320–350 / €450–490
$520–570 G(L) ☝

Set of six Burn & Co creamware plates, painted with named plants within basket moulding and arcade-pierced rim bands, early 19thC, 7¼in (18.5cm) diam.
£380–420 / €530–590
$620–690 CGC ☝

◄ **Sèvres-style plate,** decorated with a portrait of woman within a gilt-enriched border, signed 'Brun', 1850–90, 10in (25.5cm) diam.
£400–450 / €560–630
$650–730 MAA ⊞

Arita dish, Japanese, late 17thC, 8½in (21.5cm) diam.
£420–470 / €590–650
$690–770 McP ⊞

***Kraak porselein* plate,** damaged, Chinese, Wanli period, c1600, 8in (20.5cm) diam. A perfect example would cost £150 / €210 / $250 more.
£450–500 / €630–700
$730–820 McP ⊞

Imari dish, gilding worn, Japanese, c1700, 12in (30.5cm) diam. Worn gilding will lower the price of an item, and regilding is rarely successful.
£500–550 / €700–770
$820–900 G&G ⊞

***Famille verte* dish,** damaged, Chinese, Kangxi period, 1662–1722, 14in (35.5cm) diam.
£500–550 / €700–770
$820–900 McP ⊞

▶ **Set of six majolica plates,** each decorated with a vine leaf on a basketwork ground, Continental, 19thC, 9in (23cm) diam. If these plates were by a named maker such as Minton they could fetch around £1,200 / €1,650 / $2,000.
£500–550 / €700–770
$820–900 G(L) ⚒

Dutch Delft dish, polychrome-painted with lotus leaves and pine cones, rim frits, hairline crack, mark for Jan van der Laan, c1700, 8¾in (22cm) diam.
£520–580 / €720–810
$850–950 G&G ⊞

Saucer dish, painted with a warrior brandishing a sword, one figure kneeling at his feet, another beneath a table, cracked, six-character and Xuande mark, Chinese, Kangxi period, 1662–1722, 10½in (26.5cm) diam. Kangxi pieces often have earlier reign marks – particularly Xuande and Changhua. The correct Kangxi mark would double the value of this dish so beware when buying.
£550–600 / €770–840
$900–980 G(L) ↗

◄ **Pair of saucer dishes,** each painted with a fox and hounds in a landscape, Chinese, 17th–18thC, 5½in (14cm) diam.
£550–600 / €770–840
$900–980 G(L) ↗

Armorial plate, with the arms of Edward with Hanbury in presence, Chinese, Qianlong period, c1755, 9in (23cm) diam.
£580–640 / €810–890
$950–1,050 McP ⊞

◄ **Pair of Minton plates,** painted by Lucien Boullemier with classical scenes emblematic of peace and war, within gilt-enriched borders, one plate cracked, gold printed globe and crown marks, dated 1870, 9½in (24cm) diam.
£580–640 / €810–890
$950–1,050 B ↗

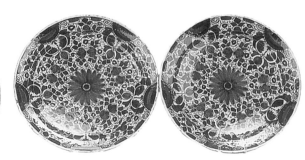

Pair of Dutch Delft plates, marked for Bartholomeus Godyn, 1675–1725, 13¾in (35cm) diam.
£610–670 / €850–930
$1,000–1,100 BERN ⚒

Armorial charger, painted with a couple beneath a tree, the girl on a buffalo, the rim with four crests, c1750, 16½in (42cm) diam. Without damage this charger could be worth £1,500 / €2,100 / $2,400.
£590–650 / €820–910
$960–1,050 S(O) ⚒

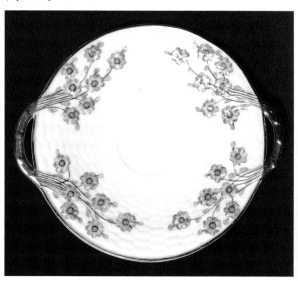

Charger, painted with deer within a rocky landscape, the rim with crickets perched on sprigs of peony, Chinese, 18thC, 15¾in (40cm) diam.
£700–770 / €980–1,050
$1,150–1,250 S(O) ⚒

Belleek bread plate, Second Period 1891–1926, Irish, 9in (23cm) diam. This plate would be attractive to collectors because it has a particularly unusual colour scheme.
£700–770 / €980–1,050
$1,150–1,250 MLa ⊞

◀ **London delft plate,** c1730, 9in (23cm) diam.
£710–780
€990–1,100
$1,150–1,250
JHo ⊞

▶ **Dutch Delft plate,** early 18thC, 13¼in (33.5cm) diam.
£800–880
€1,100–1,250
$1,300–1,450
BERN ⚒

Jars & Canisters

Staffordshire jar and cover,
19thC, 7in (18cm) high.
£45–50 / €60–70
$75–80 MCC ⊞

**Royal Worcester jar and
cover,** c1907, 4in (10cm) high.
£180–200 / €250–280
$300–330 WAC ⊞

Imari jar, moulded with dragons,
minor damage, Japanese,
19thC, 25¼in (64cm) high.
€260–290 / €360–400
$430–470 L&E ⚒

Satsuma *koro* and cover,
decorated with panels of figures,
landscapes and fans and brocade,
some rubbing to gilt finial, one
handle restuck, character mark
to base, Japanese, Meiji period,
1868–1912, 2¾in (7cm) high.
If this piece had been in perfect
condition it could have sold for
£700 / €980 / $1,150.
£520–570 / €720–790
$850–930 BR ⚒

► ***Wucai* vessel,** painted with
two five-clawed dragons on a
scrolling foliage ground, damaged
and repaired, six-character mark,
Chinese, c1620, 4½in (11.5cm)
high. If this piece were in
perfect condition it could
be worth £3,000–4,000 /
€4,150–5,500 / $4,900–6,500.
£600–660 / €840–920
$980–1,100 G(L) ⚒

The look without the price

Porcelain jar and cover,
decorated with panels of flowers,
with wooden stand and cover, neck
crack, 17thC, 7¼in (18.5cm) high.
£190–210 / €260–290
$310–340 G(L) ⚒

An undamaged jar with its
correct porcelain lid could
cost as much as £800–1,200 /
€1,100–1,650 / $1,300–1,950.

Swankalock jar, Thai, 14th–15thC,
24in (61cm) high.
£600–660 / €840–920
$980–1,100 GRG ⊞

Jugs & Ewers

Staffordshire gravy boat, decorated with Willow pattern, c1875, 8in (20.5cm) wide.
£35–40 / €48–55
$60–65 CoCo ⊞

Copeland cream jug, with a rope-twist handle, transfer-printed with a floral decoration, mid-19thC, 4in (10cm) high.
£40–45 / €55–60
$65–75 CoCo ⊞

◀ **Lustre jug,** hair crack to body, c1825, 4¾in (12cm) high. Without the crack this jug would be worth £60–70 / €85–95 / $100–115.
£45–50 / €60–70
$75–80 PSA ⊞

Wedgwood jasperware milk jug, the neck with a Pan mask to the lip, the body decorated with Classical figures, impressed mark and numerals, 19thC, 7in (18cm) high. Jasperware is still very sought-after, but this piece is affordable because the shape is not popular with collectors.
£45–50 / €60–70
$75–80 PFK ⚲

> **For more examples** of Jugs & Ewers see Silver & Plate (pages 132–165)

Miller's compares...

A. Adams milk jug, transfer-printed with Cattle Scenery pattern, 1890–1917, 5in (12.5cm) high.
£70–80 / €95–110
$115–130 CoCo ⊞

B. Milk jug, transfer-printed with a hunting scene, c1820, 7in (18cm) high.
£430–480 / €600–670
$700–780 SCO ⊞

Collectors of blue and white pottery tend to focus on the period 1800–30. Item A is later than this, is not well made and the printing is of poor quality. Item B, however, is a good shape, is from the correct period and, although the pattern is quite common, it is worth considerably more than item A.

Ironstone jug, with a domed cover and *famille rose* decoration, 19thC, 8in (20.5cm) high.
£120–130 / €165–180
$200–210 TRM ↗

Worcester milk/cream jug, transfer-printed with Three Flowers pattern, 1775–80, 5in (12.5cm) high.
£125–140 / €175–200
$200–230 WAC ⊞

Transfer-printed chintz jug, mid-19thC, 6in (15cm) high. Blue is the most common colour, and also the most desirable – this purple example is therefore more affordable.
£125–140 / €175–200
$200–230 SWN ⊞

◄ **Mason's Ironstone jug,** decorated with pheasant pattern, 1813–20, 4in (10cm) high. A later example, from c1880 could be purchased for half this price.
£130–145
€180–200
$210–230 CoCo ⊞

Two Mason's Ironstone jugs, each printed with griffin-like beasts, printed marks and numerals, 19thC, larger 6½in (16.5cm) high.
£180–200 / €250–280
$300–330 SWO ↗

Pair of Coalport porcelain jugs, each with a cartouche framing a miniature landscape, printed marks and numerals, c1900, 6¾in (17cm) high. This price would suggest that both jugs are damaged. In perfect condition they would cost £500–800 / €700–1,100 / $820–1,300.
£190–210 / €260–290
$310–350 SWO ↗

Pearlware jug, possibly by Ralph Stevenson, printed with British scenes, c1830, 5in (12.5cm) high.
£200–220 / €280–310
$330–370 DSA ⊞

▶ **Mason's Ironstone jug,** decorated with Japan pattern, impressed mark, 19thC, 7¾in (19.5cm) high.
£200–220 / €280–310
$330–370 SWO ↗

Two Mason's Ironstone jugs, decorated with Imari pattern and underglaze blue, printed mark and pattern No. B8839, 19thC, larger 6in (15cm) high.
**£210–230 / €290–320
$350–380 SWO** ⚒

Bow sauce boat, with a lobed scroll-moulded rim, painted in *famille rose* style with peony and prunus sprays, fine cracks, 1754–55, 6in (15cm) wide. In perfect condition this piece would fetch £600–700 / €840–980 / $980–1,150.
**£260–280 / €360–390
$430–460 B** ⚒

Pair of Derby porcelain sauce boats, with foliate relief decoration, hand-painted with flowers, encrusted flower and leaf to the looped handle, chips to rim and base rim, c1760, 6in (15cm) long. Without the chips this piece would be worth £500 / €700 / $820.
**£380–420 / €530–590
$620–690 B(W)** ⚒

Bow double-lipped sauce boat, with double scrolled handles, the interior painted with a bird perched in the branches of a flowering tree, within a diaper border, restored, 1749–52, 7in (18cm) long. The restoration has halved the price of this piece.
**£300–330 / €420–460
$490–540 B** ⚒

Belleek bone china jug, First Period, 1863–90, 7in (18cm) high.
**£310–350 / €430–490
$510–570 MLa** ⊞

◄ **Worcester porcelain mask jug,** with cabbage leaf moulding, printed in underglaze blue with chrysanthemums and roses, 1776–92, 9in (23cm) high.
**£420–460
€590–640
$690–750 G(B)** ⚒

What is underglaze & overglaze?

Underglaze colours are applied to the ceramic body before the piece is glazed. Cobalt blue is the best known and has been used in China since the Yuan Dynasty (1279–1368) because it tolerates a very high firing temperature. Overglaze decorating by definition is applied after the piece has been glazed. It is painted or printed and fired in a muffle kiln at a lower temperature than the underglaze colours. Some wares, such as the Chinese *doucai* and *wucai* porcelains and some Japanese *Kakiemon* and *Nabeshima* porcelains use a combination of underglaze and overglaze colours.

Belleek lily jug, Second Period, 1891–1926, 4½in (11.5cm) high.
£430–480 / €600–670
$700–780 MLa ⊞

J. Rogers & Son, Longport, ewer, decorated with a floral pattern, c1820, 8in (20.5cm) high. Rogers were noted for their floral transfer-printed everyday wares during the 19thC.
£430–480 / €600–670
$700–780 SCO ⊞

Frechen stoneware jug, German, c1660, 8in (20.5cm) high.
£440–490 / €610–680
$720–800 JHo ⊞

To find out more about antique ceramics see the full range of Miller's books at
www.millers.uk.com

Worcester porcelain jug, with cabbage leaf moulding, printed with Parrot and Fruit pattern, crescent 'C' mark, 1770, 8¼in (21cm) high.
£520–570 / €720–790
$850–930 HYD ⚒

Staffordshire pottery jug, printed and enamelled with seated musicians, inscribed 'I wish I was in Dixey land Sally is the girl for me', within a rope-twist and floral border between blue rim bands, c1835, 8in (20.5cm) high.
£560–620 / €780–860
$910–1,000 WL ⚒

Linthorpe jug, by Christopher Dresser, with flared rim and bracket handle, glazed decoration, impressed marks and numerals, 1879–89, 6½in (16.5cm) high. The fact that this jug was designed by Christopher Dresser has added a great deal to its value. Without the attribution it would be worth less than £120 / €165 / $195.
£720–800 / €1,000–1,100
$1,200–1,300 AG ⚒

▶ **Staffordshire earthenware ewer and basin,** by William Adams & Sons, transfer-printed with Athens pattern, marked, 1835–50, ewer 12in (30.5cm) high.
£620–680
€860–950
$1,000–1,100
NOA ⚒

Plaques

Miller's compares...

A. Pair of porcelain plaques, painted with young girls, Continental, c1880, 3½in (9cm) high, in gilt mantle and ebony frames.
£140–155 / €195–215
$230–250 G(B) ➚

B. Porcelain plaque, painted with a portrait of a woman, Continental, 19thC, 3¼in (8.5cm) high, in a gilt frame.
£520–570 / €720–790
$850–930 AH ➚

The quality of the painting affects the price of plaques. Item B is a superior painting and its frame is better quality than those of Item A. Had these examples been British, rather than of Continental origin, they would both have fetched higher prices.

Pair of pearlware plaques, each moulded with a bust of a Greek scholar within painted rims, one with a hair crack, 19thC, 9½in (24cm) diam. The crack has reduced the value of these plaques by around £50 / €70 / $80.
£280–310 / €390–430
$460–510 SWO ➚

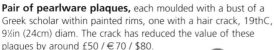

▶ **Wedgwood and Bentley blue jasper plaque,** modelled by Isaac Gosset, 18thC, 3¼in (8.5cm) high. The value of portrait plaques such as this is dictated by the date and subject.
£300–330 / €420–460
$490–540 L ➚

Set of four portrait medallions, each painted with a figure of a lady including Mme Le Brun, labels to verso, Continental, 19thC, 3¼in (8.5cm) high. Had these plaques been Berlin and by KPM, they would be worth four times as much.
£480–530 / €670–740
$780–870 AH ➚

Services

Livesley Powell & Co child's part dinner service, some pieces impressed 'Best L.P & Co', some damaged, mid-19thC. Miniature services can be very desirable to collectors. This set could have fetched £250 / €350 / $410 if it had been undamaged.
£150–165 / €210–230
$250–270 SWO 🔨

The look without the price

Nine Meissen dessert plates, outside-decorated with birds and insects, damaged, crossed swords mark, German, late 19thC, 8in (20.5cm) diam.
£160–175 / €220–250
$260–290 SWO 🔨

In perfect condition, this set of plates could be worth £300 / €420 / $490.

Coalport bone china part tea service, comprising 15 pieces, painted with a floral decoration in enamels and gilt, early 19thC.
£170–185 / €230–260
$280–300 G(L) 🔨

Staffordshire tea service, comprising 42 pieces, teapot damaged, c1850. Had this service been made by Coalport it would be worth £300 / €420 / $490.
£180–200 / €250–280
$300–330 SWO 🔨

Derby porcelain part coffee service, comprising 16 pieces, with painted and gilded decoration, red painted mark, 1800–25. Coffee cans and saucers are extremely sought-after. This set is a very low price due to the damage. A coffee can and saucer on their own could cost £50–80 / €70–110 / $80–130.
£220–240 / €310–330
$370–390 PF 🔨

Wedgwood creamware part dessert service, comprising five pieces, with finely-moulded ferns and painted details, impressed mark, 19thC.
£280–320 / €390–450
$460–520 BWL 🔨

Spode toy part tea service, comprising 11 pieces, printed with Daisy and Bread pattern, c1820, teapot 6in (15cm) wide. The fact that this is a toy service adds 15–20 per cent to the value.
£310–340 / €430–470
$510–560 SWO ⚹

Coalport part dessert service, comprising 17 pieces, damaged and repaired, c1825.
£350–390 / €490–540
$570–640 DN ⚹

Royal Crown Derby porcelain dessert service, comprising 15 pieces, decorated with pattern No. 3707, hairline crack to one plate, printed and impressed marks, date code for 1896–97. The hairline crack will have reduced the price, but only by five per cent.
£440–480 / €610–670
$720–780 SWO ⚹

Part dinner service, probably Derby, comprising 10 pieces, with richly-gilded borders, marked, 1800–25, plates 10in (25.5cm) diam.
£480–520 / €670–720
$780–850 NOA ⚹

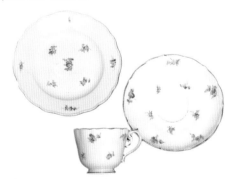

Pearlware part dinner service, comprising nine pieces, decorated with Tobacco Leaf pattern, cracks, early 19thC. This pattern is normally associated with 18thC Chinese ceramics, where it would be worth a great deal more.
£750–820 / €1,050–1,150
$1,200–1,350 SWO ⚹

Meissen part tea service, comprising 18 pieces, German, c1900, saucer 5in (12.5cm) diam.
£590–650 / €820–910
$960–1,050 BROW ⊞

▶ **Wedgwood majolica dessert service,** comprising 10 pieces, the borders moulded with a basket weave pattern, 19thC.
£750–820 / €1,050–1,150
$1,200–1,350 BWL ⚹

Stands

Teapot stand, French, mid-19thC,
7in (18cm) wide.
£65–70 / €90–95
$105–115 CoCo ⊞

◀ **Spode tureen
stand,** transfer-
printed with
Trophies Etruscan
pattern, printed and
impressed marks,
c1820, 13½in
(34.5cm) diam.
£75–85
€105–120
$120–140 SWO ⚹

Spode stand, by Lanje Lijsen, transfer-
printed with Long Elisa and Jumping Boy
pattern, printed and impressed marks, c1820,
11¼in (28.5cm) diam, together with a hot
water plate in the same pattern.
£140–155 / €195–215
$230–250 SWO ⚹

Spode eggstand, transfer-printed with Gothic Castle
pattern, 1810–20, 7¼in (18.5cm) diam.
£190–210 / €260–290
$310–350 GRe ⊞

Caughley teapot stand, painted in
underglaze blue with Tower pattern,
1785–90, 6¼in (16cm) diam. This stand
was once part of a full tea service.
£300–330 / €420–460
$490–540 LFA ⚹

The look without the price

Porcelain inkstand, probably Coalport, with two
covered compartments, space for a taperstick and two pen
trays, restored, c1840, 13¾in (35cm) wide.
£350–380 / €490–530
$570–620 S(O) ⚹

If this inkstand had been in perfect condition it
could have sold for £800 / €1,100 / $1,300. However,
it would still look very attractive on a desk.

Tea & Coffee Pots

Wedgwood stoneware teapot, relief-moulded with anthemia and flowerheads within foliate tendrils, the cover with recumbent dog finial, cracked, impressed mark, 3½in (9cm) high. This teapot would be worth more than twice this amount if it were in perfect condition.
£40–45 / €55–60
$65–75 PFK ✎

Desirable patterns of blue-printed pottery

English blue and white transfer-printed pottery is a fascinating collecting area with countless different print subjects and a great variety of shapes. It is the rare and unusual patterns that are most prized by collectors and thus the most expensive. Among the more popular subjects are Spode's Indian Sporting series, Naval and shipping scenes and, most famously, the Durham Ox series, despite being unmarked and by an unknown maker.

▶ **Ridgways child's teapot,** transfer-printed with Humphrey's Clock scenes from Charles Dickens' *Old Curiosity Shop,* c1890, 5in (12.5cm) high.
£65–70 / €90–95
$105–115 CoCo ⊞

Teapot, possibly Davenport, transfer-printed with a garden scene, c1830, 6in (15cm) wide. If this teapot were attributable to a known maker it could be worth up to 20 per cent more
£100–110 / €140–155
$165–195 SWO ✎

Miller's compares...

A. Chinese Imari teapot, decorated with figures, birds, animals and flowers, chipped, 18thC.
£130–145 / €180–200
$210–230 WW ✎

B. Chinese Imari teapot, with silver mounts, 1710–20, 4in (10cm) high.
£500–550 / €700–770
$820–900 McP ⊞

Item A is damaged, whereas Item B is not only in good condition, a better shape and with more interesting decoration, but the silver mounts make it a more desirable piece.

Meissen teapot, painted with flower sprays and with gilt decoration, cancelled crossed swords mark, German, 19thC, 9in (23cm) wide. The cancelled marks indicate that this piece is a second – in the case of Meissen this usually means that it was decorated outside the factory and thus of lower value.
£150–165 / €210–230
$240–270 WW ✣

Berlin coffee pot, moulded with rococo-style spout and handle, floral knop, German, late 19thC, 9in (23cm) high.
£180–200 / €250–280
$290–330 G(L) ✣

Redware pottery teapot, by Jack Field, decorated with a lead glaze, c1760, 5in (12.5cm) high.
£230–250 / €320–350
$380–410 JRe ⊞

Berlin coffee pot, after the Meissen example, the curved animal spout with satyr mask terminal, sceptre mark and incised and impressed marks, German, 1850–99, 6¼in (16cm) high.
£450–500 / €630–700
$730–820 S(O) ✣

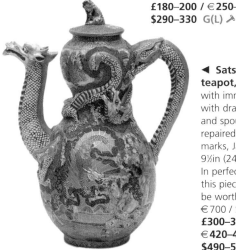

◀ **Satsuma teapot,** enamelled with immortals, with dragon handle and spout, handle repaired, character marks, Japanese, 9½in (24cm) high. In perfect condition this piece could be worth £500 / €700 / $820.
£300–330
€420–460
$490–540 G(L) ✣

Teapot, tea caddy and bowl, each painted with two reserves of an exotic bird in a garden, on a cell diaper ground, Chinese, late 18thC.
£450–500 / €630–700
$730–820 CGC ✣

Meissen teapot, painted with figures in a landscape within foliate scrollwork, trellis and floral cartouche with *deutsche Blumen*, crossed swords mark in underglaze blue, some wear, knop repaired, German, 1750–55, 4in (10cm) high. In perfect condition this teapot could have made up to £900 / €1,250 / $1,450.
£760–840 / €1,050–1,150
$1,250–1,350 S(O) ✣

Vases

Miller's compares...

A. Adams vase, transfer-printed with Cattle Scenery pattern, 1879–91, 9in (23cm) high.
£75–85 / €105–120 $120–140 CoCo ⊞

B. Pair of Arita vases, decorated with figures in a landscape, c1900, 31in (78.5cm) high.
£580–650 / €810–910 $950–1,050 BRU ⊞

Item A is small and rather late for collectors of blue and white pottery. Item B, as well as being a pair – which are worth proportionately more than singles – is also much taller, at almost three times the height of Item A, and this accounts for the higher value.

Set of three Wilton Fairyland lustre vases, one with a cover, decorated with figures in gardens on an iridescent ground, damaged, largest 8¾in (22cm) high. The damage to these vases has greatly reduced their value, which could be as high as £400 / €560 / $650.
£85–95 / €120–130 $140–155 L&E ⚒

◀ **Linthorpe glazed vase,** impressed mark and number, minor crack, 1879–89, 12¼in (31cm) high.
£90–100 / €125–140 $150–165 AG ⚒

▶ **Spode porcelain spill vase,** the rim with gilt egg-and-tongue border, painted with a bird and eggs in a nest within a gilded bead-and-billet panel, repaired chip, painted mark and pattern No. 2114, c1815, 4½in (11.5cm) high. Without the chip this piece would be worth over £150 / €210 / $250.
£100–110 / €140–155 $170–180 G(L) ⚒

Pair of Dutch Delft lobed vases, each with two handles modelled as snakes and lion masks, the bodies with landscape scenes, bases monogrammed, 19thC, 7in (18cm) high. 18thC examples would cost four or five times this price.
£120–130 / €165–180
$195–210 AMB ✂

Vase, from the *Hoi An* cargo, Vietnamese, 1450–1500, 5in (12.5cm) high.
£125–140 / €175–195
$210–230 McP ⊞

Pair of Coalport vases, painted with hawthorn blossom and butterflies, marked, c1900, 3¼in (8.5cm) high.
£160–175 / €220–240
$260–290 B(W) ✂

Ryosai *sumida gawa* vase, applied with figures of boys, Japanese, c1890, 8¼in (21cm) high. This type of pot is not especially popular, hence the low price, so if you like this work now is a good time to buy.
£155–170 / €210–230
$250–280 FU ⊞

◄ **Pair of Royal Worcester nautilus vases,** on coral stands, dated 1889, 6¾in (17cm) high.
£160–175 / €220–240
$260–290 SWO ✂

Pair of Imari bottle vases, one cracked, Japanese, 19thC, 12½in (32cm) high. In perfect condition, these vases would be worth almost twice as much.
£160–175 / €220–240
$260–290 SWO ✂

► **Pair of vases,** the shoulders with moulded dragons, decorated with shaped panels of ladies and dignitaries on a terrace, alternating with panels of exotic birds on flowering branches, Chinese, Canton, 19thC, 9¾in (25cm) high.
£160–175
€220–240
$260–290 Mit ✂

▶ Pair of Staffordshire pottery spill vases, each modelled as a peacock perched in a spill tree with shreddings, on a gilt-decorated oval base, c1860, 8in (20.5cm) high.
£260–290 / €360–400
$430–470 B(W) ⚒

Royal Worcester vase, c1902, 7in (18cm) high.
£175–195 / €250–270
$290–320 WAC ⊞

Pair of Derby vases, decorated with flowers and gilt trailing, date mark for 1887, 8¾in (22cm) high.
£280–310 / €390–430
$460–510 SWO ⚒

Linthorpe vase, with two-tone glaze, impressed mark and number, rim chip, 1879–89, 10in (25.5cm) high.
£280–310 / €390–430
$460–510 AG ⚒

Belleek vase, modelled as a nesting bird on a flower-encrusted tree stump, on a rocky base, uppermost bird missing, some restoration, black printed mark, Second Period 1891–1926, 11½in (29cm) high.
£300–330 / €420–460
$490–540 S(O) ⚒

▶ Pair of Dutch Delft covered vases, decorated with a landscape with buildings, 18thC, 17in (43cm) high.
£320–350
€450–490
$520–570 BERN ⚒

Pair of Belleek Nile vases, the neck applied with flowers and buds, above a leaf-moulded border, black printed marks, Second Period 1891–1926, 9½in (24cm) high.
£350–390 / €490–540
$570–640 S(O) ⚘

Tea dust vase, with an elongated neck, Chinese, Qianlong mark and period, 1736–95, 12½in (32cm) high. Tea dust glaze is so-called because it resembles the flecked surface of tea dust.
£400–440 / €560–610
$650–720 L ⚘

Wucai vase, with a pierced and carved wood cover, painted in the Transitional style with horses galloping among flowers and Buddhist emblems, on a ground of whorls and breaking waves, Chinese, 19thC, 11¼in (28.5cm) high. The Transitional style can be identified by shape, subject matter or decoration. In this case, the distinguishing fact is that it is *wucai* and features an amonite scroll ground.
£350–390 / €490–540
$570–640 S(O) ⚘

Minton porcelain soft glaze vase, possibly by Jessie Smith, the neck with a reticulated collar, painted with roses and birds, on a pierced foot, lid missing, drill hole to base, printed mark and painted Ermine mark, mid-19thC, 16¼in (41.5cm) high.
£380–420 / €530–590
$620–690 SWO ⚘

Pair of Worcester Flight, Barr & Barr spill vases, with everted rims and seed pearl borders, with eagle-head ring handles, the bodies painted with butterflies and flower sprays, on square bases, one rim damaged, gilding rubbed, 1813–40, 3½in (9cm) high. Without the damage these vases would be worth over £1,000 / €1,400 / $1,650.
£600–660 / €840–920
$980–1,100 G(L) ⚘

◄ **Vase and cover,** Chinese, Tang Dynasty, 618–907, 5in (12.5cm) high. Without its cover, the value of this vase would be reduced by around £200 / €280 / $330.
£630–700 / €880–980
$1,050–1,150 GLD ⊞

Miscellaneous

◀ **Staffordshire blue and white cache-pot,** 1818–60, 3½in (9cm) high.
£80–90
€ **110–125**
$130–150 CoCo ⊞

▶ **Porcelain toilet bottle,** decorated with rural scenes, French, 19thC, 5¼in (13.5cm) high.
£85–95
€ **120–130**
$140–155 SWO ↗

Porcelain snuff bottle, with stopper, moulded as a curled lotus leaf and buds, 19thC, 2¾in (7cm) long.
£90–100 / €125–140
$150–165 G(L) ↗

Locate the source

The source of each illustration in Miller's can be found by checking the code letters below each caption with the Key to Illustrations, pages 286–290.

Mason's Ironstone washstand set, comprising three pieces, decorated with a chinoiserie pattern of a grotto table and birds flying among peony and chrysanthemum, rim crack to ewer, c1860, chamber pot c1895, ewer 11¾in (30cm) high. The slightly later date of the chamber pot has not affected the price unduly.
£100–110 / €140–155
$165–180 BR ↗

Pounce pot, enamel-painted with flowers, paper label 'Royal Archaeological Institute', enamel damaged, Continental, late 18thC, 1¾in (4.5cm) high.
£170–185 / €240–260
$280–300 SWO ↗

◀ **Davenport pearlware bough pot and cover,** 1815–20, 5½in (14cm) high.
£270–300
€380–420
$440–490 DSA ⊞

Pair of J. Rogers & Son, Longport, majolica wall pockets, each modelled as a bird perched on a nest against a naturalistic tree background, chips, impressed mark to base, 19thC, 12in (30.5cm) high.
£280–310 / €390–430
$460–510 EH ⚒

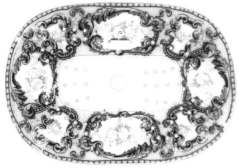

Copeland Spode flow blue drainer, c1860, 13in (33cm) wide.
£280–310 / €390–430
$460–510 CoS ⊞

Adams drainer, c1825, 12in (30.5cm) wide.
£300–330 / €420–460
$490–540 CoS ⊞

Drainer, c1820, 12in (30.5cm) wide.
£310–350 / €430–490
$510–570 CoS ⊞

Minton drainer, c1827, 10½in (26.5cm) wide.
£330–370 / €460–520
$540–610 CoS ⊞

◀ **Spode drainer,** decorated with Star pattern, gilded, c1820, 14in (35.5cm) wide.
£350–390 / €490–540
$570–640 CoS ⊞

Pair of Wedgwood Queensware pot-pourri urns, with pierced covers, damaged and repaired, c1780, 7½in (19cm) high. Without damage these items could be worth £1,500 / €2,000 / $2,450.
£380–420 / €530–580
$620–680 DN ✍

▶ *Kendi,* painted with stylized plants, Chinese, 17thC, 7½in (19cm) high.
£420–460
€590–640
$690–750 L ✍

Coalport sauce tureen, cover and stand, decorated with flowers within gilt borders, early 19thC, 7in (18cm) diam.
£420–460 / €590–640
$690–750 TRM ✍

Pair of Vienna tureens and covers, the domed covers with lemon finials, decorated with flower sprays and sprigs within gilt foliate scrollwork, rim chips, marked, mid-19thC, 8¼in (21cm) high. The damage to these tureens has reduced their value by about £100 / €140 / $165.
£450–500 / €630–700
$730–820 S(O) ✍

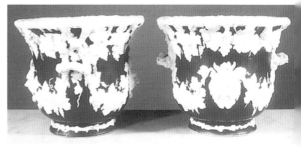

Pair of Copeland ice pails, decorated with fruiting vine and satyr masks, 19thC, 10¼in (26cm) diam.
£500–550 / €700–770
$820–900 HOK ✍

Chamberlain's Worcester inkwell, decorated with Thumb and Finger pattern, c1810, 3in (7.5cm) high.
£520–580 / €720–810
$850–950 DIA ⊞

Sets/pairs

Unless otherwise stated, any description which refers to 'a set' or 'a pair' includes a guide price for the entire set or the pair, even though the illustration may show only a single item.

The look without the price

Derby bough pot and cover, probably painted by 'Jockey' Hill, puce printed mark, minor damage and repair, c1790, 8in (20.5cm) wide.
£550–600 / €770–840
$900–980 S(O)

This bough pot has minor damage only, but in perfect condition it would be worth nearly twice as much, and is a very attractive display piece.

Copeland earthenware wash set, comprising 22 pieces, damaged and repaired, impressed and printed marks, late 19thC.
£590–650 / €820–910
$960–1,050 S(O)

Who was 'Jockey' Hill?

Thomas 'Jockey' Hill was the son of a portrait and landscape painter who worked at Derby from 1795. He specialized in landscapes in the style of Paul Sandby, a well-known 18th-century watercolour artist. The nickname 'Jockey' was acquired from his habit of riding about on his pony, Bob.

Wedgwood three-colour jasper ware 'Barber Bottle' and cover, decorated with satyrs' heads, grape festoons and rams' heads, the four cartouches with classical scenes, 1870–80, 11in (28cm) high. Three-colour jasper ware is much more sought-after than that of two colours.
£650–710 / €910–990
$1,050–1,150 SWO

Bow model of a jardinière and flowers, 1760–70, 7½in (19cm) high.
£700–770 / €980–1,050
$1,050–1,250 HYD

Paris porcelain Louis XVI-style cachepot, with drainer, marked, 1775–1800, 8¼in (21cm) high.
£870–960 / €1,200–1,300
$1,400–1,550 NOA

Silver & Plate

You don't have to be a millionaire or been born with a silver spoon in your mouth to own a piece of silver – there are plenty of affordable pieces on the market to choose from. If you are not buying purely for investment purposes, damaged or repaired items will be inexpensive to buy but will look superb displayed in the home. All they need is a gentle rub with an appropriate silver-cleaning cloth and they will glow beautifully. They will not shatter like pottery or porcelain when dropped and woodworm will not devour them.

Many people start their collection with decorative silver that has probably just been used and loved for many years and become a little too worn for the serious collector. An area often avoided by collectors is items with 'later decoration' such as a plain George II silver pint mug that has been refashioned by adding embossing, chasing and engraving of foliage and swags. The work would have been carried out by a Victorian silversmith on the instruction of the owner who wished to enhance his social status by having the 'modern design'. This type of modification is highly frowned upon by serious collectors and therefore prices are very low in comparison to an unadulterated piece. However, the workmanship of these later decorations is usually very high quality.

At the other end of the scale of affordable antiques is the perfect example that is reasonably priced. Such treasures may be difficult to find but they do exist. It is a matter of looking at the market and finding out whether there are areas that have not already been exploited. For example, many collectors do not consider 20th-century silver worthy of notice, especially pieces from the 1970s. Of course, there are collectors of this period but on the other hand there are many more ignoring it, thus allowing the possibility of great finds at antique markets, auctions and shops.

Over the last five years one of the largest areas of growth in antique silver has been that of small collectables. This is mainly due to the following reasons: there is a large variety of items to collect, such as spoons, vinaigrettes, bookmarks, snuff boxes, pencils, inkwells, nutmeg graters, miniature toys, napkin rings and items of medical, nautical and historical interest, plenty of which can be found for as little as £100 / €140 / $160. They can easily be locked away for safekeeping and are easy to maintain and keep clean.

If you would like to collect slightly larger items, domestic objects such as tea and coffee sets, cream jugs, sauce boats, sugar bowls, bonbon dishes and bread and fruit baskets are good pieces to buy at the moment. Prices have been low for quite some time now and have, in fact, fallen over the last few years. This is mainly due to a change in fashion. People no longer aspire to own – or clean – these 'luxury goods' which they feel will clutter their modern lifestyles and, as a result, silver items are no longer appearing on wedding lists. As with all fashions, this will undoubtedly change, so if you dream of a Sunday afternoon relaxing and entertaining friends, pouring that perfect cup of tea from a beautiful silver teapot, then now is the time to buy.

Daniel Bexfield

Bowls & Dishes

Silver sugar bowl, with a gilt interior, the part-lobed body with two applied rococo cartouches, on four scrolling paw feet, maker's mark part rubbed, London 1797, 4¼in (11cm) diam, 8oz.
£85–100 / €120–140
$140–165 SWO ✱

Find out more in

Miller's Silver & Plate Buyer's Guide, Miller's Publications, 2002

Miller's compares...

A. Silver cake basket, with swing handle, pierced sides and ball feet, maker's mark 'RFM', Sheffield 1907, 11½in (29cm) wide, 13oz.
£140–155 / €195–220
$230–250 WW ✱

B. Silver cake basket, by Elkington & Co, with swing handle, pierced and embossed sides and floral scroll border, Birmingham 1903, 13in (33cm) wide, 23oz.
£300–330 / €420–460
$490–540 WW ✱

Item B is by Elkington & Co, who are renowned for the high quality of their products. It is made of thicker gauge silver than Item A and also has a thick applied rim, giving it more stability.

Silver sugar bowl, with embossed and chased scrollwork, maker's mark 'D.S.', Sheffield 1862, 5½in (14cm) wide. This sugar bowl is made of thick gauge silver, and would make an ideal container for flowers today.
£150–165 / €210–230
$250–270 SWO ✱

▶ **Silver sugar bowl,** by George Fox, the sides chased with panels depicting the signs of the Zodiac, gilt interior, initialled, London 1872, 4¼in (11cm) diam, 4.75oz. The design of this bowl was influenced by Indian silversmiths.
£170–185 / €240–260
$280–300 WW ✱

Silver cake basket, by Holland, Aldwinckle & Slater, with a gadrooned border and foliate shells, London 1905, 9in (23cm) wide, 17oz. Items such as these are now often used as fruit baskets.
£170–185 / €240–260
$280–300 WW ✱

▶ Arts and Crafts silver dish, by P. F. Alexander, the rim chased with stylized trailing floral scrolls, with a stepped centre, London 1912, 6in (15cm) diam. Arts and Crafts silver is very much underrated and pieces can still be found at affordable prices.
£190–210 / €270–290
$310–350 WW ✎

Pair of silver comports, by Towle Silversmiths, the rims decorated with acanthus scrolls, swags and roses, with beaded borders, the bowls embossed, on gadrooned baluster stems on high-domed ogee feet, American, Massachusetts, c1915, 4¼in (11cm) high. The bowl of this type of comport is pressed out and then the base is applied. This pair has pretty decoration and they are in good condition.
£190–210 / €270–290
$310–350 NOA ✎

▶ Two silver-plated vegetable dishes, mid-19thC, 12½in (32cm) wide. These dishes would have originally had covers. The fact that they are missing is reflected in the price.
£210–230 / €290–320
$350–380 SWO ✎

Silver embossed rose bowl, by C. H. Cheshire, with a gilt interior, Chester 1901, 6¾in (17cm) diam, 10oz. Rose bowls were often used for presentations and engraving can lower the value.
£240–270 / €330–380
$390–440 WW ✎

Silver-plated vegetable dish, by Thomas Wilkinson & Sons, Birmingham, the domed cover with an annulated rim and spiral-fluted top, monogrammed 'MLK', the conforming base revealing two liners, one plain, the other pierced, the stand with opposing handles, four gadrooned legs and lion-paw feet, c1875, 9¾in (25cm) wide.
£250–280 / €350–390
$410–460 NOA ✎

Silver bonbon basket, with a swing handle and pierced base, Birmingham 1896, 7in (18cm) wide, 7.5oz.
£250–280 / €350–390
$410–460 WW ✎

Engraved silver sugar bowl, by George Fenwick, with a reeded border and gilt interior, Edinburgh 1806, 8½in (21.5cm) wide, 10oz. Scottish silver is popular at present, and this bowl has well executed engraving.
£300–330 / €420–460
$490–540 WW ✎

Silver bonbon dish, modelled as a boat on four spoked wheels, with an anchor, chain and working tiller and rudder, Continental, English import marks for London 1895, 8½in (21.5cm) wide, 8oz. Novelty items are popular with collectors. Dutch laws were not as strict as the British hallmarking laws and many late 19thC Dutch pieces would have copies of early 18thC Dutch hallmarks. When these pieces were imported, they would be hallmarked with import marks by one of the British assay offices, thereby fairly accurately dating each piece.
£300–330 / €420–460
$490–540 WW ✎

Silver cake basket, with a pierced swing handle, the sides pierced and embossed with swirl fluting and floral sprays, the centre engraved with a coat-of-arms, on a pierced foot, London 1766, 13¾in (35cm) wide, 21oz. If this basket had not been repaired, it could be worth at least twice the price.
£320–350 / €450–490
$520–570 WW ✎

◄ **Sheffield-plated entrée dish,** by I. and I. Waterhouse, Sheffield, with a gadrooned handle, the cover banded *en suite* with the liner, the base liner with a gadrooned edge and an acanthus and shell border, the base with acanthus and cornucopia handles, on four annular bun feet, c1835, 10in (25.5cm) wide. It is possible that the cover of this dish may have been replated. Generally it is not acceptable to replate old Sheffield plate, as this can lower the price.
£300–330 / €420–460
$490–540 NOA ✎

Silver twin-handled miniature porringer, partly wrythen-fluted and with punched decoration, London 1706, 3in (7.5cm) wide. Miniatures are very sought-after and many, being small and delicate, did not survive. These items are ideal for collectors with little space.
£350–390 / €490–540
$570–640 L&E ✎

Arts and Crafts silver bowl, by Robert Hilton, the detachable cover embossed with a rose bordered by the inscription 'fill the cup and drink with me in the name of the Trinity', Chester 1903, 4in (10cm) diam, 6oz. Ecclesiastical items do not normally sell well, but this box has an endearing inscription.
£340–380 / €470–530
$560–620 B(NW) ✎

Find out more in

Miller's Collecting Silver: The Facts At Your Fingertips, Miller's Publications, 1999

Miller's compares...

A. Silver sugar basket, with a swing handle and reeded borders, the part-fluted body with a crest, gilt interior, London 1788, 5½in (14cm) wide, 6oz.
£350–390 / €490–540
$570–640 WW ✎

B. Silver sugar basket, by Henry Chawner, with a reeded swing handle and a reeded foot, London 1791, 4¾in (12cm) wide, 5.25oz.
£650–710 / €910–990
$1,100–1,150 WW ✎

Item A has a later engraved crest and may have been regilded, which could be hiding repairs. Item B has contemporary engraving and is a more pleasing shape as well as being by a known maker, thereby increasing its value.

Silver dessert dish, by Hunt & Roskell, London 1858, 10¾in (27.5cm) diam, 20oz. Hunt & Roskell produced high-quality work and their items are much sought-after today.
£420–460 / €590–640
$690–750 S(O) 🔨

Silver sugar basket, the body with deep gadrooning and a milled floral band, the shaped rim and handle decorated with embossed bellflowers, on a waisted stem with a gadrooned foot with floral banding, French import marks, Continental, probably Austrian, c1800, 9in (23cm) high.
£460–510 / €640–710
$750–830 NOA 🔨

The look without the price

Four embossed silver-gilt dishes,
reshaped and later decorated, hallmarked London 1822, 13½in (34.5cm) wide, 69oz.
£480–530 / €670–740
$780–870 WW 🔨

It was very fashionable for the Victorians to send older plain pieces to the silver-smith to be decorated in the latest style. This does affect the price considerably.

Silver pedestal sugar vase, probably by John Wakelin & Robert Garrard I, the bowl with bright-engraved decoration, London 1794, 4½in (11.5cm) high, 9oz. This is an unusual piece in good condition.
£520–570 / €720–790
$850–930 WW 🔨

◄ **Silver entrée dish,** by William Frisbee, with a ring handle and gadrooned border, the cover with a crest, London 1805, 10¼in (26cm) wide, 50oz. Silver entrée dishes are good value compared to silver-plated ones, and are usually quite heavy.
£700–770 / €980–1,050
$1,150–1,250 B(NW) 🔨

Boxes

Silver dressing table box, maker's initials 'W.N.', Chester 1901, 5½in (14cm) wide.
£90–100 / €125–140
$150–165 SWO ⚲

Care of pressed silver boxes

Pressed silver boxes are prone to holes caused by wear which will affect the price, so check pieces carefully before buying. Also, the detailing of high relief designs can be affected by over polishing. However, these boxes will still look attractive when displayed on a dressing table.

The look without the price

Engine-turned silver snuff box, by Francis Clarke, with engraved scroll borders and gilt interior, the central cartouche inscribed 'John Lean', Birmingham 1849, 3½in (9cm) wide, 2oz.
£140–155 / €195–210
$230–250 WW ⚲

This item has been worn and has had a lead repair. If it had been perfect it would be worth twice as much.

Silver snuff box, with a gilt interior, 1824, 3in (7.5cm) wide. This box may have had the cartouche applied at a later date, perhaps to hide earlier initials.
£150–165 / €210–230
$250–270 SWO ⚲

Silver table box, with engine-turned decoration, London 1850, 3¼in (8.5cm) wide. The engine turning on the lid of this item is worn – if it were in good condition the value could be doubled.
£160–175 / €220–240
$260–285 SWO ⚲

Silver dressing table box, decorated with putti portrait medallions and floral garlands, with a gilt interior, Continental, English import marks for London 1910, 5in (12.5cm) wide, 3.5oz.
£210–230 / €290–310
$350–380 WW ⚲

PRESENTED by the J of the PEACE and ATTORNIES of the C LOTH Arthur C Macartney Esq Assistant Barrister in Testimony of the high Sense they entertain of the PURE, PROMPT AND GENTLEMANLY MANNER in which he discharges the Arduous Duties of his Station

Silver snuff box, by Samuel Pemberton, the cover with a presentation inscription dated 1805, the base with a coat-of-arms, Birmingham, 2¾in (7cm) wide. Boxes with social history can be interesting to research.
£200–220 / €280–310
$330–370 G(L) ⚲

◀ **Silver cigarette box,** in the Dutch style, the hinged cover decorated with a repoussé interior scene, Chester 1898, 4½in (11.5cm) wide, 8oz.
£230–260
€320–360
$380–430 JAd

Silver box, the cover decorated in high relief with a bacchanalian scene, the sides with a fruiting vine, with a parcel-gilt interior, Continental, import marks for London 1894, 5½in (14cm) wide.
£240–270 / €330–380
$390–440 WilP

Silver dressing table box, by Deakin & Francis, the hinged cover relief-decorated with putti, with a gilt interior, Birmingham 1902, 2¾in (7cm) diam, 2.25oz.
£240–270 / €330–380
$390–440 WW

Silver novelty string box, by W. & G. Neal, modelled as an apple, with a gilt interior, London 1900, 2½in (6.5cm) diam.
£250–280 / €350–390
$410–460 WW

Silver and cut-glass toilet box and scent bottle, by Thomas Whitehouse, the reeded mounts applied with rock crystal over an earl's coronet, London 1870, box 7in (18cm) wide.
£250–280 / €350–390
$410–460 S(O)

Silver box, by S.C., London 1885, 4in (10cm) diam.
£260–300 / €360–420
$430–490 WAC

Silver snuff box, by Louis-François Thiryfocq, engraved with a central flower-filled basket roundel, with classical wrigglework borders, French, Paris 1788, 2½in (6.5cm) wide.
£280–310 / €390–430
$460–510 S(O) 🔨

Silver snuff box, by James Wilkes, with an embossed cover and gilt interior, the base inscribed 'Ann Stevenson of Hastings, Sussex, 1753', London 1751, 2¾in (7cm) wide, 1.5oz.
£320–350 / €450–490
$520–570 WW 🔨

Silver box, by Nathan & Hayes, the hinged cover embossed with a tavern scene, Chester 1902, 4½in (11.5cm) wide. This is an English copy of a Dutch box.
£320–350 / €450–490
$520–570 B(NW) 🔨

Silver snuff box, by Joseph Preedy, the cover chased with a balcony and bird scene within rococo scrolls, base initialled, London 1776, 3in (7.5cm) wide.
£400–440 / €560–610
$650–720 S(O) 🔨

Locate the source

The source of each illustration in Miller's can be found by checking the code letters below each caption with the Key to Illustrations, pages 286–290.

▶ **Silver and agate snuff box,** the lid rim with a scroll design, c1790, 3½in (9cm) wide.
£430–480 / €600–670
$700–780 LBr ⊞

Silver-gilt snuff box, by Thomas Pemberton and Richard Mitchell, the engine-turned decoration with floral borders, the interior with an inscription, London 1817, 3in (7.5cm) wide.
£450–500 / €630–700
$730–820 S(O) ✦

► **Silver niello snuff box,** decorated with a scene after Teniers, French, Paris c1860, 4in (10cm) wide. The detail on this box is exceptional.
£520–570 / €720–790
$850–930 S(O) ✦

► **Gilt-metal and silver cagework box,** the pierced trailing flowers applied to a gilt cover and base, c1680, 2in (5cm) diam. It is difficult to find boxes of this age in such good condition. This would represent a very desirable addition to a collection.
£500–550
€700–770
$820–900 S(O) ✦

Silver counter box, the box decorated with a band of trailing flowers, the 18 counters etched with either Charles I or Henrietta Maria, and dated 1638, 1in (2.5cm) high. It is unusual to find dated counter boxes such as this.
£650–720 / €910–1,000
$1,050–1,200 S(O) ✦

➤ **Silver smelling box/spice caster,** by Lawrence & Allen, the hinged cover and base engraved with a floral motif, the sides decorated with leaf motifs and pricked dots on a hatched ground, the nozzle at one end pierced with seven holes, Birmingham 1802, 1½in (4cm) wide.
£650–720 / €910–1,000
$1,050–1,200 WW ✦

◄ **Silver-mounted snuff box,** the tortoiseshell cover moulded and carved in relief with a bust of Charles I, the base with a tortoiseshell panel, c1700, 3¾in (9.5cm) wide.
£650–720
€910–1,000
$1,050–1,200
G(L) ✦

Candlesticks & Chambersticks

The look without the price

Pair of Victorian silver-plated candlesticks, with fluted baluster columns, hexagonal bases and detachable nozzles, 8in (20.5cm) high.
£80–90 / € 110–125
$130–150 WW

Silver-plated candlesticks such as these can be reasonably priced, whereas silver examples could cost upwards of £450 / € 630 / $730 .

Pair of Edwardian silver dwarf candlesticks, with vase-shaped nozzles, reeded stems and square domed bases with chased gadrooned borders, 6in (15cm) high. The appearance of these candlesticks would be greatly improved by cleaning.
£100–110 / € 140–155
$165–180 G(L)

◀ **Pair of Victorian silver-plated candlesticks,** by Elkington, Mason & Co, with detachable nozzles, the knopped and reeded columns on square bases, 10in (25.5cm) high. A pair of similar candlesticks in Georgian silver would cost £2,500 / € 3,500 / $4,100.
£100–110
€ 140–155
$165–180 WW

Early Victorian silver-plated candelabrum, the vase-shaped sockets with scroll-edged nozzles, the centre light with a flambé finial, the three-light branch on a leaf-decorated baluster stem, on a scroll-edged multifoil foot, 22½in (57cm) high. Single candelabrum can be reasonably priced and are useful for smaller tables.
£170–185 / € 235–260
$280–300 CGC

Sets/pairs

Unless otherwise stated, any description which refers to 'a set' or 'a pair' includes a guide price for the entire set or the pair, even though the illustration may show only a single item.

◀ **Silver candlestick,** by F. Arroyo, on a stepped base, Mexican, 19thC, 6¼in (16cm) high.
£230–260 / € 320–360
$380–430 LCM

Silver chamberstick, by John Roberts & Co, with a snuffer, the base with a moulded border, Sheffield 1813, 5½in (14cm) high.
£300–330 / €420–460
$490–540 S(O) ✍

Pair of silver single-light candelabra, with S-scroll branches and decorative bases, marks rubbed, Sheffield c1803, 10in (25.5cm) high. Possibly converted from larger, twin-branch candelabra, these are ideal for a mantelpiece or piano.
£380–420 / €530–590
$620–690 WW ✍

◀ **Pair of silver-mounted ebonized candlesticks,** by George Betjemann & Sons, applied with entwined initials, London 1893, 7½in (19cm) high. These are very unusual candlesticks at a very reasonable price.
£400–440
€560–610
$650–720 S(O) ✍

Pair of silver candlesticks, by John Watson, with gadroon-shell borders, Sheffield 1822, 8in (20.5cm) high.
£400–440 / €560–610
$650–720 S(O) ✍

What are loaded candlesticks?

The development of mechanization during the Industrial Revolution resulted in a proliferation of machine-made loaded candlesticks produced to meet the growing demands of the newly affluent merchant classes. Less metal was used to make a loaded candlestick than a cast one, as the stem was hollow and filled with pitch or sand for weight and stability, and therefore loaded candlesticks could be sold for a significantly lower price. Collectors should be careful when buying filled candlesticks as they often have holes worn through on edges and corners, due to the thinness of the silver.

Pair of George II-style silver candlesticks, by Martin, Hall & Co, the shaped nozzles with shell decoration, the baluster stems on shell-decorated bases, loaded, Sheffield 1912, 12½in (31.5cm) high. These candlesticks are loaded, whereas a Georgian pair would have been cast.
£420–460 / €590–640
$690–750 L ✍

◀ **Silver chamberstick,** by Henry Chawner, engraved with an armorial, with a detachable nozzle and extinguisher, London 1793, 5¾in (14.5cm) diam, 7oz. The sconce on this item has been bent, but could be easily straightened.
£650–720 / €910–1,000
$1,050–1,200 S(O) ✍

Condiments

Four silver salts, by P. Smiley, with engraved swag decoration, London 1874, 2¾in (7cm) high.
**£80–95 / €110–130
$130–155** SWO ✗

◀ **Pair of silver salts,** by Hyam Hyams, on three feet, replaced liners, London 1859, 2¾in (7cm) high.
**£90–100 / €125–140
$150–165** SWO ✗

Silver pepper, with pierced foliate sides, on a domed foot, with a blue glass liner, late 19thC, 3¾in (9.5cm) high.
**£60–65 / €85–90
$100–105** G(L) ✗

Effects of salt on silver

Condition is vital with salt cellars – the corrosive nature of salt, particularly when damp, means that many salts are corroded or stained with black spots, which reduces the value.

▶ **Silver three-piece cruet,** by Liberty and Co, Birmingham 1937, pepper 3¼in (8.5cm) high. Names such as Liberty increase the price of silver dramatically. This set was very good value.
**£210–230 / €290–320
$350–380** BR ✗

Silver bun-top pepper, with a plain moulded girdle, London 1730–39, 3in (7.5cm) high, 2oz.
**£240–260 / €330–360
$390–430** WW ✗

The look without the price

Silver mustard pot, the cover with a ball finial, the body with a reeded border, on ball feet, the interior with traces of gilding, maker's mark partially struck, London 1810, 3¼in (8.5cm) high, 4.75oz.
**£150–165 / €210–230
$250–270** WW ✗

If the mark had been fully struck the value could increase by around 20 per cent, and if marked by a famous maker such as Hester Bateman, this piece could be worth up to four times as much.

Silver cruet, by Samuel Wood, with a central loop handle, the gallery joined to the base with a rococo cartouche and three double C-scroll supports, on shell feet, London 1768, 6in (15cm) wide, 16.5oz, with five later glass bottles, three with silver tops, Birmingham 1913. If all the bottles in this item were original, the value would have been in the region of £4,000 / €5,500 / $6,500.
£250–280 / €350–390
$410–460 PF 🪒

Regency-style silver condiment set, by Julius Rosenthal, comprising four salts, two pepperettes and a mustard pot, with leaf and shell repoussé decoration, Sheffield 1904, 15oz, in a fitted case.
£320–350 / €450–490
$520–570 L 🪒

▶ **Silver mustard pot,** by J. & J. Angell, with engraved decoration and applied husk and scroll borders, the cover engraved with a crown and bugle and the number '85', probably for the Shropshire Volunteer Regiment, with a blue glass liner, London 1846, 3½in (9cm) high, 5.5oz.
£400–440 / €560–610
$650–720 WW 🪒

Pair of late Victorian silver-plated novelty condiment sets, by Elkington & Co, modelled as riding boots and a riding hat on a horseshoe base, with a horse-shaped spice bottle, with glass liners and four spoons, one cover missing, one spoon damaged, 3¾in (9.5cm) high.
£420–460 / €590–640
$690–750 WW 🪒

Silver sugar caster, by Samuel Wood, the cover pierced with scrolls and flowerhead motifs in a wrythen pattern below a knop finial, the foot with corded borders, London 1754, 7in (18cm) high, 7oz.
£480–530 / €670–740
$780–870 WW 🪒

Silver cruet frame, with a scroll leaf handle, the eight reeded divisions gadrooned at intervals, with eight square-cut glass bottles, pots and a sifter spoon, maker's mark rubbed, London 1815, 9¾in (25cm) wide.
£580–640 / €810–890
$950–1,050 S(O) 🪒

Cups, Mugs & Tankards

Silver tankard, with an embossed cartouche, inscribed 'Mkt Harboro Quoit Club 1869', London 1869, 5in (12.5cm) high.
£160–180 / €220–250
$260–295 SWO ⚒

Silver mug, by Mappin & Webb, the bell-shaped bowl decorated with applied foliage around the lower body, with a leaf-capped scroll handle, on a cast and chased foot, London 1900, 4¼in (11cm) high, 9oz.
£160–180 / €220–250
$260–295 WW ⚒

Find out more in

*Miller's Is it Genuine?
How to Collect Antiques
with Confidence,*
Miller's Publications,
2002

Silver baluster mug, with embossed floral decoration, applied monogram and scroll handle, embossing later, London 1750, 4in (10cm) high. This mug has later Victorian decoration. Had it remained in its original plain state, this mug would have been worth three to four times this amount.
£200–220 / €280–310
$330–370 BWL ⚒

Miller's compares...

A. Silver two-handled cup, with floral-and-leaf embossed decoration, crested and monogrammed, with double scroll handles, Hibernia and Harp marked only, Irish, c1770, 7in (18cm) wide, 14oz.
£260–290 / €360–400
$430–470 B(NW) ⚒

B. Silver two-handled cup, by Matthew Walsh, with later chased decoration, on a pedestal foot, with a gilt interior, Irish, Dublin 1781, 6¼in (16cm) high, 13oz.
£680–750 / €950–1,050
$1,100–1,200 WW ⚒

Item A has later decoration and the inscription has been removed. It has then been gilded. The removal of an inscription can leave the silver very thin, which would account for this cup being lower in value than Item B.

Silver christening mug, the thistle-shaped bowl decorated with applied flowers, with a scroll handle, on a cast foot, maker's mark partially struck, London 1838, 4in (10cm) high.
£260–290 / €360–400
$430–470 WW ⚒

Silver mug, by Jason Holt, with a leaf-capped scroll handle, on a spreading foot, engraved with the initials 'RML', Exeter 1764, 4in (10cm) high, 5.75oz. Makers from the west of England are in high demand, but this mug has been severely over-cleaned, decreasing its value.
£300–330 / €420–460
$490–540 WW ⚒

◀ **Silver baluster mug,** possibly by Thomas Whipham, engraved with a contemporary coat-of-arms, with a double scroll handle, on a moulded foot rim, c1743, 4¼in (11cm) high.
£380–420
€530–590
$620–690 G(L) ⚒

Sterling silver mug, probably by Baldwin & Co, with a milled ogee rim, the body engraved in the second Egyptian Revival style with sarcophagus-mask caryatids, with an embossed and applied bust of 'Stonewall' Jackson, the sides engraved with an inscription, with an 'ear-shaped' handle, on an annulated and chevron-banded foot, American, New York, c1868, 3¾in (9.5cm) high, 8oz.
£390–430 / €540–600
$640–700 NOA ⚒

◀ **Parcel-gilt cup and saucer,** repoussé-decorated and engraved to simulate silver birch bark, Russian, Moscow 1888, saucer 5in (12.5cm) diam.
£590–650 / €820–910
$960–1,050 S(O) ⚒

Cutlery & Serving Implements

Miller's compares...

A. Silver caddy spoon, by William Pugh, with a leaf-shaped bowl and a pointed stem initialled 'R', Birmingham 1807.
£60–65 / €85–90
$100–105 WW ⚒

B. Silver caddy spoon, by Joseph Taylor, the bowl with fish scale, crosshatch and scroll decoration, Birmingham 1781.
£190–210 / €270–290
$310–350 B(NW) ⚒

Item A is quite plain, whereas Item B is much more decorative and of an earlier date, and therefore more desirable to collectors, which contributes to its higher value.

Silver tablespoon, with a wavy end and a drop on the back of the bowl, Dutch, Rotterdam 1771, 8in (20.5cm) long, 1.5oz. The marks on this spoon are excellent and would appeal to a collector of Continental silver.
£70–80 / €95–110
$115–130 WW ⚒

Set of six silver dessert spoons, decorated with maidens carrying baskets of fruit, American, 1875–1925.
£70–80 / €95–110
$115–130 G(L) ⚒

Silver spoon and fork, by Wilson & J. Langman, commemorating the Diamond Jubilee of Queen Victoria, engraved '1837–1897', London 1897, 1.5oz, cased.
£70–80 / €95–110
$115–130 WW ⚒

Silver spoon, with a stylized flower engraved on the back of the bowl, with a ball knop twisted stem, maker's mark 'IP', Norwegian, Bergen, c1820, 5¾in (14.5cm) long, 1.75oz.
£80–90 / €110–125
$130–150 WW ⚒

◀ **Set of six silver dessert spoons,** by George Angell, London 1877.
£85–110
€120–155
$140–180 SWO ✗

▶ **Pair of silver sauce ladles,** by Hayne & Carter, London 1854, 7in (18cm) long.
£90–100
€125–140
$150–165 SWO ✗

Pair of silver sardine serving tongs, by Richard Turner, with fish-shaped bowls, London 1816, 5½in (14cm) long, 1.5oz. These tongs are quite rare. However, beware – sugar tongs are sometimes converted to simulate sardine tongs.
£120–130 / €165–180
$195–210 WW ✗

Pair of silver sugar tongs, by John Bourne & Thomas Moore III, with cast pierced arms, London 1775, 5½in (14cm) long. It is important to check the arms of sugar tongs for splits and repairs.
£130–145 / €180–200
$210–230 WW ✗

Pair of silver sugar nips, possibly by William Cox III, with shell grips and ring handles, initialled 'R.M.', London c1775, 5in (12.5cm) long. Sugar nips were the forerunners of sugar tongs.
£140–155 / €195–210
$230–250 WW ✗

Silver butter spade, by George Smith & William Fearn, with a pierced blade, London 1792, 6¾in (17cm) long, 1oz. It is advisable to check butter spades for signs of conversion from tablespoons.
£150–165 / €210–230
$245–270 WW ✗

Pair of silver grape scissors, by Edward Hutton, with bead pattern handles, London 1891, 7in (18cm) long, 2.75oz.
£180–200 / €250–280
$300–330 WW ✗

▶ **Seven silver Scottish Fiddle pattern teaspoons,** including a pair probably by Adam Graham, Glasgow, c1765, another pair by Alexander Gairdner, Edinburgh, c1790, and three by Milne & Campbell, Glasgow, c1760, all initialled, 3oz.
£190–210
€270–290
$310–350 WW ✗

Miller's compares...

▶ **A. Pair of cast silver sugar nips,**
by Joseph Wilmore, with leaf grips, the
arms decorated with fruiting foliate
scrolls, Birmingham, c1840,
4½in (11.5cm) long.
£150–165 / €210–230
$245–270 WW ⚒

◀ **B. Pair of silver-gilt sugar nips,**
by Paul Storr, with leaf grips, the arms
decorated with openwork leafy tendrils
set with bees and ladybirds, with a
large floral boss, London 1835,
5¾in (14.5cm) long, 2oz.
£480–530 / €670–740
$780–870 WW ⚒

Items A and B are of a similar date, but the workmanship of Paul Storr, the maker of Item B, is
far superior to that of Item A, with the result that it is three times more valuable. The quality
of Paul Storr's workmanship is extremely high, and these sugar nips represent an excellent
opportunity to buy a top-quality piece by a well-known maker at a relatively low price.

What are mote spoons?

Mote spoons, an 18th-
century invention, were
used to remove stray
leaves from cups of tea
– the pointed stem was
used for clearing the
straining holes inside
the teapot. Most mote
spoons were made
during the mid-1700s,
and later examples had
elaborate pierced bowls.
Some have applied
shellwork, scrolls or other
motifs struck on the back
of the bowl, all of which
will increase the value.
Teaspoons were often
converted into mote
spoons but the piercing
is usually quite crude
in comparison to an
original and often the
bowl tip will show typical
wear from when it was
used as a teaspoon.

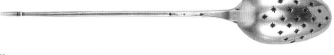

Silver mote spoon, with a turned finial, the single drop bowl pierced with a
panel of drilled holes, filed to look like mullets on the reverse, c1740,
5¾in (14.5cm) long, 0.5oz.
£210–230 / €290–320
$350–380 WW ⚒

George III silver-gilt mote spoon, the shoulders and feather-edge stem
terminating with a diamond point, the bowl pierced with a crosslet, pellets and
scrolls, 5½in (14cm) long, 0.5oz. The feather-edge decoration and shoulders
make this a rare mote spoon at a very good price.
£230–255 / €320–360
$380–420 WW ⚒

Silver mote spoon, by William Foster, with a diamond point finial, the egg-
shaped bowl decorated with a floral scroll motif and pierced scrolls, London,
c1775, 5in (12.5cm) long, 0.25oz.
£230–255 / €320–360
$380–420 WW ⚒

Silver trefid spoon, by Thomas Allen, with a ribbed rattail and a cleft terminal pricked 'TH' over 'H', marks worn, London c1680, 7½in (19cm) long, 1.5oz. There is a strong market for trefid spoons, but it is wise to be sure of good marks and condition.
£300–330 / €420–460
$490–540 WW

White metal and enamel spoon, hallmarked, Russian, 19thC, 8¼in (21cm) long.
£400–440 / €560–610
$650–720 SWO

Silver-gilt dessert service, comprising 18 knives and matching forks by Harrison & Howson, with reeded handles and fluted 'pistol' terminals, Sheffield 1897 and 18 spoons by Francis Boone Thomas, with fluted, flared terminals, London 1897, 21oz. Gilded flatware is not very popular, and this is reflected in the low price of this dessert service.
£360–400 / €500–560
$590–650 WW

Miller's compares...

A. Silver marrow scoop, by Andrew Archer, with faceted bowl, London 1722, 9in (23cm) long, 1.5oz.
£400–440 / €560–610
$650–720 WW

B. Silver marrow scoop, by James Turner, the stem shouldered where it meets the scoop, crested, marked 'IT' within a heart-shaped punch on the back of the stem, American, Boston, c1750, 8in (20.5cm) long 1.5oz.
£560–620 / €780–860
$910–1,000 WW

These are both fine examples and Item A has good marks. However, Item B is early for American silver which is rare and highly sought-after by collectors at the moment, and therefore of higher value.

Daniel Bexfield Antiques
FINE QUALITY SILVER

Specialising in fine quality silver, jewellery and objects of vertu dating from the 17th Century to 20th Century.

Web: www.bexfield.co.uk
Email: antiques@bexfield.co.uk
26 Burlington Arcade, London W1J 0PU

   Tel: 0207 491 1720
  Fax: 0207 491 1730

Silver-plated fish service, by Levesley Brothers, comprising 24 pieces, the forks engraved with a band of shamrocks, the engraved scimitar-bladed knives all with silver collars and ivory handles, 1896–97, forks 7½in (19cm) long, in original mahogany box.
£420–460 / €590–640
$690–750 NOA 🔨

▶ **Child's silver knife, fork and spoon,** by Tiffany & Co, American, c1890, fork 7in (18cm) long.
£450–500 / €630–700
$730–820 BEX ⊞

Silver-plated dessert service, by James Dixon & Sons, comprising 24 pieces, all with gadrooned mother-of-pearl handles, with silver collars by William Morton, Sheffield 1887, knives 8in (20.5cm) long, in the original inlaid mahogany case with brass plaque monogrammed 'EJR'.
£490–540 / €680–750
$800–880 NOA 🔨

▶ **Pair of cast silver-gilt salt spoons,** by J. Hunt & R. Roskell, pierced and crested, with a vine pattern and applied shield cartouches, London 1872, 4½in (11.5cm) long, 1oz.
£520–570 / €720–790
$850–930 WW 🔨

▶ **Set of six cast silver teaspoons,** with fluted bowls and leafy tendril stems, each with a ladybird and a caterpillar, maker's mark 'JD' below a trefoil, London c1745, 4¾in (12cm) long, 3.25oz.
£440–490
€610–680
$720–800 WW 🔨

What is casting?

Cast silver items are made by pouring molten silver into a cast or mould of the desired shape. When the silver has solidified the mould is broken away, leaving the casting. When a casting comes out of the mould it has a rough, unfinished appearance which has to be trimmed off or polished down.

Silver medicine spoon, by William Barber, with a gilt interior, London 1829, 5¼in (13.5cm) long, 2.25oz. Items of medical interest are very collectable.
£520–570 / €720–790
$850–930 WW 🔨

For more examples of Medical items see Scientific Instruments (pages 266–269)

Jugs & Sauce Boats

Silver hot water jug, maker's mark 'RM/EH', Sheffield 1895, 8¾in (22cm) high. This jug is reasonably priced because the handle has been broken and repaired with a silver band. In original condition it would have been of higher value.
£110–120 / €155–165
$180–195 SWO ✦

For more examples of Cream Jugs see Ceramics (pages 64–131)

Miller's compares...

A. Silver helmet-shaped cream jug, by William Sutton, on a square-based pedestal foot, 1792, 5in (12.5cm) high.
£160–175 / €220–240
$260–280 G(L) ✦

B. Silver jug, probably by Elizabeth Morley, chased with peacock scenes, with a leaf-capped scroll handle, London 1770, 4¼in (11cm) high, 4oz.
£380–420 / €530–590
$620–690 S(O) ✦

Item B is of higher value than Item A because of its fine workmanship, pleasing shape and thickness of silver. The handle of Item A may have been repaired where it joins the body, thus lowering the price.

Vase-shaped silver cream jug, probably by John Lambe, with a beaded lip and loop handle, on a square-base pedestal foot, London 1784, 3oz.
£160–175 / €220–245
$260–285 WW ✦

Silver jug, monogrammed on both sides, maker's mark for R. Garrard, dated 'February 1861', 3½in (9cm) high. The Garrard workshop was renowned for high quality silver.
£200–220 / €280–310
$330–370 SWO ✦

Silver sauce boat, double lipped, on a stand, German, late 19thC, 10in (25.5cm) wide, 21oz.
£200–220 / €280–310
$330–370 S(O)

Silver cream jug, probably by John Stoyte, fan-fluted and engraved with a foliate design below a shaped moulded edge, loop handle, Irish, Dublin 1792, 5in (12.5cm) high, 3.5oz. This is a very desirable cream jug and represents good value at this price.
£220–240 / €310–330
$370–390 CGC

Miller's compares...

A. Silver-mounted hobnail cut-glass claret jug, with a silver collar, cover and handle with chased floral decoration and a scroll finial, maker's mark 'W.D.', Birmingham 1901, 8¾in (22cm) high.
£200–220 / €280–310
$330–370 BR

B. Silver-mounted cut-glass claret jug, Sheffield 1896, 8½in (21.5cm) high.
£640–700 / €890–980
$1,050–1,150 G(L)

Item B sold for a much higher price because of its better proportions. Although unusual in style, the handle on Item A appears too large and heavy for the jug. When buying a claret jug, always check the glass for any damage, especially around the neck, as this will affect the price quite considerably.

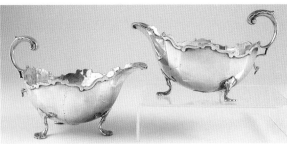

◄ **Pair of silver sauce boats,** by G. Nathan & R. Hayes, with flying scroll handles and applied scroll borders, on three cast feet, Chester 1900, 6in (15cm) wide, 10.5oz.
£260–290 / €360–400
$430–470 WW

► **Silver cream jug,** by Alexander Field, with a helmet-shaped reeded rim, reeded decoration and pricked borderwork, engraved with a crest, London 1803, 4in (10cm) high, 3.75oz.
£260–290
€360–400
$430–470 WW

Silver sauce boat, by William Justus, with an upscrolled leaf-capped handle, on three C-scroll feet, c1755, 5¾in (14.5cm) wide.
£280–310 / €390–430
$460–510 G(L)

◄ **Silver ewer,** by John Wakelin and William Taylor, with a plaited cane handle, the body embossed with floral decoration, on a gadrooned foot and rim, London 1777, 11in (28cm) high, 22oz. This item is described as a ewer but is, in fact, a hot water pot and would have belonged to a tea service. The plaited cane handle was for insulation from the heat of the water. This item has also been later decorated.
£480–530 / €670–740
$780–870 CGC ⚥

Silver helmet-shaped cream jug, by Samuel Meriton II, with a loop handle, decorated with bright-engraved borders and a wreath cartouche, initialled, on a pedestal foot, London 1795, 4¾in (12cm) high, 4oz.
£300–330 / €420–460
$490–540 WW ⚥

► **Silver sauce boat,** by William Bateman II, with a flying scroll handle and gadrooned rim, on three fluted supports with hoof feet, initialled, London 1830, 8in (20.5cm) wide, 15oz.
£500–550 / €700–770
$820–900 WW ⚥

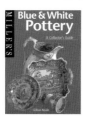
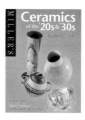

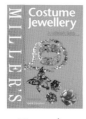

M I L L E R ' S

COLLECTOR'S GUIDES SERIES

Blue & White Pottery — A Collector's Guide

Ceramics of the '20s & '30s — A Collector's Guide

Glass of the '20s & '30s — A Collector's Guide

Goss & Crested China

Costume Jewellery

Corkscrews & Wine Antiques

Handbags — A Collector's Guide

To order any of the above call the Miller's credit card hotline on

01903 828800 (UK) 1-800-759-0190 (USA)

Alternatively visit our website and see the full range of Miller's titles available

w w w . m i l l e r s . u k . c o m

Salvers & Trays

Engraved silver salver, with a stamped border of rocaille scrolls and floral motifs, maker's mark partially struck, Birmingham 1902, 10in (25.5cm) diam, 12oz.
£140–155 / €195–210
$230–250 WW ✦

Silver-plated tray, with a pierced rim and applied grapevine edge, the base engraved with a band of C-scrolls, flowers and acanthus on a quilted field, a rococo cartouche to the centre, on four cast and applied grape-leaf feet, c1895, 16¼in (41.5cm) wide.
£160–180 / €220–250
$260–290 NOA ✦

The look without the price

Silver salver, by Robert Rew, on pad feet, with later foliate chasing, London 1768, 12in (30.5cm) diam, 24oz.
£180–200 / €250–280
$300–330 S(O) ✦

The later decoration on this piece has lowered the price and made it less desirable to the purist. In its original undecorated condition this salver could be worth as much as £500–600 / €700–830 / $800–980.

◀ **Silver waiter,** by John Carter, on pad feet, London 1770, 7in (18cm) diam, 9oz.
£320–350
€450–490
$520–570 WW ✦

▶ **Silver waiter,** by John Robertson II, on hoof feet, crested, London 1741, 6¾in (17cm) diam, 8oz.
£380–420
€530–590
$620–690 WW ✦

Silver salver, by Matthew Dixon, with a gadroon and floral scroll border, on ornate feet, the centre engraved with a coat-of-arms, the reverse with a presentation inscription, Birmingham 1822, 12¼in (31cm) wide, 22oz.
£450–500 / €630–700
$730–820 WW ⚒

▶ **Cast and embossed silver tazza,** by Frederick Elkington, the central boss depicting Medusa, bordered by three masks and angels, further surrounded by vacant cartouches and winged mythological beasts, on a spreading base, with gilt highlights, the removable base cover signed and numbered 1547, with glass cover, Birmingham 1870, 10in (25.5cm) diam, 29oz.
£560–610 / €780–850
$910–1,000 B(NW) ⚒

Silver salver, by John Carter, with a beaded border, on claw-and-ball feet, later initialled 'RMS', London 1774, 12¾in (32.5cm) diam, 32oz. This salver has lost over 3oz Troy of silver according to its scratch weight. It possibly had a family armorial that has been polished off and replaced by initials. It would have sold for at least twice the price if original.
£500–550 / €700–770
$820–900 S(O) ⚒

Silver two-handled tray, by Turner Bradbury, with a husk and scroll border and engraved central cartouche bordered by engraved scrolls, London 1903, 24in (61cm) wide, 81oz.
£820–1,000 / €1,150–1,400
$1,350–1,650 WW ⚒

Pair of silver salvers, by Charles Fox, with a lion rampant crest within flat-chased rococo decoration and conforming shell-scroll border, London 1829, 10in (25.5cm) diam, 38oz.
£850–1,050 / €1,200–1,450
$1,400–1,700 S(O) ⚒

Tea, Coffee & Chocolate Pots

◀ **Silver coffee pot,** with embossed and chased bands, Birmingham 1901, 9½in (24cm) high. Tea services have dropped from fashion, and therefore in price, over the last few years, so can be bought relatively cheaply.
£120–135
€ **165–190**
$195–220 SWO ⚹

Victorian silver-plated teapot, 9¾in (25cm) high.
£170–185 / € **240–260**
$280–300 SWO ⚹

◀ **Sheffield-plated four-piece tea and coffee service,** with foliate scroll feet, c1840.
£190–210 / € **270–290**
$310–350 WW ⚹

Silver chocolate pot, by Gibson & Langman, the stepped hinged cover with a wooden finial, wooden side handle, on a flared foot, London 1897, 16¾in (42.5cm) high, 7.75oz.
£190–210 / € **270–290**
$310–350 CGC ⚹

Batchelor's silver tea set, the tea pot with urn finial, scrolled wooden handle, faceted spout and moulded foot, with matching jug and sugar bowl, London 1906, teapot 6½in (16.5cm) wide, 10.25oz.
£190–210 / € **270–290**
$310–350 AH ⚹

Silver teapot, the cover with a flowerhead finial, the reeded body on a domed foot, London 1824.
£200–220 / € **280–310**
$330–370 AMB ⚹

▶ **Pair of silver café au lait pots,** by Holland, Aldwinckle & Slater, with carved wooden side handles, on foliate bracket feet, London 1905, 7in (18cm) high, 24oz. This pair of very stylish pots are good value.
£210–230
€ **290–320**
$350–380 WW ⚹

◄ **Pair of silver coffee pots,**
with turned ebony handles, 1907,
6in (15cm) high.
£240–260 / €330–370
$390–440 SWO ⚒

**Art Deco silver three-piece tea
service,** by H. C. Davis, the teapot with a
Bakelite handle and finial, the sugar bowl
with twin-lug Bakelite handles, Birmingham
1932–33, 27oz.
£320–350 / €450–490
$520–570 WW ⚒

**The look without
the price**

Silver teapot, by Peter and Anne Bateman, with a
pineapple finial and wooden handle, and bright-cut
engraved decoration, 1797, 6¼in (16cm) wide, 13oz.
£280–310 / €390–430
$460–510 L ⚒

This is an excellent opportunity to own a teapot by
well-known makers, which would normally sell for
three times the amount of this piece, suggesting
that the spout or base may have been repaired.

Silver coffee pot, Viennese, 1858,
9in (23cm) high.
£360–400 / €500–550
$590–650 DORO ⚒

◄ **Embossed silver teapot,** by Rebecca
Emes and Edward Barnard, with a floral
knop finial, the spout cast as a bird's neck
with a bacchanalian mask below, engraved
on one side with a coat-of-arms, London
1818, 6¼in (16.5cm) high, 27oz.
£420–460 / €590–640
$690–750 WW ⚒

Silver three-piece tea service, possibly by Charles Lamb, repoussé-decorated with animals and birds, the teapot with a swan finial, all with lion-mask and pad feet, Irish, Dublin 1906, 32.25oz.
£420–460 / €590–640
$690–750 L ⚷

Silver three-piece tea service, by Soloman Royes and John East Dix, with all-over floral and scroll embossing, the teapot with hinged cover and floral finial, an insulated loop handle applied with a thumbpiece cast as a head, London 1819, teapot 6in (15cm) high, 48oz.
£540–590 / €750–820
$880–960 CGC ⚷

Silver four-piece tea and coffee service, embossed and engraved with stylistic foliate pattern, the spout terminals leaf-cast, London 1853, coffee pot 12in (30.5cm) high, 70oz.
£580–640 / €810–890
$950–1,050 TMA ⚷

Silver three-piece tea service, by Solomon Hougham, the fluted upper bodies with borders of gadrooning and shells with acorns, with leaf-capped handles, on ball feet, London 1814–15, 40oz.
£480–530 / €670–740
$780–870 WW ⚷

◄ **George IV silver three-piece tea service,** by Henry Hyams, with gadrooned border and repoussé floral bands, on paw feet, 1822, 41.5oz.
£520–570 / €720–790
$850–930 L ⚷

For more examples
of Tea, Coffee & Chocolate Pots see Ceramics (pages 64–131)

Silver three-piece tea service, by Elkington & Co, with repoussé floral decoration, the teapot with a floral finial, Birmingham 1850, 45.5oz.
£550–600 / €770–840
$900–980 L ⚷

▶ **Silver coffee pot,** by Walter Brind, with urn finials, London 1775, 12in (30.5cm) high, 27oz. This pot benefits from not having later decoration applied by the Victorians.
£850–930
€1,200–1,300
$1,400–1,500
S(O) ⚷

Vinaigrettes

Silver vinaigrette, by George Unite, engraved with foliate scrolls, Birmingham 1834, 1in (2.5cm) wide. The engraving on the cover of this vinaigrette is sharp but its value is lowered by the fact that the hinge has come away from the body slightly.
£90–100 / € 125–140
$150–165 G(L) ✍

Silver vinaigrette, by Samuel Pemberton, the lid engraved with acorns and oak leaves, enclosing a floral grille, Birmingham 1817, 1½in (4cm) wide.
£120–130 / € 165–180
$200–210 G(L) ✍

George IV silver vinaigrette, possibly by William Parker, London 1820, 1¼in (3cm) wide.
£140–150 / € 190–210
$230–240 WW ✍

◀ **Silver vinaigrette,** by Sampson Mordan, modelled as a horn, with chain, 1871, 3in (7.5cm) wide.
£320–350 / € 450–490
$520–570 L ✍

Silver castletop vinaigrette, by John Tongue, Birmingham 1842, 1½in (4cm) wide.
£680–750 / € 950–1,050
$1,100–1,200 WW ✍

Miller's compares...

A. Silver vinaigrette, with engine-turned decoration, Birmingham, c1843, 1¾in (4.5cm) wide.
£140–155 / € 195–210
$230–250 SWO ✍

B. Silver vinaigrette, by Yapp & Woodward, the cover engraved with a lake scene with a building, pleasure boats and a setting sun, within scroll borders, Birmingham 1847, 1½in (4cm) wide.
£780–860 / € 1,100–1,200
$1,300–1,400 WW ✍

Item A has simple engine-turned decoration and is a much more common design. Item B is in very good condition and has unusual engraving, making it higher in value. Vinaigrettes engraved with scenes are always more desirable to the collector.

Miscellaneous

Silver model of a Sussex trug, by James Dixon & Sons, Sheffield 1909, 4½in (11.5cm) wide.
£45–50 / €60–70
$75–80 G(L) ✣

Silver-mounted glass preserve jar, Birmingham 1911, 2¾in (7cm) high. The lid of this preserve jar is a marriage and this has been taken into account in the price.
£65–70 / €90–95
$105–115 G(L) ✣

Silver travelling shaving brush, by Charles Rawlings, in a tubular case, engraved with the royal crown, 2¾in (7cm) long, 2oz.
£80–90 / €110–125
$130–150 WW ✣

Silver planter, by SG, the centre of the body embossed with a floral scroll and trellis pierced beneath a crimped anthemion edge, Birmingham 1903, 5¾in (14.5cm) diam, 7.75oz.
£90–100 / €125–140
$150–165 CGC ✣

◀ **Silver planter,** with lion-mask and drop ring handles, blue glass liner, English import marks for London 1903, 4¾in (12cm) high, 11oz. Continental silver is often overlooked by collectors, which may account for the low price of this elaborately pierced and embossed example.
£100–110
€140–155
$165–180 WW ✣

Late Victorian silver scent flask, with scroll decoration, 2in (5cm) high. This scent flask has lost its stopper, hence the low price.
£100–110 / €140–155
$165–180 G(L) ✣

▲ **Pair of Edwardian silver specimen vases,** by Synyer & Beddoes, pierced and repoussé decorated, on a plain pedestal foot, one with glass liner, loaded, Birmingham 1903, 4¾in (12cm) high. One of the vases has lost its glass liner, which has affected the price. However, this can be replaced without too much difficulty.
**£110–120 / € 155–165
$180–195** CGC ⚹

▶ **Late Victorian silver-plated soup tureen and cover,** part reeded, the domed cover with looped handle, the body applied with two turned wood handles, on foliate pad feet, 13¼in (33.5cm) wide, with a fiddle-and-shell patterned soup ladle.
**£140–155
€ 200–215
$230–250** BR ⚹

Silver-plated bottle stand, with glass bottle and stopper, the base with a heart-shaped cartouche inscribed 'This bottle was carried as a water bottle throughout the Ashanti Expedition of 1873–4 by Lieutenant F Jerrard, The Kings Regt Commanding Abrah Transport Levy', c1873, 11¼in (28.5cm) high.
**£120–130 / € 165–180
$195–210** WW ⚹

Silver-plated trefoil decanter stand, with three glass decanters, late 19thC, 15½in (39.5cm) high.
**£140–155 / € 200–210
$230–250** SWO ⚹

◀ **Silver tobacco 'pebble',** the hinged cover doubling as a vesta case, gilt interior, initialled and dated '1914', maker's mark 'S & Bm', Birmingham 1914, 3in (7.5cm) diam, 2oz. Combination items such as this are always sought-after by collectors.
**£170–185 / € 240–260
$280–300** WW ⚹

Silver-mounted cut-glass travelling ink pot, the screw top with a hinged locking well cover, engraved with a stag within engine-turned decoration, London 1833, 1½in (4cm) diam. This inkwell would have come from a travelling box with many other implements, but it is still highly collectable. It is advisable to check the leather seal on the lid of an item such as this, as it often perishes.
**£170–185 / € 240–260
$280–300** TMA ⚹

The look without the price

Edwardian silver bosun's whistle/call, by Hilliard & Thomason, with engraved sides, Birmingham 1902, 3¾in (9.5cm) long, 0.4oz.
£190–210 / €270–290
$310–350 WW ✐

This is a copy of a Georgian whistle. If it had been made c1810 it would be worth £400–500 / €560–700 / $650–820, and will be of interest to collectors of naval and nautical items, as well as those who collect silver.

Silver-plated centrepiece, by Henry Wilkinson & Co, modelled as a palm tree, on a lobed base with a carved and applied acanthus-and-scroll rim with integral feet, Sheffield, c1870, 9in (23cm) high.
£210–230 / €290–320
$350–380 NOA ✐

◀ **Silver patch box,** the pull-off cover inset with a portrait miniature of George II, the interior with a mirror, on a mother-of-pearl base, c1750, 1½in (4cm) diam. This is an extremely unusual patch box and excellent value at this price.
£210–230
€290–320
$350–380 WW ✐

Silver-mounted bottle, by Thomas Aldwinkle and John Slater, the glass body engraved with a starburst base, with a hinged silver collar, the lid decorated with embossed flowers and rococo scrolls with a central putto masque, London 1886–87, 4in (10cm) high.
£220–240 / €310–330
$370–390 NOA ✐

◀ **Silver travelling communion set,** by Nathaniel Mills, retailed by Reid & Sons, Newcastle, comprising a communion cup and paten, engraved with the religious sunburst emblem, Birmingham 1845, 1.5oz, in a fitted leather case.
£230–250 / €320–350
$380–410 WW ✐

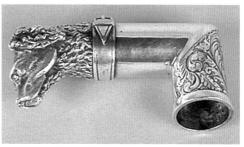

Silver-coloured metal cane handle, modelled as a spaniel with a collar, 19thC, 3in (7.5cm) long. This is an attractively cast handle, and it would not be too difficult to replace the stick.
£260–290 / €360–400
$430–470 L ⚒

Silver nutmeg grater, with removable steel grater, 1700–50, 2¾in (7cm) long. If this nutmeg grater had been marked it would have sold for two or three times as much.
£230–250 / €320–350
$380–410 WW ⚒

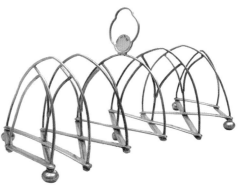

Silver vesta case/cigar cutter, by Sampson Mordan & Co, with a reeded tapering handle, hinged at one end for vestas, London 1900, 5½in (14cm) long, 2oz. Pieces by Sampson Mordan are always sought-after, as are vesta cases and cigar cutters. This item has all three elements.
£300–330 / €420–460
$490–540 WW ⚒

Silver expanding toast rack, by S. Roberts, G. Cadman & Co, with concertina action and arched wirework bars, on ball feet, initialled 'M', stamped 'R. C. & Co. Patent', Sheffield 1812, 21½in (54.5cm) wide. Expanding toast racks are great fun, but are prone to damage and repair. Always check them carefully before purchase.
£320–350 / €450–490
$520–570 WW ⚒

Child's silver rattle, by Margaret Binley, with a coral teether, the whistle terminal with chased floral scroll decoration and eight bells, engraved with the initials 'T.I.S. A.S.H.' and dated 1777, one bell replaced, London, c1770, 5½in (14cm) long. The replacement bell has halved the value of this rattle.
£420–460 / €590–640
$690–750 WW ⚒

The look without the price

Pair of Sheffield plate wine coasters, pierced and bright-cut with floral swags, c1790, 5in (12.5cm) diam.
£350–390 / €490–540
$570–640 S(O) ⚒

If these coasters had been silver rather than Sheffield plate they would have cost
£2,000–3,000 / €2,800–4,200 / $3,300–4,900.

Glass

Glass is an unusual category of antiques for several important, interrelated reasons. Unlike nearly all other antiques, most glass does not bear factory marks or signatures. As a result of this anonymity, the recognition and appreciation of a given piece rests largely in the eye of the beholder. These factors combine to leave the field abundant with potential bargains for those willing to learn and to put theory into practice.

The debutante glass collector faces an important decision when starting out: whether or not to concentrate on the classics, such as 18th-century drinking glasses or 19th-century coloured glass. These have performed well over recent decades but are relatively rare and known to be desirable even among the uninitiated. However, such 'collectables' form but a tiny minority of the available pool. For those of limited budget or prepared to be slightly speculative, British 18th-century salts, syllabubs and jellies, 19th-century drinking glasses, decanters, most cut-glass and European pieces currently remain undervalued.

Despite its fragility, huge quantities of antique glass, mostly dating from the 19th and 20th centuries, remain available at today's specialist and general fairs and flea markets. However, such is its nature that few vendors appreciate precisely what they are selling. The effect is three-fold: glasses of the type given away by petrol stations sometimes reappear labelled and priced as 'antiques', a few pieces are correctly recognized and priced accordingly, while the majority is often lumped together as 'miscellaneous', or even 'junk'.

While few specialist fields are more dependant on knowledge than glass, the rewards are potentially huge for those prepared to read and digest the available literature. However, there is little point in owning books, catalogues and articles that remain unopened or unread beyond the captions. The keys to success are of course, a retentive memory, a keen eye and the ability to prevent wishful-thinking from overtaking reality when buying.

Classic cases of over-optimism when glass-hunting include confusing Edwardian reproductions for period pieces, and the misconception that all coloured and/or textured 20th-century glass was made by Whitefriars. The former is tricky as reproductions mimicked old shapes and decorative styles. The best general rule for avoiding them is to remember that 20th-century glass is invariably better-made than earlier work, being brighter and including fewer bubbles, striations and contaminants. As for the latter, Whitefriars was a small works whose limited output was widely copied. While some of its 1960s' designs are distinctive, rival companies including Stuart and Walsh produced Art Nouveau pieces that are commonly mistaken today for the designs of Whitefriars' legendary Harry Powell.

As a result of its obvious pitfalls, glass remains the Cinderella of the antiques world, widely neglected and misunderstood. The flip-side for the potential collector is that most of it remains remarkably cheap and available, especially to those prepared to learn at least the basics and devote the time necessary to track down bargains.

Andy McConnell

Baskets, Bowls & Dishes

Glass cup plate, moulded with a named likeness of Henry Clay, c1850, 3¼in (8.5cm) diam. Pressed-glass cup plates are avidly collected in the United States. They were used to hold teacups and protect table-cloths while the tea was being sipped from a deeper saucer. Pressed-glass versions were first recorded in 1827 and those with commemorative portraits and slogans were popular. Henry Clay was a particular hero among American glassmakers as he was the driving force behind the 1824 tariff imposed on glass imports into the United States. Fragments of this particular pattern have been recovered from the site of the Boston & Sandwich factory.
£40–45 / €55–60
$65–75 SAS ⚲

What is Carnival glass?

Mass-produced kaleidoscopic carnival glass was pioneered by the Fenton Art Glass Co of Williamstown, West Virginia in 1907. It imitated the more expensive effects developed by Loetz, Emile Gallé, Louis C. Tiffany and Frederick Carder yet sold for as little as a few cents a piece. Carnival's rich shimmering colours found an eager market among the industrial world, and destroyed the market for superficially similar art glass. Carder himself lamented, 'when a maid could possess iridescent glass as well as her mistress, the latter promptly lost interest in it.'

▶ **Crimped carnival glass bowl,** the lustrous interior moulded with a fruiting vine, rim chip, early 20thC, 8½in (21.5cm) diam.
£50–55 / €70–75
$80–90 PFK ⚲

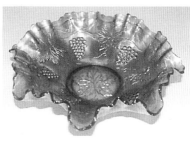

Find out more in

Miller's Popular Glass of the 19th & 20th Centuries: A Collector's Guide, Miller's Publications, 2000

Pair of cut cranberry glass salts, with ruby glass spoons, c1925, 2½in (6.5cm) diam. Cranberry glassware is being increasingly reproduced and it can be hard to differentiate between antique and modern examples. These salts are cut with notches around the rims, thumbnail 'olives' and starred bases, which suggests that they are period pieces.
£100–110 / €140–150
$165–180 GRI ⊞

◀ **Glass sugar bowl and domed cover,** late 18thC, 5½in (14cm) high. Sugar bowls of this shape, used for storing small quantities of lump sugar, were produced in England between c1780 and 1820. The dark green colour of this glass was based on iron oxide – rusty iron was added to furnace pots of colourless glass. The difficulty lay in achieving a consistent hue.
£70–80 / €95–110
$115–130 DN ⚲

Cut-glass dish, the base cut with a radial star, rim chips, c1825, 11in (28cm) diam. 'Wine suites' of decanters and drinking glasses with matching decoration date from the 1750s, followed by dining services some 50 years later. This piece, a beautiful example of the finest Georgian cut glass, would have originally been accompanied by matching bowls, decanters, glasses, jugs, salts and so on. The tiny chips around the rim barely detract from this superb quality but inexpensive piece.
£100–110 / €140–150
$165–180 WW ⚲

Lalique glass

René Lalique (1860–1945) remains the world's most famous, popular and best documented glassmaker. Originally a jeweller, in the first decade of the 20th century he changed direction to design an extraordinary range of moulded table, lighting and architectural glass, some applied with post-production techniques, including staining, sand-blasting and acid-etching. The company he founded continues to this day, so the presence of his name on a piece of glass does not guarantee its age or value. The prices commanded by Lalique glass vary according to the age, design and production method of the piece.

Late Victorian cranberry glass sugar bowl and milk jug, on clear shell feet, jug 3in (7.5cm) high. The opaque white glass trails wound around these pieces were applied by a machine invented in Stourbridge during the 1880s, and their shell-like feet are of a similar date.
**£120–130 / €165–180
$195–210** PFK ⚘

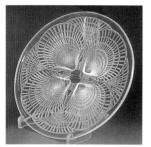

Lalique opalescent glass dish, No. 3012, 'Coquilles', engraved mark, c1930, 8in (20.5cm) diam.
**£240–270 / €330–380
$390–440** CGC ⚘

Two-part glass comport, possibly by Richardson and Co, engraved with geometric patterns and a Greek key border, the bowl supported on a bell-shaped base, 1860–75, 10in (25.5cm) high. Fine quality engraving of this style was executed in London, Stourbridge and Edinburgh, and it is impossible in most cases to attribute particular pieces to individual makers or engravers. Wheel engraving is a labour-intensive process in which the glass is lightly pressed against small copper wheels of various diameters applied with oil-based abrasives to build up a pattern. This large, imposing piece represents excellent value.
**£270–300 / €380–420
$440–490** NOA ⚘

Pair of Anglo-Irish-style glass lidded bowls, cut with strawberry diamonds, the domed lids with faceted knop finials, 1800–25, 7½in (19cm) diam. Cut glass has been out of fashion for some time, making pieces such as these available at relatively low prices.
**£290–320 / €400–450
$470–520** NOA ⚘

▶ **Cut-glass ice bucket,** mounted with a silver collar with two projecting handles by The Goldsmiths & Silversmiths Co, with matching pierced silver drainer, London 1939, 7in (18cm) diam.
**£430–475 / €600–660
$700–770** CGC ⚘

Cut glass

Most British cut glass has been unfashionable for several decades. Its combinations of geometric motifs were created freehand in three basic stages: roughing, cutting and polishing. The use of acids largely superseded the polishing processes from around 1930, although the others still require a steady hand and great precision. Too fussy for many tastes, some Regency and almost all Victorian cut glass remains remarkably cheap and available, and even slight damage can render a piece almost valueless.

Candlesticks & Lustres

Pair of Victorian glass lustres, the faceted bowls with serrated edges and gilt floral decoration, on tapering stems and domed feet, each missing four of the eight cut-glass drops, 11½in (29cm) high. The absence of four glass drops dramatically reduces the price of this piece. However, drops of this type are fairly common and can be replaced for a very small outlay. With its original eight drops it might have fetched £250–300 / €350–420 / $410–490.
£90–100 / €125–140 $150–165 PFK

Pair of cranberry glass baluster candlesticks, with gilt borders, one with rim chip, Bohemian, c1880, 8½in (21.5cm) high.
£150–165 / €210–230 $245–270 TMA

▶ **Pair of cased glass lustres,** with prism drops, 19thC, 11¼in (28.5cm) high. Pieces of this type were produced in Bohemia, England and France. They provide an imposing 150-year-old table centrepiece without costing a fortune.
£480–530 / €670–740 $780–870 SWO

Regency cut-glass candelabrum, with hobnail decoration, later drops, 18in (45.5cm) wide.
£410–450 / €570–630 $670–730 S(O)

Cut-glass candelabrum, late 19thC, 15in (38cm) high.
£500–550 / €700–770 $820–900 S(O)

Find out more in

Miller's Glass Buyer's Guide, Miller's Publications, 2001

Cut-glass five-light hung chandelier, the glass corona and baluster above joined saucers, with scrolled glass arms, with cut chains, rings and prisms, converted for electricity, 1875–1900, 34in (86.5cm) high.
£650–720 / €910–1,000 $1,050–1,200 NOA

Pair of cased glass lustres, with floral panels and cut-glass prisms, mid-19thC, 13in (33cm) high.
£950–1,050 / €1,320–1,460 $1,550–1,700 BAu

Carafes & Decanters

◀ **Glass decanter,** with a blown ball stopper, three-ring neck and kick-in base, c1770, 18in (45.5cm) high. The uppermost section of the neck and pouring lip have been lost and the neck ring polished to create a lip. The replacement stopper is around a century later than the decanter. Buyers should be aware of such extensive damage, since resale of such an item could prove difficult.
**£75–80 / €105–110
$120–130 TMA** ⚒

Pair of glass cylinder decanters, one with replacement stopper, 1835–45, 11in (28cm) high. The replacement stopper on the right-hand example keeps the price of these decanters low.
**£100–110 / €140–150
$165–180 SWO** ⚒

◀ **Glass decanter,** cut in the Empire style, with a moulded 'pinched target' stopper, probably Irish, c1820, 11¼in (28.5cm) high.
**£170–185 / €235–260
$280–300 WW** ⚒

William IV cut-glass claret decanter, the neck with vertical flutes and original stopper, the body cut with hobnails, c1840, 14in (35.5cm) high. Decanters were first fitted with handles during the 18thC and became increasingly common after c1810. However, surviving examples are rare because the point where the handle meets the body is prone to damage.
**£190–210 / €265–290
$310–350 PFK** ⚒

The look without the price

This piece offers remarkable value. The downside is that the pouring rim of one decanter is chipped, and another is of a different pattern. However, the chip could be removed, and a replacement decanter purchased for around £50 / €70 / $80. This would make a superb decorative piece.

Oak tantalus, with brass fittings, the velvet-lined fitted interior with four glass decanters with enamelled labels for 'Whiskey', 'Claret', 'Brandy' and 'Port', one decanter replaced, one chipped, 1880–1900, 9½in (24cm) wide.
**£180–200 / €250–280
$295–325 SWO** ⚒

Glass decanter, with three triple neck rings, the neck cut with flutes, the lower body cut with hollow flutes, c1795, replacement stopper c1830, 8½in (21.5cm) high. The mushroom stopper is wider than the pouring lip, indicating that it is a replacement.
£200–220 / €280–310
$330–370 Som ⊞

How to tell if a decanter stopper is original

The commercial value of most decanters is reduced when not fitted with their original stoppers. There should be no movement whatsoever if the stopper is agitated sideways, and the diameter of a stopper is almost never greater than that of its decanter's pouring lip. The stoppers in many 19th-century decanters were formed as mirror images of their decanter's shape. Above all, a stopper should look 'right' when married to its decanter.

Two glass decanters, each with three single neck rings, one plain, the other cut with broad flutes to the neck and hollow flutes around the lower body, replacement stoppers, c1820, 8½in (21.5cm) high. The left-hand example has been fitted with a lozenge stopper 1780–1820, the right-hand example has a target stopper 1785–1835.
£220–240 / €310–330
$370–390 Som ⊞

Three cut-glass decanters and stoppers, cut with vertical prisms, in a silver-plated frame, 19thC, 13½in (34.5cm) high. 18thC decanter frames produced in colourless, green or blue glass were customarily applied with gilded cartouches. Mid-19thC examples such as these are far more common, and therefore more affordable, than earlier ones.
£250–275 / €350–385
$410–450 TMA ⚹

Pair of silver-mounted glass spirit decanters, the upper bodies cut with diamonds, the bases cut with stars, both with original lapidary-cut ball stoppers, London 1902, 11½in (29cm) high.
£300–330 / €420–460
$490–540 DA ⚹

Silver-mounted glassware

The proliferation of silver-mounted glass across Britain, Europe and North America between the end of the 19th century and the 1930s was the result of the increasingly commonplace nature of glassware and, more especially, the collapse of the price of silver. Improved mining techniques and the abolition of the Silver Duty in Britain in 1890 caused its price to fall from 60d an ounce in 1870 to 24d in 1910.

Glass decanter, cut with flutes, with an engraved cartouche for 'Cloves' within fruiting vine, c1830, 12in (30.5cm) high. Extract of cloves was a common natural remedy for ulcers and other stomach disorders. This decanter may have been used to dispense them in a Victorian chemist's shop. The inscription has added to its value. A plain decanter would be worth only a quarter of the price.
£330–370
€460–520
$540–610 JAS ⊞

Looking after gilded pieces

Take care when cleaning gilded glass. Do not use detergent.

What is a tantalus?

The tantalus was the trademark of George Betjemann & Sons of Islington, founded in 1851 by the great-great-grandfather of the late Poet Laureate, Sir John Betjeman. The firm remains best known for its tantalus, patented in 1880, and defined as a 'stand for decanters, bottles and jars, to prevent surreptitious withdrawal.' A tantalus normally contains three decanters or perfume bottles, although single decanter versions were also produced. Betjemann examples are distinguished by their superior quality and ingenious mechanisms incorporating theoretically impregnable Bramah locks.

Pair of glass spirit decanters, with gilded cartouches for 'Brandy' and 'Rum', fitted with gilt lozenge stoppers, c1790, 7¼in (18.5cm) high. Reproduction decanters of this type were also made in dark green and cobalt blue and usually fitted in threes into brass-fitted papier mâché stands. Significant numbers were produced during the early 20thC by London retailers including Thomas Goode and Droods and are difficult to discern from the original, but are of lower value.
£360–400 / €500–560
$590–650 Som ⊞

Edwardian oak tantalus, with silver-plated strapwork, fitted with three cut-glass decanters, the lid with mirrored back, with a cigar section and secret drawer to front, 15in (38cm) wide.
£340–380 / €470–530
$560–620 AMB 🔨

Liqueur set, containing four decanters, six glasses and five matched glasses on a lift-out stand, French, 19thC, in an oak case 13in (33cm) wide. Boxed sets of decanters and glasses from the 18thC were used by travellers, military officers and colonial officers who were often away from home for long periods of time. Late 19thC versions were generally finer and used exclusively in the home. The glassware in this set is acid-etched with a Greek key pattern and would have been considerably more expensive in real terms at the time of its manufacture than it is today.
£420–460 / €590–640
$690–750 SWO 🔨

Miller's compares...

A. Pint-sized glass tapered decanter, engraved with a rococo-style cartouche for 'Port', with replacement stopper, c1800, 7in (18cm) high.
£400–440 / €560–610
$650–720 Som ⊞

B. Glass decanter, engraved 'Port' within a cartouche, with a faceted disc stopper, mid-18thC, 9¼in (23.5cm) high. Dealers and collectors generally call this shape 'mallet'. However, recently-published research has revealed that 18thC glassmakers and merchants referred to it as 'sugarloaf'.
£800–880 / €1,100–1,250
$1,300–1,450 Som ⊞

Bladder-shaped glass wine bottle, with applied string rim and base pontil, all-over patination to body, 1710–20, 8¼in (21cm) high. Wine bottles of this shape are known in the US as 'kidney' bottles, and in the UK as 'Hogarths' because of the frequency with which they appear in the artist's caricatures of 18thC life. The presence of a dated seal on this bottle would increase its value as much as tenfold.
£520–570 / €720–790
$850–930 BBR ⚒

The fact that Item B is more expensive than Item A is due to rarity. Item B is a sugarloaf shape dated 1765–70 and Item A is a taper shape dated 1780–90. While 20 years is little in historical terms, the period witnessed an explosion in British manufacturing and consumerism. This revolution transformed decorative wares such as porcelain and glass from luxuries for the affluent to objects found in even middle-class homes. The result being that later pieces are more common than earlier ones, a fact reflected in today's prices.

Labelled decanters

Decanters from the middle of the 18th century are rare today, largely because relatively few were made. However, some of the survivors are engraved with cartouches in the shape of contemporary silver 'bottle tickets'. Common inscriptions include Ale, Burgundy, Champagne, Cider, Beer, Hock, Lisbon, Madeira, Punch, Rum and various forms of wine, and at least two examples are known for milk.

Cased and cut-glass decanter, cut with hobnail diamonds, the shoulder with prisms, with a star-cut base, Continental, 1875–1925, 8½in (21.5cm) high.
£600–660 / €840–920
$980–1,100 S(O) ⚒

Drinking Glasses

The look without the price

The Edwardian craze for antiques caused a shortage of genuine pieces. To meet this demand, Britain's finest glassworks produced extensive ranges of reproduction 'Georgian' vessels which now outnumber the originals. However, many of them are now 100 years old and genuine antiques, yet when correctly identified sell for a fraction of Georgian pieces. Ironically, the Edwardian pieces can be discerned from earlier ones because they are invariably better made and in a clearer, brighter glass.

Glass rummer, with a funnel bowl, on a thick stem and a plain foot with pontil mark to underside, early 20thC, 5½in (14cm) high.
£25–30 / €35–42
$40–50 PFK 🔨

Glass rummer, with an ovoid bowl, c1800, 4½in (11.5cm) high.
£45–50 / €60–70
$75–80 JHa ⊞

Miller's compares...

A. Dwarf ale glass, with wrythen-moulded decoration, on a plain conical foot, c1810, 4¼in (11cm) high.
£65–70 / €90–95
$105–115 Som ⊞

B. Dwarf ale glass, with wrythen flammiform-moulded decoration, on a plain conical foot, c1740, 4¾in (12cm) high.
£320–350 / €450–490
$520–570 Som ⊞

The difference in price between Item A and Item B is the result of age and technique. Item B dates from c1740, Item A is c1810. While the decoration appears similar, Item B is more complex and was achieved by blowing the plain part of the bowl into the moulded section. The bowl of Item A was blown into a ribbed mould before being twisted to achieve the effect.

Glass rummer, with an ovoid bowl, on a capstan stem, c1800, 5in (12.5cm) high.
£50–60 / €70–85
$80–100 RUSK ⊞

Sets/pairs

Unless otherwise stated, any description which refers to 'a set' or 'a pair' includes a guide price for the entire set or the pair, even though the illustration may show only a single item.

The look without the price

Intaglio is a traditional glass-decorating technique midway between wheel engraving and cutting. When demand for labour-intensive cameo glass waned from 1890, the legendary Stourbridge glass decorator John Northwood (1836–1902) revived intaglio to safeguard the employment of his staff. Executed on small stones rather than copper wheels, intaglio is characterized by larger, more expansive designs than engraving. The use of powerful lathes and acid polishing made it relatively faster and thus cheaper than previous techniques. Intaglio-cut colourless glass has yet to take off among modern collectors and so still provides high quality at affordable prices.

White wine glass, with intaglio-engraved ribbed bowl, c1910, 5in (12.5cm) high.
£30–35 / €42–48
$50–60   JHa ⊞

Glass goblet, with diamond-cut ovals and engraved panel, c1900, 7in (18cm) high. The introduction of electrical cutting wheels from the late 19thC enabled the application of crisp, complex motifs now known as brilliant cutting. This goblet is typical of the type found in rich Edwardian homes, with cutting applied to the bowl, stem and foot and engraved panels on the bowl.
£50–55 / €70–75
$80–90   G(L) ↗

Four glass rummers, with capstan stems and plain conical feet, c1820, largest 5¼in (13.5cm) high.
£70–80 / €95–110
$115–130 each   Som ⊞

What are rummers?

The generous-bowled rummer was Britain's most popular form of wine glass between c1785 and 1830, yet the derivation of its name remains uncertain. It was first mentioned in 1684 when the Scottish Earl of Breadalbane bought a dozen 'flint purld rummers' for ten shillings. It probably took its name from the *roemer*, an archetypal German white wine glass with a globular bowl and conical foot which dates from the middle ages. However, some believe it took its name from the naval rum ration which was diluted one-to-six in water after 1740 to reduce drunkenness aboard Britain's fighting fleet.

George III punch glass, the 'custard cup' body with a clear handle, on an opaque-twist stem and plain foot, damaged, 4½in (11.5cm) high. A crack at the junction of the bowl and handle dramatically reduces the value of this rare and desirable piece. In perfect condition it would be expected to fetch £650 / €900 / $1,050.
£90–100 / €125–140
$150–165   PFK ↗

Pair of conical wine glasses, the wheel-engraved decoration commemorating the Battle of the Boyne, on a double-knopped stem and circular foot, Irish, late 19thC, 6in (15cm) high. The engraving is possibly by the Dublin-based Bohemian engraver Franz Tieze.
£90–100 / €125–140
$150–165 JAd ✎

For more examples of
Irish see Silver & Plate (pages 132–165)

Beware 'Williamite' glassware

'Williamite' glasses and decanters were engraved in Ireland, supposedly during the 18th century, in honour of protestant King William's victory at the Battle of the Boyne in 1690. However, they have under-performed during the boom market for 18th-century drinking glasses. This is largely because recent research has shown that most were faked by Franz Tieze, a Dublin-based Bohemian engraver, between 1896 and 1913. A famous pair of Prussian-shaped decanters at the Victoria & Albert Museum bearing the motto 'Success To The Waterford Volunteers, 1782' and previously considered genuine, has been found to bear the telltale initials 'FT' among their shamrock garlands.

Eight wine glasses, with frosted bowls, probably French, late 19thC, 5¼in (13.5cm) high. The bowls were frosted by immersing them in hydrofluoric or 'white' acid, the clear lips having been protected by a waxy 'resist'. It would be difficult to buy eight modern wine glasses of this quality for as competitive a price as these antiques.
£100–120 / €140–165
$165–195 SWO ✎

Glass rummer, the bucket body engraved with a thistle spray and monogram 'TSG' within a shield flanked by barley sheaves, on a ball knop stem, c1830, 6½in (16.5cm) high. The engraving on this piece, while not of the highest quality, would have been laborious to apply, and doubles the value of this glass.
£100–120 / €140–165
$165–195 Som ⊞

Wine glass, with a funnel bowl, on a facet stem and plain conical foot, c1770, 5¾in (14.5cm) high. 18thC drinking glasses with facet-cut stems have traditionally been undervalued when compared to twist-stemmed examples of a similar date. Facet-cut stems were produced between 1740–80, and are beginning to rise in value, making this a good time to buy.
£145–160 / €200–220
$235–260 Som ⊞

Glass tumbler, wheel-engraved with Masonic symbols, the base cut with lozenges, Bohemian, c1820, 6½in (16.5cm) high. Masonic glassware is highly collectable.
£150–165 / €210–230 $245–270 G(L) 🖊

Wine glass, the ovoid bowl on an opaque-twist stem, c1765, 5½in (14cm) high.
£160–175 / €220–245 $260–285 WW 🖊

Set of eight glass Champagne flutes, cut with bands of diamonds, ovals and flutes, on square bases, Continental, 19thC, 7in (18cm) high. These are cut in the English style or *façon d'Angleterre*.
£160–175 / €220–245 $260–285 WW 🖊

Flutes versus *coupes*

Champagne flutes are currently more fashionable, and thus more expensive, than bowls, or *coupes*. Both were produced in Renaissance Venice and each has enjoyed periods of supremacy over the other. Flutes were the traditional 18th-century form while *coupes* were the most popular during the Victorian and Edwardian eras.

Set of 15 overlay glasses, with knopped slice-cut stems, initialled 'GS', Bohemian, late 19thC, 4¾in (12cm) high. These glasses were intended for white wine. Their quality is high and they represent great value for money at about £10 / €14 / $15 each.
£160–175 / €220–245 $260–285 CGC 🖊

▶ **Wine glass,** the drawn trumpet bowl on a short faceted stem and conical foot with pontil mark, c1790, 5in (12.5cm) high. The cut and engraved border applied below the lip of this glass comprises alternate crosses and polished circles figuratively known as an OXO border. It was part of the standard repertoire of neo-classical motifs commonly applied to English glassware between 1770 and 1790.
£160–175 / €220–245 $260–285 PSA ▦

Wine glass, the bowl engraved with a fruiting vine and a pineapple, on a square lemon squeezer base, c1800, 6in (15cm) high. The base was formed by pouring molten glass into a mould, before manually decorating it with a hand-held squeezer.
£180–200 / €250–280 $295–330 WW 🖊

Firing glass, engraved with a Roman bust within an inscription, on a short drawn foot, c1820, 4½in (11.5cm) high.
£200–220 / €280–310
$330–370 Som ⊞

Glass rummer, diamond point-engraved with a band of stylized flowers, above 'BB' within an oval panel, on a short stem, 19thC, 8¾in (22cm) high.
£200–220 / €280–310
$330–370 WW ⚒

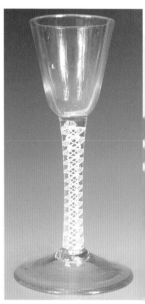

George III wine glass, the bell-shaped bowl on an air-twist stem and plain conical foot, 6½in (16.5cm) high.
£210–230 / €290–320
$350–380 SWO ⚒

Miller's compares...

A. Sweetmeat glass, with a shaped rim, faceted bowl, hexagonal section stem and domed foot, 18thC, 6¼in (16cm) high.
£220–240 / €310–330
$370–390 WW ⚒

B. Sweetmeat glass, with a shaped rim, flat-cut bowl and moulded stem, on a domed moulded foot, 18thC, 6¾in (17cm) high.
£400–440 / €560–610
$650–720 WW ⚒

The development of English cutting during the 18thC remains a grey area among glass academics and historians, and the price difference between these sweetmeat glasses provides a perfect case in point. Item B sold for a higher price, presumably because of its moulded pedestal stem, which many collectors regard as earlier than the cut version seen in Item A. Yet moulded stems were produced between 1720–80 and it is likely that both examples were made between 1750–60.

Wine glass, the funnel bowl on a double series opaque-twist stem and plain conical foot, c1760, 5½in (14cm) high.
£230–260 / €320–360
$380–430 Som ⊞

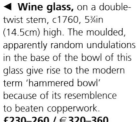

◄ **Wine glass,** on a double-twist stem, c1760, 5¾in (14.5cm) high. The moulded, apparently random undulations in the base of the bowl of this glass give rise to the modern term 'hammered bowl' because of its resemblence to beaten copperwork.
£230–260 / €320–360 $380–430   CHAC ⊞

Set of four Victorian glass goblets, the bowls cut with flutes, on knopped stems with plain conical feet, 7¼in (18.5cm) high.
£250–280 / €350–390 $410–460   Som ⊞

Gilt- and pebble-decorated glass beaker, with oval panels depicting goldfish, Bohemian, 19thC, 4½in (11.5cm) high. This piece demonstrates part of the range of extraordinary skills possessed by central European glass decorators, and is still relatively affordable. The goldfish, depicted within lens-cut panels, are painted in fine detail in yellow and orange enamels, and the surrounding gilding carefully scratched with a stiletto into a series of fine circles or bubbles.
£260–290 / €360–400 $430–470   SWO ⋏

Pair of Venetian glass goblets, on clear glass stems with moulded hollow knops, early 20thC, 7in (18cm) high. Venetian glassmaking, once the envy of the world, endured a prolonged recession during the supremacy of the Bohemian, then English styles between 1700–1900. However, its renaissance dates from the establishment of the Venice & Murano Glass Co which opened a London shop selling its authentic reproductions during the 1870s. An original late 17thC glass would cost in the region of £10,000 / €14,000 / $16,300.
£250–280 / €350–390 $410–460   G(L) ⋏

Central European beakers

Highly-decorated beakers, intended as souvenirs and collectors' pieces, have played a leading role in the central European glassmaker's repertoire for over three centuries. They have been applied with all known decorative forms including engraving, cutting, flashing, gilding, jewelling, casing and vitreous, translucent and *Schwartzlot* (black lead) enamels. Values range from tens to thousands of pounds, with the finest examples by the leading artists, painted in transparent enamels with subjects including insects, land- and townscapes, and themes from folklore.

◄ **Wine glass,** the bowl with neo-classical engraved stars, on a facet-cut stem, c1780, 5in (12.5cm) high.
£270–300 / €380–420 $440–490   PSA ⊞

Pair of cordial glasses, with engraved bowls, on double-series opaque-twist stems, with conical feet, 18thC, 5¾in (14.5cm) high. The pattern engraved around the rim of these English glasses is from the Bohemian repertoire, but is also found on mid-18thC English glass and early 19thC American and Irish pieces. In Ireland it is known as the 'Vessica' pattern and is closely associated with the Cork and Waterloo glass companies. It is evidence of the presence of Bohemian engravers in most important glassmaking centres.
£290–320 / €400–450
$470–520   G(L) ⚘

▶ **Set of five wine glasses,** engraved and polished with OXO bands, the stems cut with hexagonal facets, on conical feet, damaged and restored, c1780, 5in (12.5cm) high. The damage and restoration to these glasses has kept the price down. A matching set of glasses would add to their value – costing what one would expect to pay for eight to ten unmatched glasses.
£300–330 / €420–460
$490–540   DN ⚘

Glass beaker, the bowl with a gilt rim and enamel floral decoration, 1860, 5¾in (14.5cm) high. This piece is embellished with three decorative forms: casing, gilding and translucent polychrome enamels. The foot is cased in opaque white, then cut through to reveal the colourless glass beneath, with each panel framed with finely-gilded lines. The cased bowl, with its all-over decoration of blue, red, green, yellow and purple flowers framed by gilt rococo scrolls provides a mass of flamboyant colour, but is not suited to everyone's taste.
£290–330 / €400–450
$470–540   DORO ⚘

Friendship glass beaker, engraved with symbols for friendship, trust, hope, love, health and luck, Bohemian, 1860, 5¼in (13.5cm) high.
£290–330 / €400–450
$470–540   DORO ⚘

Firing glass, the funnel bowl on a double-series opaque-twist stem and thick firing foot, c1760, 4¼in (11cm) high.
£340–380 / €470–530
$560–620   Som ⊞

Wine glass, the opaque-twist stem with a double knop, c1760, 6½in (16.5cm) high.
£340–380 / €470–530
$560–620 CHAC ⊞

Wine glass, the plain drawn trumpet bowl above a plain stem with basal knop, c1740, 6¾in (17cm) high.
£400–440 / €560–610
$650–720 BrW ⊞

Glass rummer, engraved with Sunderland Bridge and an inscription, the reverse with initials 'J.B.B.' within a floral surround, on a bladed knop stem and plain foot, c1825, 5½in (14cm) high. While glasses engraved with ships are always popular, Sunderland rummers are common compared with shipping tumblers, and rarity always enhances the price.
£400–440 / €560–610
$650–720 Som ⊞

◀ **Wine glass,** on an opaque-twist stem, c1760, 5¾in (14.5cm) high. This is an English wine glass but with engraving by a Bohemian working in Britain.
£400–440
€560–610
$650–720 CHAC ⊞

▶ **Glass beaker,** engraved with a two-masted ship, the reverse with a diamond point, the initials 'GL', 'Junior' and 'Leeds' within a wheel-engraved surround, c1800, [...]in (10cm) high.
[...]450–500
[...]630–700
[...]730–820 Som ⊞

Stephen Hearn

TringMarket Auctions

AUCTIONEERS AND VALUERS OF ANTIQUE FURNITURE, COLLECTABLES AND FINE ART

FINE ART SALES

FORTNIGHTLY SALES OF ANTIQUE FURNITURE AND EFFECTS

TOTAL AND PART HOUSE CLEARANCE SPECIALISTS

VALUATIONS FOR SALE, PROBATE & INSURANCE

A pair of early Staffordshire spill figure groups, sold £750

Brook Street, Tring, Herts HP23 5EF
Telephone: 01442 826446
Email: sales@tringmarketauctions.co.uk
www.tringmarketauctions.co.uk

◀ **Glass beaker,**
with a gilt rim and
gilt floral decoration,
Bohemian, 1840,
4¾in (12cm) high.
£450–500
€630–700
$730–820 DORO ⚒

19th-century Bohemian glass

Bohemian-style, or *façon de Bohème* glassware, dominated the European trade during
the late 17th and most of the 18th century
before being eclipsed by English-style cut glass
from c1775. However, Bohemia retained its
pool of talent and enjoyed a renaissance from
the 1840s. By the end of the 19th century
its local glass industry employed thousands
of men, women and children, many of the
latter occupied in gilding and enamelling
vessel glass. While some of their work
appears ostentatious or stiff to British eyes, it
remains popular in other parts of the world.

Collectable twisted stems

The most collectable air-
twist glasses are those
with coloured twists, the
rarest being the most
collectable. The most
rare are yellow twists,
followed by green, blue,
'tartan' (mixed colours)
and red. Yellow twists
have recently fallen
back from a peak of
around £11,000 /
€15,300 / $17,900.

Miller's compares...

A. Wine glass, the cup-shaped
bowl engraved with a three-
masted sailing vessel and
inscription, on a multi-knopped
baluster stem enclosing a tear,
and a folded conical foot, Dutch,
mid-18thC, 8¾in (22cm) high.
£520–570 / €720–790
$850–930 CHAC ⊞

B. Wine glass, the drawn
trumpet bowl finely engraved
with fruiting vine, on a spiral
air-twist stem, c1750,
6¾in (17cm) high.
£800–880 / €1,110–1,230
$1,300–1,440 BrW ⊞

Item A is finely engraved with a popular subject and is
larger than Item B. However, the lower price of Item A
reflects the fact that collectors tend to be patriotic in their
buying habits and the depressed state of the continental
European economy of recent years has resulted in a low
demand. The English economy has not been affected in
the same way and so Item B has maintained its value.

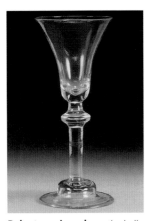

Baluster wine glass, the bell-
shaped bowl above a plain stem
with shoulder knop, on a domed
foot, c1730, 7in (18cm) high.
£470–520 / €650–720
$770–850 S(O) ⚒

What are sulphide inclusions?

Sulphides are white or coloured three-dimensional siliceous motifs inserted into the walls of various forms of glassware. The technique was perfected by Sèvres sculptor Barthelemy Desprez from the late 18th century and patented by his son in Paris in 1819. It was adopted in Britain by Apsley Pellatt and John Ford, and in the United States by Bakewell's of Pittsburgh. However, it remains most closely associated with Baccarat, which inserted all manner of white or coloured floral motifs and heroic busts into glass plaques, tumblers and paperweights.

◄ **Wine glass,** the ogee bowl on an air-twist stem with a single knop, on a folded foot, c1740, 7½in (19cm) high.
£520–570 / €720–790
$850–930 CHAC ⊞

Set of six blown glass and parcel-gilt Champagne flutes, German, Karlsbad, late 19thC, 6½in (16.5cm) high.
£500–550 / €700–770
$820–900 NOA ✦

▶ **Baccarat cut-glass beaker,** inset with a sulphide of a pansy on gilt foil, the reserve cut with raised diamonds, above a cogwheel foot with a radial-cut base, c1850, 3½in (9cm) high.
£530–580 / €740–810
$870–950 S(O) ✦

The look without the price

Mid-18thC drinking glasses can command very high prices. This goblet, in the Anglo-Venetian style associated with George Ravenscroft (1618–81), one of Britain's greatest glassmakers, is therefore remarkably good value for a historic drinking vessel.

Glass goblet, in the Ravenscroft style, the bowl with a fluted base above a hollow stem with a bun knop, on a folded foot, 18thC, 10¼in (26cm) high.
£580–640 / €810–890
$950–1,050 CGC ✦

Set of ten cut-glass wine goblets, with ruby overlay and vermicelli gilding, Bohemian, 1875–1900, 5¾in (14.5cm) high.
£540–600 / €750–840
$880–980 NOA ✦

Jugs

Satin glass ewer, the three-lobed crimped rim on a balustroid neck and melon-lobed body overpainted with cream blossom within foliate scrolls, with a frosted handle, 19thC, 8¾in (22cm) high. The value of Victorian frilled and crimped glass has fallen owing to its decrease in popularity.
£25–30 / €35–40
$40–50 PFK ✎

Victorian glass jug, with engraved decoration of leaves, 7in (18cm) high.
£50–55 / €70–75
$80–90 TOP ⊞

Cut-glass cream jug, c1825, 4in (10cm) high.
£130–145 / €180–200
$210–240 JAS ⊞

Zipper-cut glass claret cup jug, possibly by T. G. Hawkes, with silver rim and spout by Tiffany & Co, minor chip to base, American, c1900, 13¼in (33.5cm) high. Claret cup was a punch based on Bordeaux red wine, fruit and herbs, enjoyed on both sides of the Atlantic around the end of the 19thC.
£280–300 / €390–420
$460–490 BAu ✎

► Pair of bronze and opaline glass ewers, with foliate-cast mounts, the bodies painted with flowers, French, mid-19thC, 11½in (29cm) high. The price of these ewers would have been higher had the original stoppers not been missing.
£300–330 / €420–460
$490–540 G(L) ✎

◄ Glass iced drinks jug, brilliant-cut with Double Hobstar-and-Fan decoration, with ribbon-cut lip and lapidary-cut handle, American, 1875–1900, 10in (25.5cm) high. Examples of brilliant-cut glass made before c1890 are particularly sought-after in the United States.
£550–600 / €770–840
$900–980 NOA ✎

Paperweights

The look without the price

Glass paperweight, with scrambled canes in floral and spiral designs, probably French, mid-19thC, 2½in (6.5cm) diam.
£60–65 / €85–90
$100–105 G(L) 🔨

As this interesting scrambled cane paper-weight has not been attributed to a specific factory or maker it is very affordable.

Glass paperweight, possibly by Clichy, enclosing a sulphide portrait, 19thC, 3½in (8.5cm) diam. The fact that neither maker nor subject is identifiable makes the price of this paper-weight very reasonable.
£90–100 / €125–140
$150–165 WW 🔨

Miller's compares...

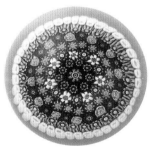

Clichy swirl glass paperweight, set with a central composite cane, minor surface abrasions, c1850, 2½in (6.5cm) diam. The swirl paper-weight is a Clichy classic. This piece has an off centre millefiori set-up which has kept the price at an affordable level. Perfect weights can range in price from £800–3,500 / €1,100–4,900 / $1,300–5,700 according to size, colour and craftsmanship.
£400–440 / €560–610
$650–720 B 🔨

A. Murano millefiori glass paperweight, with four rows of complex canes, 19thC, 3in (7.5cm) diam.
£90–100 / €125–140
$150–165 L&E 🔨

B. Clichy concentric millefiori glass paperweight, with five rows of pastrymould canes, one with alternating Clichy roses, c1850, 2in (5cm) diam.
£800–880 / €1,110–1,230
$1,300–1,440 B 🔨

The workmanship in Item A is inferior to that in Item B, and there is less variety in the canes. The colours are also rather weak in Item A. Although Item B is less beautifully coloured than many Clichy paperweights it is still an outstanding example with superior workmanship.

▶ **Baccarat faceted glass paperweight,** set with a pansy and leaves encircled by canes, with a star-cut base, mid-19thC, 2½in (6.5cm) diam. It is rare to see a Type II pansy (Type I is the rarest and Type III the most common), especially coupled with a beautiful garland and multi-faceting. A paperweight such as this would normally sell for five times this price, which makes this piece a very good buy.
£400–440 / €560–610
$650–720 WW 🔨

The look without the price

John Deacons 'J' Glass paperweight, Camomile, 1983, 2¼in (5.5cm) diam.
£115–130 / €160–180
$190–210 SWB ⊞

John Deacons is an admirer of classic French paperweights and their inspiration can be seen in his work, which at first glance could be mistaken for Baccarat. This example features a fine camomile or pompom garlanded with perfect canes. Camomiles are challenging to make and yellow is a difficult colour to handle in glass. It was also made by John Deacons' firm 'J' Glass (1978–83) which is very collectable today.

◀ **Clichy glass paperweight,** set with a central composite cane bordered by four clusters of canes and four smaller canes, minor wear, c1850, 2½in (6.5cm) diam. Although this paperweight has a poor colour ground, the pattern is off centre and the four cane rondellos are badly placed, it is still a good opportunity to purchase a relatively low price Clichy paperweight. Good examples can fetch six times this amount.
£500–550 / €700–770
$820–900 B 🔨

Baccarat facet and garlanded clematis glass paperweight, the dome cut with six printies and a top window to reveal a flower, star-cut base, chips and surface wear, c1850, 2in (5cm) diam. This burgundy double clematis paperweight has a beautiful alternating cane garland and the star-cutting is reflected in the facets in an attractive way. The poor condition of this piece has kept its value down from £1,600 / €2,200 / $2,600.
£550–610 / €770–850
$900–1,000 B 🔨

Paul Ysart glass paperweight, with flowers in a basket, with PY cane, c1960, 2¾in (7cm) diam.
£590–650
€820–910
$960–1,050 SWB ⊞

Sweetbriar ✿ Gallery
Mrs Anne B. Metcalfe, B.A. Mr Peter Metcalfe, B.A. **Paperweights Ltd.**

Here's our new shop at
3 Collinson Court,
off Church Street,
Frodsham, Cheshire, WA6 6PN
England

Too far? See our vast stock on our website then – www.sweetbriar.co.uk

Or – send for our free colour literature

Phone: 01928 730064 Fax: 01928 730066
Email: sales@sweetbriar.co.uk

How to identify Paul Ysart fakes

Paul Ysart paperweights in particular have been the subject of fakes. The first series is easy to recognize – the Y cane is dropped lower than the P in the PY signature cane. The second series is more difficult. The Y is not dropped but is a different colour from the P; additionally the PY cane itself has 20 ribs, whereas the genuine article would have only 16.

Scent Bottles

Double-ended cut-glass scent bottle, with gilt-metal mounts, c1900, 5½in (14cm) long. This is a typical example of the high quality craftsmanship achieved by Victorian silversmiths and glassmakers. The small size and wide variety of styles and colours make examples such as this favourites with collectors.
£75–85 / €105–120
$120–140 SWO ⚹

Pair of silver-mounted glass scent bottles, Birmingham 1894, 6in (15cm) high. Silver-mounted glassware commands a price greater than the value of the metal. Without silver mounts, this piece would probably be worth less than half the price.
£220–240 / €310–330
$370–390 G(L) ⚹

Flashed glass scent bottle, the faceted stopper containing a second perfume container, with Biedermeier-style cutting, with a scalloped rim and a fluted body, Bohemian, c1845, 4¾in (12cm) high. The Biedermeier period witnessed an explosion in tinting and production techniques, many derived from the hundreds of glasshouses and decorating shops scattered across Bohemia. Amber and a mid-green were two of the earliest new colours, and were widely adopted across Europe.
£80–90 / €110–125
$130–150 AH ⚹

▶ **Opaline glass scent bottle,** with a silver top, Continental, c1870, 4in (10cm) high. Moulded examples of opaline glass are invariably cheaper than cut ones and the presence of an original silver cap in good condition can more than double the value.
£350–390 / €490–540
$570–640 CoS ▦

◀ **Alabaster and glass scent bottle,** with gilded highlights, Bohemian or French, 1820–30, 5in (12.5cm) high. Fine quality scent bottles of this type are highly sought-after, but the price can be affected dramatically by the condition of the gilding.
£290–320 / €400–450
$470–520 DORO ⚹

Glass scent bottle, with a painted female portrait plaque, within gilded foliage, 19thC, 4¾in (12cm) high. Entirely hand-made, and decorated to a high standard in great detail, this is a fine quality piece, despite the wear to the gilding. Its low price is attributable to taste as busy decoration is currently unfashionable.
£150–165 / €210–230
$245–270 G(L) ⚹

Vases

Pair of opaque glass vases, with shaped beaded borders, enamelled with flowers, late 19thC, 4in (10cm) high. Vivid decoration such as this is still applied to coloured glassware in Bohemian decorating shops today, making it difficult to distinguish the antique from the modern.
**£40–45 / €55–60
$65–75 L&E** ✂

What is flashed glass?

Flashing is an ancient technique that involves dipping a fully-formed vessel into a furnace pot containing molten glass of a contrasting colour. The full bi-tonal flashed effect is achieved by selectively removing the outer layer by cutting or engraving. Flashing was the standard method of medieval window staining and was revived in Bohemia from c1835 from where it spread across Europe and to the United States.

Glass vase, with raised, gilded and enamelled oak-leaf decoration, Continental, 19thC, 8¾in (22cm) high. This shape dates from the 18thC when it would have been known as a guglet and used for dispensing water. Such high-relief decoration is considered gaudy by today's standards and keeps the vase affordable.
**£40–45 / €55–60
$65–75 WilP** ✂

▶ **Vaseline and green glass
épergne,** with frilled rims, 19thC, 20in (51cm) high. These delicate pieces, produced in a rainbow of differing colours and effects, are extremely prone to damage and missing elements are difficult to replace. However, they make a bold decorative statement and are superb value at this price.
**£220–240 / €310–330
$370–390 G(L)** ✂

◀ **Ruby-flashed glass vase,** the flared goblet bowl on a knopped stem and flared foot, Bohemian, c1900, 12¼in (31cm) high. This vase is of good quality and size which makes it excellent for use as interior decoration.
**£220–240 / €310–330
$370–390 B(W)** ✂

Engraved glass trumpet vase, held by a carved wood bear, Swiss, mid-19thC, 15¼in (38.5cm) high. Thousands of these tourist-quality pieces were sold in Switzerland during the late 19thC although this may have been made in Bohemia where labour was relatively cheap. Without close inspection, modern copies made in composite plastics are easily confused with the original wooden versions.
**£160–175 / €220–250
$260–285 G(L)** ✂

Pair of Victorian Stourbridge-style glass Jack-in-the-pulpit vases, with clear glass frilled ornamental rims and bases, 5¾in (14.5cm) high. This type of applied spiked decoration has become associated with Stourbridge, c1880, but the Jack-in-the-pulpit shape will always be associated with Louis C. Tiffany, who produced it at his New York glassworks around 1900.
£240–270 / €330–380
$390–440 PFK ✍

How Victorian rock crystal glass was made

Victorian rock crystal glass was deliberately formed and decorated to resemble the natural transparent mineral quartz carved into vessels and static objects for royal and wealthy patrons during the Middle Ages. The late 19th-century equivalents were formed in normal free-blown, thick-sectioned lead glass into which profiles and patterns were cut, engraved and acid-etched. The labour-saving methods that followed saw blanks forced against moulds indented with pillars, plumes and ovals. Released from the mould, the partially-shaped blank was reheated, tooled and blown to size. In both methods undulations were exaggerated to produce a carved effect, as if hewn from a solid chunk. Rock crystal glass is now highly sought-after.

Pair of glass vases, with folded flared rims, gilt with Vermicelli pattern to the shoulders, mid-19thC, 11¼in (28.5cm) high. The pattern is known as Vermicelli after its resemblance to the fine spaghetti. These large, high-quality pieces with fine decoration are an excellent example of late Victorian glassmaking at an affordable price.
£260–285 / €360–400
$430–470 SWO ✍

Pair of glass vases, the tulip-shaped bodies decorated with alternate spear-shaped panels of hand-painted flowers on a white ground and panels of hatched diamonds, the edges with gilt scrolls, on knopped stems and spreading circular bases decorated with flowers, late 19thC, 10in (25.5cm) high.
£350–390 / €490–540
$570–640 B(W) ✍

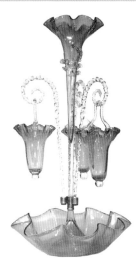

Stourbridge rock crystal glass vase, engraved with pheasants among scrolling foliage, on a petal-cut foot, c1900, 8¾in (22cm) high. This vase is excellent value.
£280–310 / €390–430
$460–510 B(Kn) ✍

◀ **Cranberry glass *épergne*,** with a trumpet-shaped central glass vase and three clear glass branches, each holding a basket, all with ruffled rims, 19thC, 21in (53.5cm) high.
£480–530 / €670–740
$780–870 BAu ✍

Miscellaneous

Glass tray, with gilded border and Mary Gregory-style decoration, 19thC, 10½in (26.5cm) diam. There is more reproduction than original Mary Gregory glass to be found in today's antique shops and fairs. The cut border around this tray would be expensive to reproduce, and suggests an earlier example. Buyers should inspect the base for signs of random wear as a further indication of age.
**£85–95 / € 120–130
$140–155 TMA** ⚲

► **Three Nailsea-style glass pipes,** late 19thC, largest 18in (45.5cm) long.
**£90–100
€ 125–140
$150–165 G(L)** ⚲

The myth of Nailsea glass

British coloured 'folk glass' takes its generic name from the Nailsea Crown Glass & Bottle Company, founded in 1788 at Nailsea, near Bristol which, as its name suggests, produced crown glazing glass and bottles. The misconception that colour-splashed oddities formed a part of Nailsea's production stems from several articles written by the curator of Taunton Museum, St George Gray, between 1911 and 1925. Gray based his work on a collection of such pieces, falsely assuming that they had been produced at Nailsea. Colourful glass novelties, including hats, rolling pins and pipes, have been produced as standard commercial lines by numerous British and European glassworks since at least the 18th century.

Cameo glass snuff bottle, the snow-storm ground with two coiled dragons and lion-mask ring handles, Chinese, 19thC, 2½in (6.5cm) high. These items are still made today and expert knowledge is required to date them accurately.
**£120–135 / € 165–190
$195–220 G(L)** ⚲

◄ **Cranberry cut-glass *épergne*,** terminating in a gilt-brass lady's hand, on an agate base, late 19thC, 6¾in (17cm) high. The function of this unusual type of *épergne* is unclear. It was possibly intended as a decorative piece for a hall table. The junction between the glass and the gilt-brass handle is prone to damage.
**£150–165 / € 210–230
$245–270 AMB** ⚲

Find out more in

Miller's Chinese & Japanese Antiques Buyer's Guide,
Miller's Publications, 2004

► **Glass pot,** the amethyst glass lid with Mary Gregory-style opaque-white enamelled decoration of a young girl framed by a gilt band, c1890, 2½in (6.5cm) high.
**£160–175 / € 220–245
$260–285 GRI** ⊞

Cranberry glass cruet, cut with flutes, with silver-plated stand, c1920, 5in (12.5cm) high. The presence of cranberry glass in this piece makes it considerably higher in value than a similar example with colourless fittings.
£250–280 / €350–390
$410–460 GRI ⊞

Find out more in

Miller's Collecting Glass:
The Facts At Your Fingertips,
Miller's Publications, 2000

▶ **Historismus-style glass jar and cover,** painted with a coat-of-arms, initialled 'I.G.H.Z., S.G.C.V.B.', German, dated 1637, 23in (58.5cm) high. Historismus was a late 19thC central European style that reproduced earlier forms and decoration. In glass terms, large beer Humpen and storage jars, usually in green and amber, were typically enamelled with armorial crests, portraits of military heroes and dates. The finest pieces, particularly those made for the Viennese retailer J. & L. Lobmeyr, are now sought-after and fetch high prices. If marked with the distinctive Lobmeyr cross-hatched logo, often applied to the centre of the base in white enamels, this piece would demand a five-figure sum.
£250–280 / €350–390
$410–460 L ▶

◀ **Cranberry and clear glass model of a horse,** possibly Continental, c1885, 6in (15cm) high. Pottery and glass shaped as animals have been produced across Europe for centuries and dating a given example can be difficult.
£270–300
€380–420
$440–490 GRI ⊞

Leaded and stained glass panel, depicting a three-masted man-o'-war, late 18thC, 11¾in (30cm) high.
£520–570 / €720–790
$850–930 RTo ▶

Set of five cut-glass and gilt-bronze table stands, by F. & C. Osler of Birmingham, one leg broken, stamped under feet, mid-19thC, largest 9in (23cm) high. Oslers, established in 1803, became one of the leading Victorian glass chandelier makers. The company exhibited the famous glass fountain for the centrepiece of the Crystal Palace exhibition in 1851 and among their commissions was a pair of sixteen feet high candelabra for Ibrahim Pascha, the ruler of Egypt, c1845.
£660–730 / €920–1,020
$1,100–1,200 S(O) ▶

Clocks, Watches & Barometers

For thousands of years man has attempted to mark the passing of days in divisible units of time. The ancient Egyptians had sundials and the Greeks devised the Clepsydra or water clock. However, these were scientific instruments unavailable to all but the highest circles of society. It was not until the medieval period in Europe that the first truly mechanical clocks were created and these were merely weight-driven machines to toll a bell at regular intervals. The 17th century was probably the greatest period of clock-making and saw important advances in technology. However, it was the industrial revolution of the 18th and 19th centuries and the coming of the railways that created a need for standardized timekeeping and the advent of mass-production brought clocks and watches to the people.

Barometers have a far shorter history. The principles were discovered in Italy by Torricelli in the 17th century and became commercially available in the early 18th century. The British fascination with the weather over the last 200 years has made the UK one of the leading manufacturers of barometers, with many Italian immigrant glass-makers using their skills to make the glass tubes. The aneroid barometer first appeared in the 1840s and by the end of the 19th century had all but replaced the mercury barometer due to its portability and lack of size restriction. Victorian wheel barometers are particularly good value but check when buying that the tube is intact and that there are no air bubbles in the mercury. Remember that you must never lay a mercury barometer flat – move and transport it carefully to avoid spillage.

Examples from the mid-19th century to the present day are most likely to fall into the categories of this book. With the age-old laws of supply and demand dictating price, it is the earlier and rarer clocks and barometers that are fetching increasingly high prices. For instance, a fine table clock by Thomas Tompion was sold in London in 2003 for over £900,000 / €1,251,000 / $1,467,000.

Whether setting out to form a collection or just wishing to purchase an individual clock to complete the furnishing of a room, there is an enormous range to choose from. The category giving the widest choice is probably French mantel clocks. With their good-quality movements and variety of styles and materials, there will be something for everyone. You will, of course, find worthy examples in every category. Look for attractive longcase clocks where the movement and dial have been married to the case. This is a common occurrence and can result in a marked reduction in value – great if you are searching for a 'look without the price'.

Wristwatches have been steadily increasing in price for a number of years but watches from WWI are still good value. Beware of movements with damaged or missing parts. Many are now obsolete and, while parts can be made, it may be prohibitively expensive to do so. Many pocket watches can be bought for little more than the scrap metal value of the cases and it is still possible to form an interesting and varied collection for very little outlay.

When buying a clock or a watch you are gaining both a decorative piece and a working instrument. If you wish to keep it in working condition, treat it like a vintage car and have it serviced regularly. However, if the costs of restoring the movement prove too high you can still enjoy the look of the case. **Jonathan Hills**

Carriage Clocks

◄ **Silver carriage/boudoir timepiece,** with an enamel dial, the rectangular movement with lever platform escapement, the case with spiral-fluted columns to each corner enclosing foliate engraved panels, hallmarked London 1891, 3½in (9cm) high. This timepiece has an English silver case with a French movement. The price is very reasonable, but the case is rather worn and dented.
£200–220 / €280–310
$330–360 B(Kn) ➤

Buying tips

The majority of carriage clocks are French and are found in brass cases, although some were produced in silver and gold. Look out for maker's marks – usually on the backplate of the movement. Names on the dial are nearly always the retailer rather than the maker. The main makers to look for are Henri Jacot, Drocourt and Margaine. English carriage clocks are rare and of extremely fine quality – you would need to be extremely lucky to find one for under £1,000 / €1,400 / $1,650. Look for clocks that are as original as possible and check to see if the platform escapement has been replaced. Travelling cases and keys with numbers to match the clock are always nice to have, but do not add a great deal to the value.

Miller's compares...

A. Brass travelling timepiece, the signed silvered dial with a concentric date hand, winding from the front, the watch movement with a quarter repeat striking on a coiled gong, the case with a recessed handle, Austrian, 19thC, 4in (10cm) high.
£200–220 / €280–310
$330–360 B(Kn) ➤

B. Carriage clock, signed for the retailers E. J. Dent, London, engraved gilt dial with moon hands and subsidiary, the signed silvered lever platform with an alarm, push repeat and striking on a gong, in a one-piece case with foliate corners and base, French, mid-19thC, 5½in (14cm) high.
£420–460 / €590–640
$690–750 B(Kn) ➤

Both these clocks are engraved and of a similar date, but Item A has a watch movement which requires winding every day. Item B is much more desirable as it has an eight-day movement and is also retailed by Dent, a highly regarded English maker.

Brass carriage timepiece, retailed by Butt & Co, Chester, with an enamelled dial, eight-day movement, c1900, 5in (12.5cm) high. This timepiece has been restored and cleaned so, providing this work has been guaranteed, it is a good price.
£240–260 / €330–360
$390–420 K&D ⊞

Silver carriage timepiece, by J. C. Vickery, the case with ribbon-tied reeded banding, 1911, 2¾in (7cm) high. Miniature carriage timepieces are always popular, and those in silver cases are particularly collectable. However, the case of this example has been over-cleaned and a lot of the detail has been lost. In less worn condition the value would be nearer £400 / €560 / $650.
£250–280 / €350–390
$410–460 G(L) 🔨

What is a timepiece?

Put very simply, a timepiece is a clock that doesn't strike or chime.

Brass carriage clock, with a gilt-engraved dial and mask, hands missing, the movement in need of restoration and repair, platform and gong loose, French, late 19thC, 7½in (19cm) high. French carriage clocks have high quality movements, but the condition of this example requires a major overhaul and repairs. This would mean expensive work in the hands of a restorer. Once repaired, the value would be around £700 / €980 / $1,150.
£300–330 / €420–460
$490–540 B(Kn) 🔨

Brass carriage timepiece, with an eight-day movement, in a serpentine case, on bun feet, c1900, 5in (12.5cm) high. This clock is in a popular doucine or serpentine-shaped case.
£310–340 / €430–470
$510–560 K&D ⊞

► **Gilt-brass carriage clock,** the silvered dial with numerals within reserves, with a pierced central boss and a plain gilt mask, the silvered lever platform escapement striking and repeating on a gong, in a corniche case, French, late 19thC, 6¾in (17cm) high. Repeating the last hour by means of the button on the top of the case is an added bonus for this clock, but the Arabic numerals make it less popular than if it had an enamel dial with Roman numerals.
£360–400 / €500–560
$590–650 B(Kn) 🔨

Brass carriage clock, by G. S. & Co, movement No. 5839, the enamel dial with outside minute track, the silvered lever platform escapement with a bimetallic, cut-compensated balance, striking on a gong, in a plain corniche case, French, late 19thC, 6¼in (16cm) high. This clock is good value, with a perfect enamel dial and the original platform escapement. After a light clean it would be a usable everyday clock.
£360–400 / €500–560
$590–650 B(Kn) 🔨

◀ **Brass carriage clock,** the cast and silvered dial with moon hands, with a silvered lever platform escapement, the case decorated with masks, figures and foliate scrolls, alarm and push-repeat on the gong possibly later, French, 19thC, 7in (18cm) high. This good value carriage clock has an attractive cast case with the extras of repeating and alarm functions.
£380–420 / €530–590
$620–690 B(Kn) 🔨

Brass carriage clock, inscribed 'Lepaute, Paris', the silvered dial with single hands for minutes, hours and seconds, the later lever platform escapement striking on a bell, the fixed back with winding apertures, French, 19thC, 7¼in (18.5cm) high. This early carriage clock has a most unusual dial, but the replaced platform escapement has reduced the price by at least £150 / €210 / $250.
£480–530 / €670–740
$780–870 WW 🔨

Engraved brass carriage clock, by A. Margaine, the hour-repeating mechanism with an alarm, striking the hours and half-hours on a gong, replacement lever escapement and compensated balance, French, c1900, 7in (18cm) high. Margaine is one of the better-known carriage clock makers and one of the few who marked their work. This clock is in generally good condition, although the case is dirty and has lost most of the gilding and the escapement has been replaced. A perfect example would be worth £800 / €1,100 / $1,300.
£500–550 / €700–770
$820–900 G(L) 🔨

Gilt-brass combination travelling clock, made for the Italian market, the clock with an engraved gilt mask enclosing an ivorine dial, the lever platform escapement with a compensated balance, with a subsidiary alarm dial striking on a bell, the aneroid barometer numbered from 69 to 80, surmounted by a compass and flanking a thermometer, in a shaped, numbered case with column supports, French, late 19thC, 6¼in (16cm) high. An attractive and popular desk compendium, but the damage to the enamel alarm dial and the Italian legend on the barometer has reduced the price by half. An English example in good condition would cost at least £800 / €1,100 / $1,300.
£400–440 / €560–610
$650–720 B(Kn) 🔨

▶ **Brass-cased carriage clock,** the signed dial with outer minute track, moon hands and alarm dial, the movement signed 'Howell James & Co', the Jules-type lever platform with a helical spring and repeat button striking on a bell, dial cracked, French, c1850, 8in (20.5cm) high. Howell James were retailers of fine clocks in London and a good cast case and original escapement make this clock of interest to collectors. However, the dial damage does slightly affect the price.
£600–660 / €840–920
$980–1,100 B 🔨

Longcase Clocks

Miller's compares...

George III longcase clock, with an arched brass dial and eight-day movement, in need of restoration, dial 11in (28cm) diam. While the case of this clock is in poor condition and needs a lot of restoration, the movement and dial are late 18thC, of good quality and worth saving. The dial should be silvered and the hands appear to be original. At this price it would be worth the restoration cost of £1,500 / €2,000 / $2,500.
£520–570 / €720–790 $850–930 SWO ⚒

A. Carved oak longcase clock, with a copper and brass dial, late 18thC.
£500–550 / €700–770 $820–900 BERN ⚒

B. Carved oak longcase clock, with an engraved copper and pewter dial, late 18thC.
£760–840 / €1,050–1,200 $1,250–1,400 BERN ⚒

Continental oak longcase clocks have a limited appeal compared to the more conventional English styles. Item A has a plain case and a badly fitting dial and is probably a marriage. The more ornate case of Item B is of better quality, but the three winding holes may indicate a later movement. The dial fits the aperture and is aesthetically more pleasing.

▶ **Oak longcase clock,** the brass dial with cast spandrels, silvered chapter ring and a single hand, inscribed 'Joseph Beaumont Allerthorpe', with a 30-hour movement striking on a bell, 18thC, 80¼in (204cm) high. This is a marriage of a dial and an unusual-shaped case. The style of the case is later than the dial, which is interesting, the ring turning being typical of Quaker makers.
£660–730 / €920–1,000 $1,100–1,200 DD ⚒

Buying tips

Walnut, mahogany and oak are the major woods used for longcase clocks with walnut being the most expensive. Cases that have been reduced at the base or the top can be expensive to restore.

Brass dials are more popular than painted ones, although when painted dials were first introduced in the late 18th century they were more expensive than brass. Victorian dials tend to be less well painted and are consequently cheaper.

Marriages in longcase clocks can be difficult to determine. If the dial and case appear to be of the same period, the first thing to look at is the dial and whether it fits well within the hood surround or mask. Remove the hood and look at the seatboard (the movement is fixed to this). Check to see if the seatboard has been replaced or whether the cheeks on which it sits have been reduced or extended. Look at the dial feet which fix the movement to the dial to ensure they have not been moved or altered and that there are no unused or spare holes in the movement plates.

Oak longcase clock, by M. A. Bartley, with a subsidiary seconds dial, the movement striking a bell, face and movement contemporary but possibly associated, 19thC, 85¾in (218cm) high. This clock is of good proportions and the dial is charming. It is an attractive, good value clock.
£820–900 / €1,150–1,250 $1,350–1,450 NES ➤

Mahogany and satinwood-strung longcase clock, with an enamelled dial and a subsidiary dial, the spandrels painted with the seasons below an arched scene of a horse and plough, with an eight-day movement, c1800, 83in (211cm) high. This longcase clock has a typically Scottish dial and case and is probably from the west coast. The painted scenes in the corners depict the four seasons. This item is good value at this price.
£800–880 / €1,100–1,200 $1,300–1,400 WL ➤

◄ **Oak longcase clock,** 18thC. The case of this clock is complete to the base and has good carving. The 30-hour movement and dial seem to fit the aperture, making this a very stylish piece.
£950–1,050 / €1,300–1,500 $1,500–1,700 BERN ➤

Mantel Clocks

Marble and gilt bronze clock, by Japy Fils, with an enamelled dial, the eight-day movement striking on a bell, mid-19thC, 12½in (32cm) high. This clock is onyx rather than white marble, which is a far less desirable material as it marks very easily. It is lacking its stand and glass dome but is still a reasonably priced decorative clock.
£120–130 / €165–180
$195–210 CGC ➴

Mahogany timepiece, the painted dial signed 'Greenway, Chippenham', with a convex glass, brass bezel and steel hands, single fusee movement, the case with carved floral applied decoration, c1850, 13in (33cm) high. This is a rather faded example of a typically Victorian mantel timepiece. The dial is worn and the case has a crack. The movements of these timepieces are comparatively simple and should not be too expensive to service.
£300–330 / €420–460
$490–540 TMA ➴

Gilt-spelter mantel clock, with a chiming Japy Frères movement, under a glass dome, late 19thC, 15¾in (40cm) high. Gilt spelter was used in the 19thC to produce clocks which looked impressive but were far less expensive than gilt bronze. Spelter will oxidize if exposed to the air. This one has its dome, but the dial is damaged around the winding holes.
£130–145 / €180–200
$210–240 SWO ➴

Gilt and alabaster mantel clock, with an urn surmount, under a glass dome, French, 19thC, 11½in (29cm) high. This is a decorative clock with the original stands and dome, which has preserved the decoration. At half the price of a comparable marble example, this is good value.
£300–330 / €420–460
$490–540 WilP ➴

Marble mantel clock, with a silvered-brass dial and a serpent bezel, the countwheel striking on a bell, the case with a bronze bird group surmount, 19thC, 18½in (47cm) high. This attractive mantel clock dates to the second quarter of the 19thC and appears to be very good value. The bird group on the top looks out of place and may be a later addition, accounting for a very reasonable price.
£220–240 / €310–330
$360–390 G(L) ➴

Gilt-bronze mantel clock, with a drum movement, on a wooden base, French, 19thC, 15¾in (40cm) high. This clock was originally gilt but it has been cleaned and polished, removing the original finish. It should also have another stand and a glass dome. It is of mainly decorative value.
£320–350 / €450–490
$520–570 SWO ➴

Miller's compares...

A. Gilt-spelter and Sèvres-style porcelain-mounted three piece clock garniture, the clock with a drum-cased eight-day movement striking on a bell, supported by four pillars, and a pair of three-light candelabra, French, late 19thC, clock 19in (48.5cm) high.
£320–350 / €450–490
$520–570 BR ✗

B. Ormolu and Sèvres-style porcelain mantel clock garniture, by Henri Marc, Paris, the clock with a drum movement and urn finial, and a pair of three-light candelabra, French, 19thC, clock 13in (33cm) high.
£700–770 / €980–1,070
$1,150–1,250 G(B) ✗

The clocks in both Item A and Item B would originally have had stands and glass domes. Item A is less well finished and the porcelain panels are not as well painted as Item B. Spelter is never as popular as gilt bronze, making Item B the higher value.

Wooden mantel calendar clock, by the Ithaca Clock Co, with an eight-day movement, restoration and losses, c1880, 26in (66cm) high. This is an interesting variation on the calendar clock made popular by Seth Thomas, and is a reasonable price.
£320–350 / €450–490
$520–570 ROSc ✗

Slate mantel clock, retailed by Foord, Hastings, the movement striking on a bell, the case with a cast-bronze sphinx surmount, 19thC, 15in (38cm) wide. This mantel clock is very stylish in the Egyptian revival manner and the movement is of good quality.
£340–370 / €470–520
$560–610 G(L) ✗

Gilt-metal and porcelain mantel clock, the outside countwheel striking on a bell, the case surmounted by an urn, 19thC, 15¼in (38.5cm) high. This clock should have the original glass dome and stands. It has attractive panels and is half the price of a gilt-bronze example.
£480–530 / €670–740
$780–870 Bea ✗

Buying tips

With such an enormous variety to choose from, there is something for everyone in this category. French clocks from the 19th century have very standard, good quality movements with most of the value being determined by the case. Bronzed and gilt-spelter clocks are less desirable than bronze and gilt-bronze examples but can be excellent value if they are in good condition. However, broken spelter is very difficult and costly to repair.

With wooden cases the more exotic woods such as rosewood and burrwoods are keenly sought-after. Look at the fineness of any inlay and details. Timepieces are the simplest of movements and are consequently the least expensive to maintain. A mass-produced chiming clock may be cheap to buy initially, but the cost of cleaning, servicing and restoration may well be two or three times the original purchase price.

Gilt-metal and Sèvres-style porcelain mantel clock, by Japy Frères, the case surmounted by an urn, French, 19thC, 14¼in (36cm) high. The dial and panels of this clock are in good condition. The original stands and glass dome are missing, but this is a good buy at this price.
£480–530 / €670–740
$780–870 L&E ✐

◄ **Rosewood portico clock,** with a silvered dial and subsidiary seconds dial, the case decorated with floral marquetry, 19thC, 19in (48.5cm) high. This style of portico clock was popular during the first half of the 19thC in France. This example dates to c1830 and is good value.
£500–550 / €700–770
$820–900 Mit ✐

Gilt-metal mantel timepiece, with an enamelled dial and eight-day single-train movement, lacks pendulum, French, 19thC, 8¾in (22cm) high. This gilt-metal timepiece is typical of the early 19thC. The lack of a pendulum means that it would need some restoration. The case looks dull and may have been painted with gold paint.
£500–550 / €700–770
$820–900 DN ✐

Find out more in

Miller's Clocks & Barometers Buyer's Guide, Miller's Publications, 2001

▶ **George III mahogany timepiece,** by Turner, London, with a painted dial and eight-day movement, the arched case inlaid with boxwood and cut brass work, with scale sound frets, 16in (40.5cm) high. This timepiece is looking quite tired. The dial is worn but is probably best left alone. The English fusee movement should not be expensive to clean and the case needs a little attention. This is good value and an attractive piece.
£550–600 / €770–830
$900–980 G(B) ✐

Alabaster and gilt-metal mantel clock, the enamel dial signed 'Leroy à Paris', the circular movement with an outside countwheel striking on a bell, the case decorated with applied gilt foliate banding, surmounted by a classical figure of a seated female reading, French, 19thC, 17¾in (45cm) high. This style of clock is typical of France in the third quarter of the 19thC. The case is good quality and clocks of this type are very good value.
**£560–620 / €780–860
$910–1,000** Bea ✎

▶ **Regency mahogany bracket clock,** retailed by Grohe of Wigmore Street, London, with a silvered dial, the twin fusee movement with anchor escapement and striking on a gong, the case with ebony stringing, signed dial and backplate, 17½in (44.5cm) high. The rather tired appearance and crack to the front of the case hold the value down, but this clock has a good quality English fusee movement and Grohe is known to have retailed fine clocks.
**£580–640 / €810–890
$950–1,050** G(L) ✎

The look without the price

Gilt-bronze Louis XV-style mantel clock, signed Thomas Dean, London, the enamel cartouche dial in a waisted rococo foliate case, c1830, 13¾in (35cm) high.
**£590–650 / €820–910
$960–1,060** S(O) ✎

The rococo style of the early to mid-18thC was revived in the mid- and late 19thC, the later examples being very decorative but less interesting horologically. An 18thC example would cost at least £2,500 / €3,500 / $4,100.

Gilt-bronze mantel clock, retailed by Cresson Fleurbe, Calais, with a silvered dial, the eight-day striking movement with silk suspension, the case surmounted by a seated figure of a Nubian female, 19thC, 21¾in (55.5cm) high. Well finished castings, fine gilding and an attractive subject make this clock a desirable decorative piece. The movement would have been made by an unknown factory c1840.
**£600–660 / €840–920
$980–1,100** NES ✎

▶ **Gilt-metal and Sèvres-style porcelain garniture,** the drum dial flanked by Corinthian columns and putti, the case surmounted by an urn and putti, together with a pair of urns, 19thC, clock 21in (53.5cm) high. This well-known model dating to the late 19thC is always made in gilt spelter. It is large and showy and, if complete, comes with stands and glass domes. Unfortunately the damaged dial is not worth repairing.
**£600–660 / €840–920
$980–1,100** L&E ✎

Skeleton Clocks

Brass skeleton timepiece,
with single chain fusee
movement, on a marble base,
under a glass dome, 19thC,
13¾in (35cm) high.
**£460–550 / €640–770
$750–900 SWO** 🔨

Brass skeleton timepiece,
the fusee movement with
pierced roman silvered chapter
ring, on an ebonized base,
under a glass dome, French,
19thC, 17in (43cm) high. This
clock would be worth more if
it were on a marble base.
**£480–530 / €670–740
$780–870 G(B)** 🔨

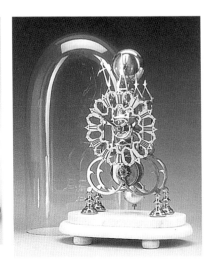

Brass skeleton timepiece, with passing
strike and painted Roman pierced dial, the
anchor escapement with four spoke wheels,
wire fusee with closed-end barrel, on a later
marble base, under a glass dome, 19thC,
15½in (39.5cm) high.
**£520–570 / €720–790
$850–930 B(Kn)** 🔨

◀ **Brass skeleton time-
piece,** with passing strike, the
fusee movement with anchor
escapement, on a later ebonized
base, under a glass dome,
repainted chapter ring, c1870,
15½in (39.5cm) high. The value
of this clock has been enhanced
by its unusual painted dial and
original dome.
**£700–770 / €980–1,050
$1,150–1,250 S(O)** 🔨

Buying tips

The majority of skeleton clocks available at under
£1,000 / €1,400 / $1,650 are English and date
from the second half of the 19th century. Look for
replaced bases and domes. It can be difficult to find
a replacement glass dome, and the original marble
bases were often replaced with skimpy ebonized
ones taken from other ornaments. The quality of the
finishing to the skeletonized frame and movement
parts will also affect the price. Skeleton clocks are
very rarely signed by the maker, so a signed example
will be more popular with collectors.

Gilt-brass skeleton timepiece, with
pierced silvered dial and fusee movement,
on a marble base, under a glass dome,
19thC, 21in (53.5cm) high. This clock has
an elegant tall frame that shows the
skeleton movement to good effect.
**£750–820 / €1,050–1,150
$1,200–1,350 WilP** 🔨

Wall Clocks

Rosewood and white-metal-inlaid drop-dial clock, with a painted dial, the two-train movement striking on a bell, the glass panel inscribed in gilt 'Champion Regulator', late 19thC, 28in (71cm) high. This is a mass-produced wall clock. The movement is far from regulator quality – it was a marketing term used for this style of clock.
£120–130 / €165–180
$195–210 DN ⚘

Miller's compares...

A. Victorian papier mâché and mother-of-pearl-inlaid wall clock, with an enamel dial, the pendulum revealed below in a glazed arch, 25½in (65cm) high.
£170–190 / €230–260
$280–310 WL ⚘

B. Ebonized mother-of-pearl-inlaid wall clock, with a two-train fusee striking movement, 19thC, 25in (63.5cm) high.
£400–440 / €560–610
$650–720 BWL ⚘

Both Item A and Item B have very similar cases and date to the third quarter of the 19th century. However, the English fusee movement of Item B makes it much more unusual as a striking clock. Item A has a mass-produced American movement whereas Item B is more collectable and good value at the price.

◀ **Oak Norwich-style wall timepiece,** retailed by Boxell, Brighton, the painted dial signed and with a cast bezel, single fusee movement, lens missing, late 19thC, 59in (150cm) high. This is a trunk dial version of a wall timepiece with a standard fusee movement and oak case. Thomas Boxell of Brighton was a retailer selling all manner of good quality clocks and timepieces.
£320–350 / €450–490
$520–570 B(Kn) ⚘

Find out more in

Miller's Clocks Antiques Checklist, Miller's Publications, 2000

▶ **Hand-painted porcelain hanging timepiece,** by E. N. Welch Mf. Co, with bevelled glass over the repapered dial, American, c1889, 6in (15cm) diam. This item is very much one for the American purist collector. An English or Continental version of this timepiece might well cost less than £100 / €140 / $165.
£320–350 / €450–490
$520–570 ROSc ⚘

Mahogany wall timepiece, with fusee movement, 19thC, dial 10in (25.5cm) diam. The standard size of dial for these timepieces is 12in (30.5cm). Smaller or significantly larger dials command a premium in price. There is a well-moulded surround to this case and the clock dates from c1850.

£500–550 / €700–770
$820–900 BR ✎

Buying tips

English wall clocks and timepieces of the 'school' or 'kitchen' type have become much more popular in recent years. Look for pre-1900 examples with original dials. The most collectable of these date to the early 19th century and have convex dials and glasses. Dials smaller than 12in (20.5cm) are particularly sought-after. Vienna-style wall clocks made in Germany have also increased in value of late. The most popular types are weight-driven and have slim and elegant cases. Watch for damage to the enamel dials. Movements by Lenzkirch and Becker are well-regarded but spring-driven movements and heavily turned cases are less popular.

► **Walnut and ebonized 'Vienna' wall timepiece,** with a two-piece enamel dial and weight-driven movement, signed 'Lenzkirch', with tapered plates, deadbeat escapement with adjustable pallets and maintaining power and a wood rod pendulum, German, c1890, 45¾in (116cm) high. This is an elegant Vienna-style wall clock by one of the more highly regarded 19thC German factories and is closer to the true Vienna regulator than the later striking examples.

£590–650 / €820–910
$960–1,060 S(O) ✎

Mahogany drop-dial wall clock, the dial with blued steel hands, the bezel on a convex moulded frame fixed to the case by four wooden pegs, the gut fusee movement with anchor escapement, the trunk with a glazed aperture and carved foliate ears, some repairs, mid-19thC, 19¾in (50cm) high. This timepiece has had some sympathetic restoration. It has attractive and unusual hands and the case is of fine quality.

£750–830 / €1,050–1,150
$1,100–1,350 B(Kn) ✎

◄ **Mahogany longcase wall clock,** the dial signed 'Thomas Moreland, Chester', with subsidiary seconds, the rack and bell-striking eight-day movement fixed with a false plate, c1860, 63¾in (162cm) high. This is a fine, mid-Victorian example by this well-known Chester maker, with well figured veneers and rich colour. It is good value at this price and an alternative to a more expensive longcase clock.

£850–940 / €1,200–1,300
$1,400–1,550 B(NW) ✎

Miscellaneous

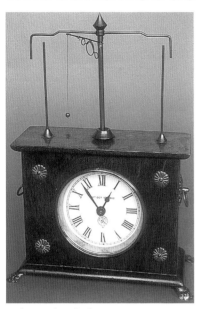

Oak novelty clock, decorated with brass roundels and surmounted by a brass swing mechanism, American, 19thC, 9¾in (25cm) high. This is a cheaply-made but fun timepiece by the American manufacturer Jerome & Co. The ball wraps the string around the vertical rods and the timepiece releases as it unwinds and moves to the next rod.
£160–180 / €220–250
$260–300 AMB ⚹

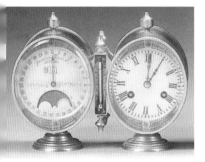

Desk clock and perpetual calendar, the clock with a silvered dial and engraved and silvered mask, the movement with cylinder platform escapement and outside countwheel striking on a bell, the perpetual calendar movement with silvered dial apertures for years, months, days and moon-phase, centred by a centigrade/Réaumur thermometer, lacking a base, French, 1825–75, 5½in (14cm) high.
£620–680 / €860–950
$1,000–1,100 B(Kn) ⚹

► **Carved walnut cuckoo clock,** German, Black Forest, late 19thC, 29½in (75cm) high. The details on this cuckoo clock are finely carved, but dead game is not popular with everyone, making this a good buy for those of a less squeamish disposition.
£600–660 / €840–920
$980–1,100 S(O) ⚹

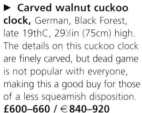

◄ **Pendule d'officier,** with a signed enamel dial, the twin-train movement with a silvered lever platform escapement and outside countwheel striking on a gong, on four eagle-claw feet, late 19thC, 5in (12.5cm) high. The *pendule d'officier* first appeared in France in the late 18thC as an early carriage clock. Originals in good condition are rare. This is an attractive revival piece at a tenth of the price of an original.
£350–380 / €490–530
$570–620 B(Kn) ⚹

The look without the price

Iron and brass lantern clock, with pewter chapter ring and posted movement, anchor escapement with silk suspension, passing strike at the half hour and rack-striking at the hour, the frame with a top-mounted bell, French, provincial, late 17thC, 12¼in (31cm) high.
£840–920
€1,150–1,300
$1,350–1,500 S(O) ⚹

There are very few late 17thC clocks that can be bought for under £1,000 / €1,400 / $1,650, and an English lantern clock would cost at least twice as much as this French example. However, only buy from a reputable source as there are many 'made-up' and fake clocks in circulation.

Pocket Watches

Lady's gold-filled pocket watch, by Hampton Watch Co, American, c1900. Produced in vast numbers at the turn of the 20thC, American ladies' watches such as this can be bought at a low price.
£25–30 / €35–42
$40–60 DuM ⚲

What is gold-filled?

Gold-filled provides the look and tarnish resistance of solid gold but at a fraction of the cost. It is made by using heat and pressure to bond a layer of gold alloy to brass or another base metal, then rolling it into a sheet or drawing it into wire to the required thickness. It is much more durable than gold plate and will not flake or peel and, with reasonable care, can last for generations.

Silver cylinder watch, by Stauffer, Geneva, the enamel dial with sweep seconds and gold hands, the gilt bar movement with a plain three arm balance and steel scape wheel, the case with a glazed cuvette and engraved decoration, with a stop button, Swiss, 19thC, 2in (5cm) diam. The crisp, clear enamel dial and sweep seconds hand make this an attractive alternative to a standard Swiss pocket watch.
£140–155 / €195–215
$230–250 B(Kn) ⚲

18ct gold lever watch, by Reid & Sons, Newcastle-on-Tyne, the signed enamel dial with sunk subsidiary seconds, the three-quarter plate movement with a cut and compensated bimetallic balance, in an engine-turned case, maker's mark for Richard Macair Ball, London 1866, 1¾in (4.5cm) diam. This watch an attractive dial with the added quality of a sunk seconds dial. The case, however, is rather tired looking, indicating that it has had a lot of wear.
£170–185 / €235–260
$280–300 B(Kn) ⚲

Buying tips

By the middle of the 19th century, the railways had caused the standardization of time across Britain, and being able to tell the time was becoming important to more and more people. The era of the pocket watch had truly arrived and they were produced in enormous quantities. Silver was the most common material for the case with gold, in general, being reserved for the more expensive models. Look for examples with more unusual dials or particularly those with complications such as repeating work, chronographs, calendars etc. Both the Swiss and Americans were masters of mass production, making good-quality watches in a variety of forms. Look for English watches with fine fusee movements and beautifully finished escapements.

◀ **18ct gold keyless lever watch,** by K. Zimmerman, Liverpool, No. 15346, with an enamel dial, the gilt three quarter plate movement with a cut and compensated bimetallic balance, case hallmarked Chester, 2in (5cm) diam. This watch has a lovely dial but sadly the missing bow and general distress to the case make this an unattractive restoration proposition.
£190–210 / €265–290
$310–350 B(Kn) ⚲

Enamel-decorated keyless cylinder watch, by Escot a Angouleme, the enamel dial within a cast bezel, with a gilt movement, the cover decorated with an iris, French, late 19thC, 1¼in (3cm) diam, together with an associated bar brooch. This watch has an attractive Art Nouveau influenced enamel case and a basic Swiss movement. Always check the enamel carefully as damage is expensive and difficult to repair.
£230–250 / €320–350 $380–410 B(Kn) ✎

Silver dual time watch, the enamel dial with sweep and subsidiary seconds with two subsidiary chapters, the gilt bar movement with compensated balance and double duplex escapement, 19thC, 2in (5cm) diam. While ordinary silver pocket watches can often be bought for less than £100 / €140 / $165, the unusual dual time dial of this watch makes it an interesting collector's item and is good value at this price.
£320–350 / €450–490 $520–570 B(Kn) ✎

18ct gold open-faced pocket watch, by W. Lanquetin, Pontatilier, the enamel dial with subsidiary seconds dial and Louis XV hands, with a Swiss keyless bar lever movement, in a monogrammed four-piece hinged case, together with a curb chain and coin fob, c1890.
£350–380 / €490–530 $570–620 DN ✎

Verge Oignon watch movement, by Ourry, Paris, the enamel dial with a single hand, in an associated engraved brass case, French, early 18thC, 2½in (6.5cm) diam. Although attractive, this is a marriage of dial, movement and case. The dial was originally intended to be a two-handed movement, as indicated by the minute markings. However, it is an early and interesting movement.
£350–380 / €490–530 $570–620 B(Kn) ✎

Gold verge watch, by Liebold, Strasbourg, with an enamel dial with polished steel bezel and signed gilt movement, in an engraved consular case, maker's mark DPN, French, early 19thC, 1¾in (4.5cm) diam. The case of this watch has survived in very good condition and assuming that the dial is perfect, this is good value.
£350–380 / €490–530 $570–620 B(Kn) ✎

14ct gold-filled pocket watch, the porcelain dial with a subsidiary seconds dial, with a Waltham keyless wind movement, the case back engraved with a stag, the sides with flowers and filigree patterns, American, 1893. The case of this watch is very attractive, but the fact that it is gold-filled makes it less desirable.
£350–380 / €490–530 $570–620 Bns ▦

◀ **Silver repeating watch,** by Paul Du-Pin, London, with an associated enamel dial, the gilt movement repeating via two hammers, in an associated two-colour gold and silver French case decorated with musical trophies, 18thC, 2in (5cm) diam. With an associated and damaged dial, the value of this watch lies in the repeating movement and the finely decorated case.
£450–500
€630–700
$730–820   B(Kn) ⚲

Silver and gold hunting-cased lever watch, the signed enamel dial with subsidiary seconds, with a nickelled split three-quarter plate keyless movement, the silver hunter case with a chased and engraved gold centre, maker's mark 'CWC Co', American, late 19thC, 2in (5cm) diam.
£470–520 / €650–720
$770–850   PT ⚲

Miller's compares...

A. Enamel-decorated gold verge watch, by Isaac Soret et Fils, the dial with fancy hands and bezel, the rear cover set with an enamel portrait of a young lady within a stone-set border, French, late 18thC, 1½in (4cm) diam.
£520–570 / €720–790
$850–930   B(Kn) ⚲

B. Enamel and diamond-set verge watch, by Francois, Metz, the enamel dial with pierced gold hands, movement signed, the case decorated with an enamel portrait of a young lady in a diamond-set surround, French, late 18thC, 2in (5cm) diam, with a gilt-metal and shagreen protective case.
£650–720 / €910–1,000
$1,050–1,200   B(Kn) ⚲

Item A and Item B are very similar decorative watches, but Item B has retained its outer case and is therefore complete, which explains its higher value.

18ct gold open-faced duplex watch, by Barwise, London, with a gold engine-turned dial, signed full plate gilt duplex movement, in an engine-turned case, 1830, 2in (5cm) diam, with key. This is a fine English watch with a relatively rare escapement. It has a fine dial and hands and the case is not too worn, making this piece a good buy.
£540–590 / €750–820
$880–960   S(O) ⚲

Silver pair-cased verge watch, by John Moon, Bristol, No. 363, with an enamel dial, the inner case with maker's mark LRR, with obscured hallmarks for London 1776, 2in (5cm) diam, in a later underpainted horn outer case. This watch, despite a hair crack to the dial and case, has good original hands and is a fine example of provincial watchmaking in the 18thC.
£550–600 / €770–840
$900–980 B(Kn)

Pair-cased verge watch, by Edward Smith, Dublin, with an enamel dial and signed movement, the case marked 'J.B.', Irish, 18thC, 2in (5cm) diam. The missing minute hand is a problem with this watch, as a new one would need to be made to match the hour hand. The dial has an early use of Arabic numerals, but has a hair crack.
£580–640 / €810–890
$950–1,050 B(Kn)

18ct gold pair-cased watch, by Barraud, London, the later enamel dial with later hands and sweep seconds, movement signed, the case with maker's mark I.P., London 1787, 2in (5cm) diam. This is an attractive watch by a highly regarded maker. The stop watch is an added feature, making this item good value.
£580–640 / €810–890
$950–1,050 B(Kn)

Three-colour gold enamel and diamond consular cased watch, by Leger, Paris, the signed enamel dial with winding aperture and diamond-set hour hand and bezel, signed full plate verge movement, the case with applied gold decoration centred by a portrait of Marie Antoinette surrounded by a diamond-set border, with a gilt outer-glazed protective cover, later minute hand, French, c1790, 1½in (4cm) diam. This pretty watch represents a good buy.
£600–660 / €840–920
$980–1,100 S(O)

Gilt pair-cased verge watch, by Thomas Windmills, London, the enamel dial with blued steel beetle and poker hands, with a signed and numbered full gilt plate verge movement, later gilt cases, the outer case stamped 'AM' under a bird, c1720, 2¼in (5.5cm) diam. Although this watch has a later case, it is by a well-known and important maker. It is a reasonable buy for a collector wanting a watch by a famous maker.
£600–660 / €840–920
$980–1,100 S(O)

Gold quarter-repeating open-faced watch, by Le Roy et Fils, with a silver engine-turned dial, a gilt cylinder movement, the polished case with an engine-turned band, push plunge repeat, cuvette signed and numbered, French, c1810, 2in (5cm) diam. This is a typical early 19thC French-style watch with clean lines, fine dial and hands. It is in need of careful cleaning, but is a fine watch at a very reasonable price.
£720–790 / €1,000–1,100
$1,200–1,300 S(O)

Wristwatches

Jule Jurgensen 14ct gold automatic wristwatch, with jewelled movement, Swiss, 1960s, 1½in (4cm) diam.
£200–220 / €280–310
$330–370 B(Kn) ✏

Locate the source

The source of each illustration in Miller's can be found by checking the code letters below each caption with the Key to Illustrations, pages 286–290.

Miller's compares...

A. Rolex stainless steel wristwatch, with 15 jewel movement, case, dial and movement signed, 1950s, 1¼in (3cm) diam.
£200–220 / €280–310
$330–370 B(Kn) ✏

B. Rolex Oyster Perpetual stainless steel automatic wristwatch, with centre seconds, the 26 jewel movement adjusted to five positions and temperature, case, dial, movement and bracelet signed, 1962, 1½in (4cm) diam, with original box and papers.
£600–660 / €840–920
$980–1,100 B(Kn) ✏

Item A and Item B are both Rolex wristwatches. However, Item A is a standard model with a later bracelet, whereas Item B is an Oyster Perpetual with its original bracelet. It also has its original box and papers which makes it of greater interest to collectors.

The look without the price

Rolex Oysterdate Precision stainless steel wristwatch, with centre seconds and 17 jewel movement, case, dial, movement and bracelet signed, 1962, 1½in (4cm) diam.
£320–350 / €450–490
$520–570 B(Kn) ✏

This watch represents very good value. In looks it is very similar to the Rolex Perpetual automatic wristwatch, which would cost about £200 / €280 / $330 more.

Rolex Oyster Speedking stainless steel wristwatch, the dial with sweep centre seconds and 17 jewel Super Balance movement, case, dial and movement signed, 1940s, 1¼in (3cm) diam.
£320–350 / €450–490
$520–570 B(Kn) ✏

Omega 9ct gold cushion-cased wristwatch, the 15 jewel movement adjusted to two positions, case, dial and movement signed, case marked for Birmingham 1934, 1¼in (3cm) wide. This watch is in good condition and with its classic 1930s cushion case is a very good buy.
£340–370 / €470–520
$560–610 B(Kn) ⚒

Universal stainless steel wristwatch, with 17 jewel movement, case, dial and movement signed, 1960s, 1in (2.5cm) wide. This watch is of a stylish design which is equally at home in the 21stC as it was in the 1960s.
£400–440 / €560–610
$650–720 B(Kn) ⚒

Miller's compares...

A. Jaeger-LeCoultre Memovox gold-plated automatic calendar wristwatch with alarm, with centre seconds and nickel lever movement, case, dial and movement signed, Swiss, c1960, 1½in (4cm) diam.
£360–400 / €500–560
$590–650 S(O) ⚒

B. Jaeger-LeCoultre Memovox 18ct pink gold calendar wristwatch with alarm, with centre seconds, nickel lever movement and monometallic compensation balance, case, dial and movement signed, Swiss, c1950, 1½in (4cm) diam.
£660–730 / €920–1,000
$1,100–1,200 S(O) ⚒

Item A and Item B are both by Jaeger-LeCoultre, the well-known maker of good-quality watches. However, the solid gold case and earlier date of Item B make it much more appealing to collectors, hence its higher value.

International Watch Co stainless steel automatic wristwatch, with centre seconds and 21 jewel movement, Swiss, 1950s, 1½in (4cm) diam. By a highly regarded maker, this watch is in good original condition and is good value.
£400–440 / €560–610
$650–720 B(Kn) ⚒

Girard Perregaux Grande Calender stainless steel calendar wristwatch, with subsidiary seconds and 17 jewel movement, case, dial and movement signed, 1950s, 1in (2.5cm) wide. The interesting calendar on this wristwatch makes it sought-after by collectors. The design is very modern and shows how fast styles changed after WWII.
£400–440 / €560–610
$650–720 B(Kn) ⚒

Rolex stainless steel automatic wristwatch, with centre seconds and jewelled movement, case, dial and movement signed, 1960s, 1½in (4cm) diam.
£420–460 / €590–640
$690–750 B(Kn) 🔨

Jaeger-LeCoultre stainless steel military wristwatch, with jewelled mechanical movement, Swiss, 1940s, 1½in (4cm) diam.
£420–460 / €590–640
$690–750 B(Kn) 🔨

Omega steel wristwatch, with seconds dial, Swiss, 1930s.
£500–550 / €700–770
$820–900 TEM ▦

Find out more in

Miller's Watches: A Collector's Guide,
Miller's Publications, 1999

Longines silver wristwatch, with seconds dial, 1920s.
£530–580 / €740–810
$870–950 TEM ▦

Omega Constellation gold automatic calendar wristwatch, with centre seconds and 24 jewel pink gilt movement, monometallic balance adjusted to five positions and temperature, with later added lugs, case, dial, crown and movement signed, Swiss, c1966, 1¼in (3cm) diam. This watch has been fitted with unusual later lugs. Good quality modifications can increase variety and hence value, making this watch double the price of a standard model.
£540–590 / €750–820
$880–960 S(O) 🔨

Rolex silver cushion-cased wire lug wristwatch, the dial with luminous numerals and subsidiary seconds, with 15 jewel polished nickel movement, one lug replaced, case and movement signed, case marked for London 1917, 1½in (4cm) wide. This wristwatch is typical of those worn during WWI by officers who were required to wear a wristwatch rather than carry a pocket watch.
£550–600 / €770–840 $900–980 B(Kn) ☞

International Watch Co stainless steel wristwatch, with centre seconds, nickel lever movement and monometallic compensation balance, case, dial and movement signed, Swiss, c1949, 1½in (4cm) diam. This wristwatch, with its black dial, was produced to appeal to ex-servicemen who might have been attached to their service watches.
£580–640 / €810–890 $950–1,050 S(O) ☞

International Watch Co 18ct gold automatic calendar wristwatch, with nickel level movement and monometallic balance, with 18ct gold bracelet, case, dial and movement signed, Swiss, c1963, 1½in (4cm) diam. This is a classic early 1960s design which could easily be worn as a dress watch today.
£600–660 / €840–920 $980–1,100 S(O) ☞

Rolex silver-cased hunter wristwatch, with luminous numerals and subsidiary seconds and 15 jewel polished nickel movement, the screw-down back inscribed 'W. J. Witchell, Weston Super Mare from Mother 1917', case and movement signed, case marked for London 1916, 1½in (4cm) diam. This is an historically interesting watch and the inscription has added to its value.
£650–710 / €910–990 $1,050–1,150 B(Kn) ☞

International Watch Co 18ct gold automatic calendar wristwatch, with centre seconds and 21 jewel movement, Swiss, 1960s, 1½in (4cm) diam. This is an elegant watch by a good maker.
£700–770 / €980–1,050 $1,150–1,250 B(Kn) ☞

Rolex Oyster Perpetual DateJust stainless steel automatic wristwatch, with centre seconds, 21 jewel nickel lever movement, monometallic compensation balance, adjusted to five positions and temperature, case, dial and movement signed, c1956, 1½in (4cm) diam, with Rolex Oyster stainless steel bracelet.
£840–920 / €1,150–1,300 $1,350–1,500 S(O) ☞

Barometers

◄ **Aneroid barometer,** c1900, 9in (23cm) diam. Aneroid barometers were introduced in the mid-18thC, bringing about the possiblity of mass production, and by 1900 they were being made in a variety of styles. This example is of a common design.
£140–155
€ **195–210**
$230–1250 AB ⊞

The look without the price

Victorian gilt-metal desk timepiece/barometer, on a marble base.
£140–155 / € **195–210**
$230–250 HOLL ⚲

Although this desk set is good value, a better quality example would be worth nearer £400 / € 560 / $650.

Miller's compares...

A. Mahogany and inlaid wheel barometer,
by P. Corti, with five dials, 19thC, 40¼in (102cm) high.
£150–165 / € **210–230**
$250–270 B(Kn) ⚲

B. Mahogany and inlaid wheel barometer,
the pediment with urn finial, dial signed, early 19thC, 39in (99cm) high.
£600–660 / € **840–920**
$980–1,000 B(Kn) ⚲

Item A is the most widely available form of mid-Victorian wheel barometer – the five dials being hygrometer, thermometer, convex mirror, barometer dial and bubble level. Item B has a much higher quality case, is a more unusual design and, being earlier in date, is more popular with collectors.

► **Mahogany wheel barometer,**
by Usher & son, Lincoln, c1900, 26in (66cm) high. The late Victorian style of this barometer is not very popular with collectors, hence its low value.
£180–200
€ **250–280**
$295–330 FHF ⚲

Aneroid barometer, in an arch-topped case, c1890, 32in (81.5cm) high. Over the last ten years aneroid barometers have become more collectable.
£230–250 / €320–350
$380–410 FHF ⚶

◀ **Mahogany banjo barometer,** with ebony and boxwood stringing, mid-19thC, 46½in (118cm) high. This barometer is in need of some work, but the restoration will double its value.
£280–300
€390–430
$460–510
B(NW) ⚶

▶ **Oak stick barometer,** by Mark Hill, Birmingham, the carved and pierced case surmounted by a cross, 42in (106.5cm) high. This barometer would complement a Victorian-style interior.
£300–330
€420–460
$490–540 FHF ⚶

◀ **Mahogany-veneered banjo barometer,** level plate inscribed 'P & A Comolli, Dudley', stain to case, mirror cracked, 19thC, 38½in (98cm) high. Prices for these, the commonest form of early Victorian wheel barometers, vary with quality and colour of the mahogany. Look for examples in good, original condition. The damaged mirror of this example would not be expensive to replace.
£320–350
€450–490
$520–570 WW ⚶

Find out more in

Miller's Antiques Price Guide, Miller's Publications, 2004

WANTED
BAROGRAPHS

IN ANY CONDITION!
BOUGHT BY COLLECTOR

AND ALL OTHER TYPES OF METEOROLOGICAL INSTRUMENTS.

WILL TRAVEL.

CONTACT:
RICHARD TWORT

TEL/FAX 01934 641900
MOBILE 07711 939789

Mahogany banjo barometer,
early 19thC,
39in (99cm) high.
£340–370
€470–520
$560–610 EH ⚲

Walnut aneroid barometer, by Aitchinson, London, 1870–1900, 35in (89cm) high.
£500–550
€700–770
$820–900 AB ⊞

Miller's compares...

A. Walnut Gothic-style stick barometer, cistern cover missing, German, 19thC, 41¼in (105cm) high.
£360–400
€500–560
$590–650 B(Kn) ⚲

B. Mahogany stick barometer, with chequered stringing, the brass scales signed 'Torre and Co, London', early 19thC, 38¼in (97cm) high.
£460–500
€640–700
$750–820 Bea(E) ⚲

The Gothic revival design of Item A has limited appeal at present, whereas the classic early 19thC-style of Item B is very popular with collectors, hence its higher value.

▶ **Mahogany banjo barometer,** by Adie & Son, Edinburgh, in a scrolled case, dial signed, mid-19thC, 34in (86.5cm) high. Alexander Adie was an innovative Scottish instrument maker and highly regarded for his barometers. This item was made towards the end of his life and is a fine example with beautiful veneers. The small dial makes it rare and sought-after, and it is very good value at this price.
£580–630 / €810–890
$950–1,050 B(NW) ⚲

Mahogany wheel barometer, by Edwards, London, c1840, 42½in (108cm) high.
£460–510 / €640–710
$750–830 S(O) ⚲

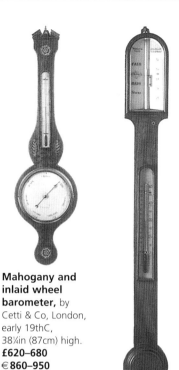

Mahogany and inlaid wheel barometer, by Cetti & Co, London, early 19thC, 38¼in (87cm) high.
£620–680
€860–950
$1,000–1,100
B(Kn) ✦

▶ **Victorian carved oak barometer,** by Primavesi Bros, Bournemouth, with lion-mask cover, inner barometer tube damaged, mercury missing, 41¾in (106cm) high.
£720–790 / €1,000–1,100
$1,200–1,300 WW ✦

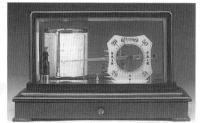

Mahogany combination barograph and barometer, by J. Lizars, Glasgow & Edinburgh, with single recording arm and seven-tier vacuum, with lift-off lid and frieze drawer, c1900, 8¾in (22.5cm) high. Barographs, or recording barometers, are very popular with amateur meteorologists. They record the barometric pressure for a week onto a paper chart. This is a good example with bevelled glass to the covers and a drawer for new and used charts.
£750–820 / €1,050–1,150
$1,200–1,350 B(Kn) ✦

◀ **Stick barometer,** by Marratt & Ellis, London, with glass scales, late 19thC, 37½in (95.5cm) high. Glass scales are less popular than silvered plates.
£620–680 / €860–950
$1,000–1,100 WW ✦

▶ **Victorian oak stick barometer,** by Potter, London, with ivory registers, 39½in (100.5cm) high. Beware of heavy staining to ivory plates – it is caused by mercury vapour and is impossible to remove.
£700–770 / €980–1,050
$1,150–1,250 G(B) ✦

▶ **Rosewood stick barometer,** by Crighton Brothers, London, the case with foliate-carved cresting, cistern cover missing, signed, c1870, 38½in (98cm) high. This barometer needs some restoration to the case but the ivory plates are in good condition. The cistern cover is well worth replacing.
£840–920 / €1,150–1,300
$1,350–1,500 S(O) ✦

Other Antiques

This section covers decorative antiques and furnishings and a variety of other collecting areas. There are many wonderful pieces available to collectors at prices that will not break the bank, although this does not mean that affordability comes at the expense of quality. The craftmanship and quality of materials used in antiques under £1,000 / €1,400 / $1,650 is usually far superior to modern, often mass-produced equivalents. Although the antiques market as a whole has seen a decline in value, this sector has maintained steady prices, especially for rarer pieces. The most common items are still inexpensive, such as the Victorian officer's sword illustrated on page 234. This is not to say that rarer items should be beyond your pocket as long as you are prepared to accept some damage or restoration. Some rare items are inexpensive because they are in low demand, for example the gilded bronze boss brooch on page 219.

The value of decorative antiques and furnishings is determined by fashion. If you are prepared to buy what you like and ignore the short-term trends there are marvellous bargains to be had. These include Roman and Saxon jewellery, plain 19th-century boxes, German bisque-headed dolls, Victorian copper and brass wares and 19th-century lace and linen.

There are certain factors that have a great bearing on value. Well-known and respected manufacturers, craftsmen and artists will command higher prices, especially if they were pioneers in their field, such as the German firm of Steiff, whose early teddy bears are generally expensive to buy. As a consequence interest has grown in early English teddy bears which are far more affordable. Often the quality of pieces by lesser makers will be near to that of the best firms but at a fraction of the cost.

It is adivsable to buy items with original features – for instance, antiquities, architectural antiques, arms and armour, metalware, sculpture, textiles and wooden antiques are more desirable and hence more valuable when they have original colour or patination. It is important when collecting arms and armour, toys and scientific instruments to check that there are no missing parts – a microscope is not useable if key accessories are missing. A good provenance is worth its weight in gold as an object may have belonged to a famous person or come from an important collection. For instance, a sword may have been awarded to a soldier who gained medals for gallantry in the field and therefore has an interesting history.

Another area to explore is 'the look without the price'. The best examples of this are 17th- and 18th-century designs such as the fire surround and overmantel mirror on page 231 and architectural antiques produced in the Victorian era.

The only note of caution is to avoid fakes and modern reproductions. Whether you are deciding what to collect or are looking for a piece to decorate your home, it is important to visit as many antiques shops, fairs and auctions as possible. Always seek the advice of a reputable dealer or auctioneer if you are unsure about a piece. You will quickly learn which items are common and the average price you would expect to pay. Most auctioneers and dealers are contactable via the internet and it is possible to view online, giving you access to more items across the country. They will be happy to provide you with a condition report, but always remember that there is no substitute for handling a piece yourself. You will soon become adept at spotting desirable features and damage or restoration. **Daniel Bray**

Antiquities

Six pottery ushabti figures, with moulded detail, Egyptian, Ptolemaic Period, 332–30 BC, 2in (5cm) high. Ushabtis were mass-produced throughout ancient Egypt in the later periods. These examples are not of great quality and are suffering from extensive wear, therefore they are consequently unlikely to increase in value.
£10–15 / €14–20
$20–25 each HEL ⊞

Buying tips

When buying antiquities always ask about provenance, keep all documentation and be aware of export and import regulations – some items will require a passport and this should be available at the time of purchase. It is advisable to buy from dealers who are members of a trade association such as the Antiquities Dealers Association (ADA) and the International Association of Dealers in Ancient Art (IADAA), as this ensures protection. For a list of members visit www.the-ADA.org. Alternatively, buy from auction houses, as they will be able to provide the necessary documentation.

◀ **Pottery bowl,** Levantine, early Bronze Age, 3rd–2nd millennium BC, 7in (18cm) diam. This was an everyday domestic pottery bowl used for a variety of household duties. Undecorated bowls like this were used all over the ancient world and are purely functional.
£55–60 / €75–85
$90–100 HEL ⊞

Gilded bronze boss brooch, with spring and catch-plate, glass central boss damaged, found in Gloucestershire, late 3rd–early 4thC AD, 1¼in (3cm) wide. It is rare to find a brooch such as this with the pin and glass centre intact, as well as with a known find spot, making this item a good buy.
£60–65 / €85–90
$100–105 ANG ⊞

ANCIENT & GOTHIC
(Chris Belton)

Tel: 01202 431721

ANTIQUITIES FROM BEFORE 300,000 B.C. TO ABOUT 1500 A.D.

Bi-monthly sales lists include:
STONE AGE ANTIQUITIES FROM THE EARLIEST TIMES

BRONZE AGE, IRON AGE
& ROMANO-BRITISH ANTIQUITIES

GREEK, ROMAN, ETRUSCAN
& EGYPTIAN ANTIQUITIES

DARK AGES, ANGLO-SAXON,
MEDIEVAL & BYZANTINE ANTIQUITIES

28th year – everything guaranteed

PLEASE PHONE 1PM TO 7PM MON TO SAT FOR COPY OF LATEST LIST – no ansafone. If no reply please try again an hour or so later (apart from annual 2 week holiday) or write to:
P.O. BOX 5390, BOURNEMOUTH BH7 6XR

HUNDREDS OF ITEMS ON EVERY LIST – from under £5 to about £500 MANY FROM £10 TO £50

The logo is an Anglo-Saxon Pagan period bronze 'small-long' brooch, 7cm long, 6th century A.D. sold from the list for £95

Miller's compares...

B. Bronze reliquary cross, with suspension loop and hanger, Bulgarian, 10thC, 2½in (6.5cm) long. Byzantine bronze reliquary crosses such as this would have once been worn around the neck, making them intimate objects with a close connection to our ancestors. They would have contained some kind of religious relic, such as the hair of a saint, for protection. This is a worn example but is almost complete.

£110–120 / €155–165
$180–195 AnAr ⊞

A. Bronze reliquary cross, depicting Christ crucified with Our Lady and St John the Evangelist to either side, with suspension loop, back part and bottom of cross missing, Bulgarian, 10thC, 2in (6cm) long. This piece was probably once a reliquary cross box, and too much is missing to make it worth restoring. If it were intact it would probably be worth £160 / €220 / $260.

£60–65 / €85–90
$100–105 ANG ⊞

Although both Item A and Item B are of the same period, Item B has a higher value because it is far more complete, and still has its hinges and the underside.

Pottery vessel, decorated with incised circular bands, with twin lug handles, Israeli, 2ndC AD, 3in (7.5cm) high. This small piece would be a good starting point for collectors of ancient vessels.

£65–70 / €90–95
$105–115 Sama ⊞

▶ **Bronze vessel mount,** in the form of the head of Serapis, Balkan, 1st–3rdC AD, 1in (2.5cm) long. The god Serapis was a hybrid of the Egyptian gods Osiris and Apis and the Greek gods Dionysus and Hades. It was hoped that this new god would appeal to a cross-section of the populace, and indeed the cult of Serapis became hugely popular in the Hellenistic and Roman periods in Egypt and beyond.

£65–70 / €90–95
$105–115 ANG ⊞

Small bronzes

Small bronzes are currently hard to sell, so large groups of relatively good pieces can be bought at very low prices. They would make a good subject for a new collector with a low budget who is not looking to make an instant return on investment.

Terracotta ridged jug,
Roman, 3rd–4thC AD,
5½in (14cm) high. This vessel
is an attractive shape and is
quite contemporary in design.
€75–85 / €105–120
$120–140 AnAr ⊞

Pewter pilgrim badge, in
the form of the Virgin and Child
on a crescent moon, complete
with pin, London area, early
16thC, 1in (2.5cm) wide. These
pilgrim badges were based on a
miracle-working statue, thought
to be a now unknown shrine in
the London area, possibly Our
Lady of Willesden. All but five
of the 320 known examples
were found in the London area.
£85–95 / €120–130
$140–155 ANG ⊞

◄ **Chancay painted pottery
vessel,** decorated with appliqués
representing pelicans, Peru,
1200–1400, 9in (23cm) high.
£110–125 / €155–175
$180–200 HEL ⊞

► **Buff ware jug,** recovered
from Tunisia, Roman, 2nd–3rdC
AD, 8in (20.5cm) high. This
undecorated jug is a good piece
for those wanting to buy an
impressive-looking Roman
vessel, but not wanting to
spend too much money.
£130–140 / €180–195
$200–230 OTT ⊞

► **Faïence shabti
figure,** Egyptian,
Ptolemaic period,
c500 BC, 5in (12.5cm)
high. This item has a
good strong colour
which is indicative
of better quality
pieces but the
hieroglyphs on the
lower body are worn.
£110–120
€155–165
$180–195 AnAr ⊞

Bronze model of a rearing lion, on a
wooden plinth, 2nd–3rdC AD, 2½in (6.5cm) high.
£135–150 / €190–210
$220–240 B 🔨

► **Gilt-bronze model of an
eagle,** Lincolnshire, 13th–14thC,
2½in (6.5cm) high. This item was
possibly once attached to a
casket or shrine. It was found by
a metal detector. With all such
finds it is important to check that
the piece has been recorded at
the local museum – this gives the
museum the chance to buy the
item if it is of national importance.
£150–165 / €210–230
$250–270 B 🔨

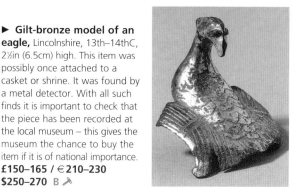

Horse-shaped brooch, some decorative enamel remaining, complete with pin, foreleg missing, Roman-Celtic, East Anglian, c2nd–3rdC AD, 1¼in (3cm) long. This type of stylized animal brooch was popular in ancient Roman Britain. Although it is damaged, it is an attractive item with lots of charm and would make a good and interesting buy.
£130–140 / €180–195
$200–230 A&O ⊞

◄ **Gnathian ware trefoil-lipped oinochoe,** with traces of painted vine decoration, worn, Greek, 4thC BC, 5in (12.5cm) high. This item would originally have been decorated in white, with the finer details of the grape bunches and vine tendrils in applied crimson and ochre. If all the decoration had been perfect this item could cost up to £400 / €560 / $650.
£180–200 / €250–280
$300–330 HEL ⊞

Glass juglet, Roman, 4thC AD, 3½in (9cm) high.
£200–220 / €280–310
$330–370 B ⚒

◄ **Two terracotta lamps,** decorated with actor's masks, one inscribed with maker's mark, Roman, 1st–2ndC AD, 3¼in (8.5cm) wide. Decorated Roman lamps are fun to collect – the decorated scenes are not only attractive but also historically interesting.
£180–200 / €250–280
$300–330 B ⚒

The Greek influence

Greek colonies were founded in southern Italy and Sicily in the 6th century BC. Pottery was originally imported from Greece, but by the mid-5th century BC a pottery industry had grown up separate from native manufacturers. The most important areas of production were Apulia, Lucania, Campania, Paestum and Sicily.

Bichrome ware chalice, with a swastika in the central panel on each side and bands of umber around the interior, on a low stemmed foot, with two lug handles, base chipped, Cypriot, Iron Age, 750–600 BC, 2¾in (7cm) high. Cypriot pottery has a contemporary feel that suits different environments from old-fashioned country cottages to modern minimalist designer flats. This is a fine example and is in good condition.
£270–300 / €380–420
$440–490 A&O ⊞

◄ **Black-glazed guttus,** with a lion's head spout, Campanian, Greek south Italian, 3rdC BC, 4¾in (12cm) wide. This oil lamp filler is an attractive piece with provenance from the early 19thC, which adds to its value.
£320–350
€450–490
$520–570 HEL ⊞

What were amulets used for?

Amulets were used as charms and would have been placed on the body to bring luck and success in the afterlife. Anubis is the god of embalming and mummification, a process practised by the ancient Egyptians, who believed that life was merely a preparation for the afterlife. Among the bandages of mummies large numbers of amulets were carefully placed where priests deemed they would offer the greatest magical protection.

◄ **Amulet of Anubis,** with a human body and head of a jackal, wearing a short kilt, on a base, the back pillar pierced for suspension, Egyptian, Late Period, post-500 BC, 2½in (6.5cm) high. This amulet retains a strong colour, indicating high-quality faïence.
£390–430 / €540–600
$640–700 A&O ⊞

Carved wood mummy mask, originally painted, Egyptian, 332–30 BC, 9½in (24cm) high. These masks can be very decorative and look good in a contemporary setting.
£450–500 / €630–700
$730–820 HEL ⊞

Painted pottery bowl, with two lug handles, Cypriot, Geometric Period, 1050–650 BC, 10in (25.5cm) diam.
£500–550 / €700–770
$820–900 HEL ⊞

Bronze figure, either of Papposilenos or an actor in the guise of Papposilenos, wearing a cloak and shoes, his head with a wreath of ivy berries, on a pedestal, Roman, c1stC AD, 2¾in (7cm) high.
£600–650 / €840–910
$980–1,050 S(NY) ⚒

◄ **Marble triple head from a Hectaeon,** Roman, 2ndC AD, 4in (10cm) high. The piece is from the Erlenmeyer Collection, which is well known in Antiquities circles. With this provenance it will retain its value and therefore be a good investment.
£630–700 / €880–980
$1,050–1,150 HEL ⊞

Pottery vase, with turquoise glaze, Parthian or Sasanian, c2nd–3rdC AD, 7in (18cm) high.
£660–730 / €920–1,000
$1,100–1,200 S(NY) ⚒

Architectural

Two-colour embossed tile, by Sherwin & Colton, c1885, 6in (15cm) square.
£9–10 / €12–14
$13–15 SAT ⊞

Aesthetic Movement tile, with floral decoration, c1890, 6in (15cm) square. Because this tile is not embossed it would make an attractive coaster.
£20–25 / €30–35
$30–40 C&W ⊞

▶ **Victorian tile,** with floral decoration, 6in (15cm) square. This tile is clearly part of a larger scheme and therefore more difficult to use. However, its attractive design offsets this disadvantage.
£10–15 / €14–20
$15–25 TASV ⊞

◀ **Floral embossed tile,** with central roundel, c1890, 6in (15cm) square.
£30–35 / €42–48
$50–60 C&W ⊞

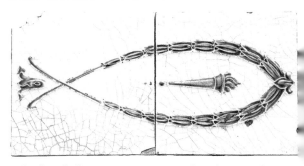

Pair of wall tiles, damaged, c1900, 6in (15cm) square. The damage can be repaired and the colour matched, although refiring and reglazing are not practical due to the expense. Using tiles should not affect the value, as long as the condition does not suffer.
£45–50 / €60–70
$75–80 C&R ⊞

Cast-iron door porter, modelled as a dog, 1870, 5in (12.5cm) high.
£50–55 / €70–75
$80–90 GBr ⊞

Cast-iron door porters

Cast-iron door porters were made in large quantities during the late 19th and early 20th centuries, and a wide range of designs produced. They were robustly constructed so many have survived to the present day, making them relatively inexpensive – only the rarest and most decorative examples command high prices. Some models, such as Mr Punch, have been reproduced, so it is advisable to purchase from a reputable dealer.

Pair of stove tiles, by Trent Tile Co, American, c1880, 3in (7.5cm) diam. The figures depicted are wrapped up against the cold, making these tiles perfect for a stove. The figures are also facing each other, indicating that the tiles are a genuine pair.
£75–85 / €105–120
$120–140 KMG ⊞

Miller's compares...

B. Coalbrookdale cast-iron door porter, modelled as a sentry in a portal, 1850–95, 17in (43cm) high.
£160–175 / €220–245
$260–285 RPh ⊞

A. Brass and cast-iron door porter, by Kenrick & Son, 1870, 15in (38cm) high.
£105–115 / €150–160
$170–190 GBr ⊞

Item B is of an unusual design and was made by one of the finest cast-iron founders. Item A is a more common shape and not so decorative.

Victorian terracotta roof finial, incomplete, 21in (53.5cm) high. This finial is missing the top part, which may have been a cross knop finial/pineapple, or something similar.
£75–85 / €105–120
$120–140 WRe ⊞

Cast-iron foot scraper, 1880, 9in (23cm) high. The unusual lyre design and good condition make this foot scraper a good buy.
£85–95 / €120–130
$140–155 SMI ⊞

► **Pair of Victorian cast-iron garden urns,** 20in (51cm) high. The urns retain their crusty old paint which is an advantage as it helps to prove the age of the piece in a market where there are increasing numbers of reproductions.
£110–120 / €155–165
$180–195 SWO 🖉

Cast-iron basket-shaped foot scraper, 1880, 13in (33cm) high. Additional features such as the lion-paw feet and basket handle make this a desirable piece.
£110–120 / €155–165
$180–195 SMI ⊞

Cast-iron door porter, modelled as Mr Punch, 1860, 14in (35.5cm) high. Mr Punch has been widely reproduced. Beware of examples which appear too fresh – rust pitting and layers of old paint are good indicators of an original piece.
£130–145 / €180–200
$210–230 GBr ⊞

▶ **Cast-iron door knocker,** by Kenrick & Sons, No. 173000, modelled as the head of Mercury, c1880, 11in (28cm) high.
£145–160 / €200–220
$240–260 OLA ⊞

▶ **Intaglio tile,** by Villeroy & Boch, German, c1880, 6in (15cm) square. Portrait tiles are quite rare and this is an attractive example in good condition.
£120–130
€165–180
$195–210 KMG ⊞

The look without the price

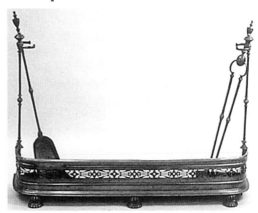

Georgian polished steel fender, with openwork decoration, fitted stands for tongs and a shovel, on paw feet, 33in (84cm) wide.
£140–155 / €195–220
$230–250 BR ⚒

A large amount of fireplace furniture was made to Georgian designs in the first half of the 20th century. If you require a genuine George I to George III set, expect to pay about ten times as much as this. 'Georgian' in this case probably applies to George V or George VI.

Painted cast-iron door porter,
modelled as an eagle, 1880, 13in (33cm)
high. The numerous layers of paint on this
decorative door porter provide useful clues
as to its age.
£150–165 / €210–230
$250–270 GBr ⊞

Wrought-iron door knocker, c1770,
7in (18cm) high. Door furniture such as
this knocker is still comparatively cheap,
and an attractive piece makes a good first
impression for visitors.
£170–185 / €240–260
$280–300 SEA ⊞

Find out more in

Miller's Antiques Price Guide,
Miller's Publications, 2004

◀ **Iron lark spit,**
by Harking, 18thC,
14in (35.5cm) long.
These spits were
used in Victorian
times for cooking
larks and other small
birds, which were
hung in pairs on the
hooks, then placed
over an open fire.
£150–165
€210–230
$250–270 KEY ⊞

▶ **Wall-mounted**
marble sundial,
inscribed 'Appleyard,
Leeds, 1893', 18in
(45.5cm) high. Wall
sundials are easier
to place than the
horizontal types which
require pedestals. The
date, and the fact that
it is made from marble,
make this piece
particularly desirable.
£160–175
€220–250
$260–290 G(L) ⌒

Late Victorian cast-iron
letter plate, by Kenrick
& Sons, No. 4, 10 x 5in
(25.5 x 12.5cm). Many antique
letter boxes are smaller in size
compared to modern ones.
£180–200 / €250–280
$300–330 OLA ⊞

▶ **York stone ball pillar top,**
19thC, 25in (63.5cm) high. Care
should be taken not to chip
weathered old stone, as it can
take years to mellow. The use of
a proprietary ageing substance
will accelerate the process.
£200–220 / €280–310
$330–370 WRe ⊞

Wrought-iron harnen, Irish, c1830, 16in (40.5cm) high. A harnen is an Irish toasting device that would have stood in an inglenook fireplace.
£220–250 / €310–350
$370–410 MFB ⊞

► **Coalbrookdale cast-iron eagle,** c1880, 10in (25.5cm) high. Antique cast-iron pieces usually have diamond registration marks and pattern numbers as well as the maker's name.
£220–250
€310–350
$370–410 OLA ⊞

Brass log/coal bin, embossed with windmills and figures, with lion mask ring handles, on claw feet, Dutch, 18thC, 11¾in (30cm) high.
£230–250 / €320–350
$380–410 SWO ⚒

Pair of Victorian cast-iron urns. Old cast-iron urns are often cheaper than modern alternatives and are more likely to maintain their value than modern reproductions.
£250–280 / €350–390
$410–460 B(Kn) ⚒

Edwardian terra-cotta roof finial, by Royal Doulton, modelled as a stylized owl, 19in (48.5cm) high. Stylish sculptural pieces such as this can be put to decorative use either inside the house or out of doors.
£240–260
€330–360
$390–430 EH ⚒

Cast-iron umbrella stand, No. 266, c1880, 25in (63.5cm) high. Before buying an umbrella stand, check that the tray matches the piece as many have been damaged and replaced over the years.
£250–280 / €350–390
$410–460 RPh ⊞

◄ **Pair of fog horn bellows,** by Alldays & Onion, restored, 1880s, 33in (84cm) long.
£250–280 / €350–390
$410–460 OLD ⊞

Miller's compares...

A. Wrought-iron and brass pot hook,
c1770, 44in (112cm) long.
£250–280 / €350–390
$410–460 SEA ⊞

B. Iron pot hook, with brass and copper
decoration, c1770, 34in (86.5cm) long.
£430–480 / €600–670
$700–780 SEA ⊞

The surface of Item A appears pitted, thus reducing the value. Item B is in better
condition and is smaller in size, making siting much easier and increasing its value.

Pair of brass roll-top bath taps, fully
reconditioned, 1890s, 6in (15cm) high.
£290–320 / €400–450
$470–520 WRe ⊞

Iron lock, Continental, mid-18thC, 9½in (24cm) wide. Locks were
very collectable during the 1920s, but have since gone out of
fashion and are reasonably priced as a result.
£300–330 / €420–460
$490–540 Penn ⊞

Brass and mirrored fire screen, with
applied brass decoration, 1880–1900,
30in (76cm) high.
£310–340 / €430–470
$510–560 RPh ⊞

Pair of brass bath taps, by Shanks & Co, fully reconditioned,
1895, 1¼in (3cm) thread. Antique taps are much more stylish than
modern ones. Make sure that the threads are a standard size. If
not, ask the dealer to recommend a plumber who will provide an
estimate and fit them for you.
£330–350 / €460–490
$540–570 WRe ⊞

Miller's compares...

A. Pair of carved oak panels, French, 17thC, 21in (53.5cm) high.
£360–400 / €500–560
$590–650 SEA ⊞

B. Pair of carved oak panels, French, 16thC, 22in (56cm) high.
£590–650 / €820–910
$960–1,050 SEA ⊞

Although similar in appearance, the panels in Item B are of a superior colour to those in Item A, and are also considerably older, therefore increasing their value.

Wrought-iron toasting fork, c1770, 17in (43cm) long.
£360–400 / €500–560
$590–650 SEA ⊞

Ceramic high-level cistern, chipped, c1900, 22in (56cm) wide.
£360–400 / €500–560
$590–650 C&R ⊞

Pair of cast-brass fireside implement rests, 1840–50, 10in (25.5cm) wide.
£400–440 / €560–610
$650–720 RGe ⊞

► **Brass ash basket,** with a tin liner, Dutch, 19thC, 22¾in (58cm) wide.
£420–460
€**590–640**
$690–750 S(O) ⚒

◄ **Steel lock,** with chased decoration, German, Nuremberg, 17thC, 13in (33cm) wide.
£430–480
€**600–670**
$700–780 KEY ⊞

Studded door, 18thC, 89in (226cm) high. This studded door would add character to a period property for a modest sum.
£400–440 / €**560–610**
$650–720 PAS ⊞

Painted pine and gesso fire surround and overmantel mirror, c1900, 59¾in (152cm) wide. Check the mouldings carefully as they can be difficult and expensive to restore. On pieces such as this stripping moulding is not as easy as stripping carved wood chimney pieces.
£440–480 / €**610–670**
$720–780 SWO ⚒

◄ **Caen stone finial,** the semi-fluted campana body carved in high relief with ribbon-tied flowers beneath a rising beaded top, French, c1900, 28in (71cm) high. Caen stone is a very fine limestone, so takes detail well and weathers beautifully. This decorative finial is not too large and could be used in a modest garden as a centrepiece. A pair of finials would cost more than twice this price.
£460–510 / €**640–710**
$750–830 S(S) ⚒

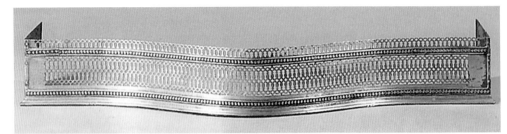

Steel fender, c1800, 45¾in (116cm) wide. Traditional English steel fenders and tools are currently more popular than their brass or French equivalents, possibly because they complement plain wood and stainless steel interiors better. Polished steel was designed for use with Georgian chimneypieces and brass became more popular later in the 19thC.
£470–520 / €650–720
$770–850 S(O) ✗

Fireclay bowl-on-stand, the acanthus-cast lobed bowl with everted egg-and-dart-moulded rim, on a baluster acanthus-cast column and base, probably Scottish, late 19thC, 38in (96.5cm) high. This rare, beautifully designed bowl-on-stand would make an impressive bird bath or planter. If you use it as a bird bath remember to empty it if frost is likely, to avoid further damage. The damage to this piece has kept the price down.
£480–530 / €670–740
$780–870 S(S) ✗

▶ **Three terracotta ball-and-spire finials,** 19thC, 28¾in (73cm) high. Architectural ornaments such as these were made in massive quantities, which is why they are still affordable.
£550–600 / €770–840
$900–980 SWO ✗

Victorian glazed copper bracket lantern, with a cut-out foliate crown over pierced quatrefoil banding, with glazed faceted sides, on scrolled supports and a shaped wall bracket, 44in (112cm) high. Had there been a pair of these lanterns, the price would have been more than double.
£500–550 / €700–770
$820–900 AH ✗

Wrought-iron trivet and long-handled frying pan, c1770, pan 51in (129.5cm) long.
£540–600 / €750–840
$880–980 SEA ⊞

Find out more in

Miller's Garden Antiques: How to Source & Identify, Miller's Publications, 2003

Pair of alabaster urns, with fluted and stiff-leaf banding, the everted rim with egg-and-dart moulding, 19thC, 37in (94cm) high.
£580–640 / €810–890
$950–1,050 AH 🎣

Cast iron

Antique cast-iron pieces usually have diamond registration marks and pattern numbers as well as a maker's name. Examine the piece closely and if no marks are present, it could indicate that it is foreign – cast iron was popular in the USA and Europe. Antique pieces are usually well finished and prominent scar marks or casting bubbles are unusual. Any rust should be hard and brown – the more orange it is, the more recent the item.

Looking after alabaster

Alabaster is very fragile and can easily be damaged by over-vigorous cleaning. If the piece is valuable, always consult a specialist restorer. If the item is already damaged and of little value, try cleaning with distilled water and cotton wool. Apply the water sparingly initially in an inconspicuous place. Alabaster should be dusted regularly with a soft duster, and protected from a smoky atmosphere as nicotine staining is almost impossible to remove.

Pair of Coalbrookdale cast-iron bench ends, in Osmundia Fern pattern, No. 273254, with diamond registration stamp, c1870. These bench ends were inexpensive despite being one of the rarest Coalbrookdale patterns. They originally had a metal back and seat rail, and to remake the bench would be costly – it would also remain a 'made up' piece thus reducing its value.
£600–660 / €840–920
$980–1,100 S(S) 🎣

Pair of Victorian stoneware jardinières-on-stands, by J. M. Blashfield, with flared rims, the bodies decorated with acanthus, the bases inscribed '17.2.60, No. 451, JM Blashfield, Stamford', 14¾in (37.5cm) high. Blashfield was one of the best makers of stoneware in the mid-19thC. This is an inexpensive price for a highly desirable pair of planters with original trays.
£600–660 / €840–920
$980–1,100 WW 🎣

Cast-iron bath, by Saracen, feet missing, enamel requires repair, 1900, 61in (155cm) long. Re-enamelling can be prohibitively expensive so check the condition before purchasing. Copper baths are more desirable than cast-iron ones, hence the low price.
£680–750 / €950–1,050
$1,100–1,200 C&R ⊞

▶ **Pair of stone-ware architectural finials,** each on a moulded base, late 19thC, 44in (112cm) high. These finials are in good condition and are likely to remain so. They are good value when compared to modern reproductions.
£900–990
€1,250–1,400
$1,500–1,600
S(S) 🎣

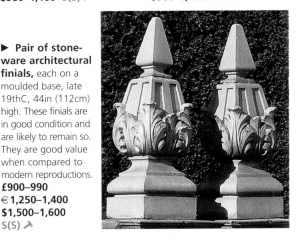

Arms & Armour

Welsh Division pouch, bullion-embroidered with the Royal coat-of-arms above a gilt-metal cannon, 19thC, 6¼in (16cm) wide.
£80–90 / €110–125
$130–150 G(L) ➹

▶ **Silver-mounted swordstick,** with a triple-edged blade, rootwood shaft and handle, inscribed 'Otto Munck', Swedish, 19thC, 37½in (95.5cm) wide. It should be noted that the swordstick is classed as an offensive weapon when carried in public.
£150–180 / €210–250
$250–300 G(L) ➹

Victorian officer's 1822 pattern sword, the blade by Timewell, with etched decoration including Royal cypher, the brass guard with 'VR' cypher, folding half-guard and rayskin grip, grip mostly missing, 30¼in (77cm) long. This unrestored sword would make an attractive wallhanger. The brass hilt is particularly attractive.
£50–60 / €70–85
$80–100 G(L) ➹

▶ **William IV light cavalry officer's 1821 pattern sword,** with steel hilt and shagreen- and wire-covered grip, the blade etched with Royal cypher and 'Prosser', with scabbard overall, 42in (106.5cm) long. The pipe back blade and scabbard make this sword desirable to the collector. These are commonly available, hence the modest cost.
£170–190 / €240–270
$280–310 G(L) ➹

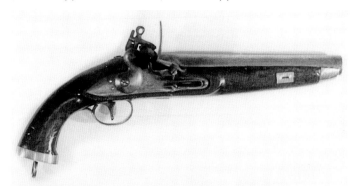

Flintlock holster pistol, with walnut full stock, brass-mounted fore end trigger guard and grip cap, steel lanyard ring, Belgian, 19thC, 15½in (39.5cm) long. This Belgian pistol is much cheaper than the British equivalent which would cost at least five times this amount.
£200–220 / €280–310
$330–370 AH ➹

Locate the source

The source of each illustration in Miller's can be found by checking the code letters below each caption with the Key to Illustrations, pages 286–290.

► **Pair of ceremonial halberds,** with iron blades and wooden shafts, French or German, early 19thC, 100in (254cm) long. These halberds would make a dramatic wall decoration and are excellent value at this price.
£220–240 / €310–330
$350–390 G(L) ⚖

Steel-hilted small sword, the guard, ferrule and pommel pierced and engraved, coliche-marde blade end damaged, mid-18thC, 27in (68.5cm) long. The original, unrestored state, the broken blade and poor condition keep this sword affordable.
£240–270 / €330–380
$390–440 G(L) ⚖

Rifled 70 bore cannon-barrelled flintlock sidelock pocket pistol, the striped walnut full stock with floral carving around breech tang, the barrel with octagonal breech and turn-off section, the plain flat lock with squared pan, plain steel mounts including long-spurred butt cap, French, c1780, 7¼in (18.5cm) long. This pistol is in poor condition but if it had been in good to excellent condition, one could expect to pay £600–800 / €840–1,100 / $980–1,300.
£250–280 / €350–390
$410–460 WAL ⚖

Percussion holster pistol, with walnut stock, chequered grip, side-by-side barrels, ramrod, brass mounts and trigger guard, with hinged brass butt cap container, 19thC, 15in (38cm) long.
£260–290 / €360–400
$430–470 AH ⚖

◄ **Silver-mounted small sword,** the coliche-marde blade etched with a trophy of arms and face within a sunburst, the silver shell guard and pommel pierced, mid- to late 18thC, 32¾in (83cm) long. The knucklebow has been replaced and is not in keeping with the rest of the hilt. A more sympathetic restoration would have added to the value of this sword.
£280–310
€390–430
$460–510 G(L) ⚖

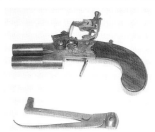

WEST STREET
Antiques

• ANTIQUE ARMS & ARMOUR † PERIOD FURNITURE •

A Fine O/U Tap Action Pocket Pistol
1½" turn off barrels, with post 1813 B'Ham proofs boxlock, action engraved within trophies of arms 'H. Nock' & 'London' (on obverse). Top slide safety which locks steel. Folding trigger, walnut slab sided butt, with its combined muzzle key and bullet mould.

c1815 Very good condition (much original finish) £995

An example of our stock of fine antique arms and armour catering for collectors of all levels of experience

63 West Street • Dorking • Surrey RH4 1BS
Tel: 01306 883487 • Fax: 01306 883487
Email: weststant@aol.com
Website: antiquearmsandarmour.com

Flintlock pocket pistol, with folding bayonet, c1820, 8in (20.5cm) long. The spring bayonet is a bonus on this piece and with good restoration it could be worth £400–600 / €560–840 / $650–980.
£300–330 / €420–460
$490–540 MDL ⊞

Naval cutlass, with adapted bone grip, the single-edged blade with a figure-of-eight guard, the spiral grip carved with discs, damaged, late 18thC, 25¼in (64cm) long. With a sailor's self-made scrimshaw grip this makes a superb conversation piece.
£300–330 / €420–460
$490–540 G(L) ⚒

Remington over-and-under Derringer, top rib of barrels stamped 'Remington Arms Co. I.L., N.Y.', c1860, 5in (12.5cm) long. These small pocket breech-loading pistols, single or multi-barrel, were very popular as self-defence weapons and are often depicted in American Western films as gamblers' guns.
£330–370 / €460–520
$540–610 MDL ⊞

▶ **Steel and brass armour backplate,** French, c1840, 17in (43cm) high. Backplates are less desirable than breastplates.
£350–380 / €490–530
$570–620 ARB ⊞

Hunting hangar, the saw-backed blade with maker's mark of three stars, the ivory handle carved as a lion's head and with figures on horseback above a silver collar and crossguard, damaged, German, late 18thC, 17¼in (44cm) long. The price of this sword has been kept down by the extensive damage. In good condition it might fetch twice as much.
£320–350 / €450–490
$520–570 G(L) ⚒

Breech loading pocket pistols

A vast field of small American pocket pistols commonly known as Derringers developed from Henry Deringer's original single-shot percussion pistol of c1840. His design was copied by many manufacturers who produced thousands of these popular self-defence weapons which continued into breech-loading self-contained cartridge weapons with various calibres and numbers of barrels. They were still being produced well into the 20th century and Colt and Remington are well-known makes. Value depends on the materials used on the grips, such as plating, ivory or mother-of-pearl, but an interesting or historical provenance can affect the price enormously. Derringers tend to be of more interest to American collectors, as Abraham Lincoln was assassinated by John Wilkes Booth in 1865 using a Derringer percussion pocket pistol.

Regency officer's sabre, the flat-backed and curved blade acid-etched and gilt with 'GR' cypher, trophies, foliage and traces of blueing, with gilt-metal hilt, wire-bound ivory handle, 30in (76cm) long. This was once a lovely sword, but the poor condition reduces its desirability considerably. In good condition it would have cost upwards of £1,200 / € 1,700 / $2,000. Restoration is not feasible as the process involves the use of toxic chemicals which are no longer in use.
£380–420 / € 530–590
$620–690 G(L) ➤

.577 1856 pattern rifled cavalry pistol, with Tower proofs, lock marked with crowned 'VR Tower 1857', regulation brass mounts, lanyard ring on butt cap, swivel ramrod, wear and restoration, rear sight leaf missing, 15½in (39.5cm) long. This is a rare and desirable pistol, keenly sought after by collectors of military weapons. The regimental markings make it particularly interesting – however the wear and over-cleaning have kept the price down. In good condition this pistol could sell for £1,200–1,500 / € 1,600–2,000 / $2,000–2,500.
£500–550 / € 700–770
$820–900 WAL ➤

Harper's Ferry model 1821 converted musket, with bayonet and sling, rusting, crack to stock, broken sling and front swivel, dated 1827, barrel 42in (106.5cm) long. Damage commensurate with field service is acceptable in military weapons. Harper's Ferry is particularly desirable for its connections with John Brown and the start of the American Civil War.
£570–630 / € 790–880
$930–1,050 JDJ ➤

Who was John Brown?

John Brown, immortalized in the song 'John Brown's body...' was a Baptist minister virulently opposed to slavery, whose preaching upset many of the Southern plantation owners who sought his arrest. Brown was finally apprehended at Harpers Ferry, West Virginia, in North America and tried and convicted of high treason by the State and executed – a martyr to the cause of abolition. Among the arresting officers was Robert E. Lee, the famous Confederate general.

Tower flintlock blunderbuss, c1800, iron barrel 15in (38cm) long. Blunderbusses can vary enormously in quality. Brass barrels are more desirable and those with spring bayonets can cost in excess of £3,000 / € 4,200 / $5,000.
£660–720 / € 920–1,000
$1,100–1,200 B(Kn) ➤

What is the Tower stamp?

'Tower' is stamped on the lockplates of British service firearms and refers to the Tower of London, the arsenal and accepting house for all British naval and military regular service weapons from the early 18th century. The component parts (locks, barrels, brass furniture etc) were delivered to the Tower from the various specialist outworkers, where they were examined and passed for service. Standards were strict and, although such pieces appear plain and rugged in construction, the quality was always high. The Tower stamp was accompanied by the cypher of the reigning monarch, together with the inspector's stamps on the component parts. Until 1764, 'Tower' was often substituted by the maker's name and date, eg 'Galton 1742', but such weapons had still been subjected to Tower inspection. In Ireland, 'Dublin Castle' is found, rather than 'Tower'.

Boxes

Miller's compares...

A. Porcupine quill and ebony box, c1900, 5in (12.5cm) wide.
£20–22 / €30–32
$30–35 AL ⊞

B. Wood and quill desk box, the interior of the cover with a bone inlaid ebony plaque, on brass ball feet, East Indian, late 19thC, 4½in (11.5cm) wide.
£65–70 / €90–95
$105–115 NOA ⚲

Carved ivory powder box, Japanese, c1880, 2½in (6.5cm) diam.
£70–80 / €95–110
$115–130 MB ⊞

Item A is a small example of a common box but with a sliding, rather than the more usual hinged cover. Item B, although still a common item, is of an earlier date and therefore commands a higher price.

◄ **Tortoiseshell trinket box,** with a domed cover, on bone ball feet, two feet missing, 19thC, 3½in (9cm) wide.
£80–90
€110–125
$130–150 TMA ⚲

Tunbridge ware rosewood box, the cover with floral inlay, 19thC, 6in (15cm) wide. This is an attractive box, but check the condition carefully when purchasing Tunbridge ware.
£85–95 / €120–130
$140–155 L&E ⚲

◄ **Victorian needle box,** with ivory-lined interior and a silver thimble, 5½in (14cm) high.
£90–100
€125–140
$150–165 G(L) ⚲

Endangered species

As with all objects that are the product of endangered species, the trade in modern items made of ivory and tortoiseshell is banned in many countries. Pieces over 100 years old may be imported and exported provided they have the correct paperwork. For example, in the UK pieces need a licence from the Department of the Environment and a certificate of authenticity from BADA (the British Antique Dealers Association). More details can be found on the CITES website (www.cites.org), which has full information regarding the individual requirements of most countries.

◄ **Tortoiseshell and ivory snuffbox,** c1780, 4in (10cm) wide.
£90–100
€125–140
$150–165 MB ⊞

Ivory powder box, the cover engraved with a panther, Japanese, 1880, 2½in (6.5cm) diam.
£90–100 / €125–140
$150–165 MB ⊞

► **Regency pen-work casket,** the sloping cover decorated with foliage, 9in (23cm) high. This box is very good value – it would be in keeping with today's fashionable 'shabby chic' interiors. However, the poor condition has brought the price down.
£95–105
€130–150
$155–170 G(L) ⋌

Birch bark and quill box, Native American, c1900, 5½in (14cm) wide.
£120–130 / €165–180
$195–210 DuM ⋌

◄ **Compressed horn table snuff box,** French, 19thC, 3½in (9cm) diam.
£110–120
€155–165
$180–195
MB ⊞

Painted pine trinket box, inscribed, Scandinavian, late 19thC, 8¼in (21cm) wide.
£120–130 / €165–180
$195–210 SWO ⋌

Alan & Kathy Stacey
Tea Caddies & Fine Boxes

The Finest Antique Boxes from the UK's Leading Specialists

Quality Tortoiseshell, Ivory,
Mother of Pearl, Shagreen, Horn, Exotic Timber,
18th & 19th Century Tea Caddies, Boxes, Objects

UK Tel 44 (0) 1963 441333   USA Tel 905 529 3613
44 (0) 7810 058078
LAPADA MEMBER   www.antiqueboxes.uk.com   LAPADA MEMBER

Burr-walnut and inlaid tea caddy, with
two compartments, c1860, 7½in (19cm) wide.
£130–145 / € 180–200
$210–235 TMA ↗

Condition of boxes

When selecting boxes for purchase carefully examine
all hinges, handles, locks and feet for signs of damage
or poorly-executed restoration. Check the cover to
make sure that it closes tightly. A gap between the
body and the cover is known as a 'smile' and can be
costly to repair, although this is not always possible.

Burr-walnut stationery box, decorated
with studded cut brass mounts, with a
hinged cover, 19thC, 7½in (19cm) wide.
£130–145 / € 180–200
$210–235 TMA ↗

Palais Royale gilt-metal and enamel box, embossed with
bands of *guilloche*, the matted cover with a Limoges enamel
medallion of a woman's head, c1880, 4¾in (12cm) wide.
£140–155 / € 195–215
$230–250 G(L) ↗

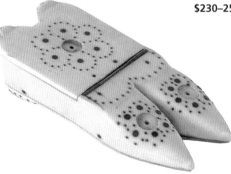

Ivory snuff box, carved as a pair of shoes, early
19thC, 3in (7.5cm) wide.
£140–155 / € 195–215
$230–250 G(L) ↗

Locate the source

The source of each illustration in Miller's
can be found by checking the code letters
below each caption with the Key to
Illustrations, pages 286–290.

Lacquered box, the cover hand-painted with figures
in a cart pulled by three horses, Russian, printed mark
to interior, late 19thC, 2¾in (7cm) diam.
£150–165 / € 210–230
$250–270 SWO ↗

Satinwood tea caddy, with double crossbanding and stringing, the cover with a brass ring handle and backplate, the divided interior with a pair of satinwood lidded boxes on one side, the other with a bowl aperture, key plate inlay, bowl and one inner lid missing, late 18thC, 12¼in (31cm) wide. This is a good caddy with original patination and colour, but the damage and missing items have reduced the value.
£160–175 / €220–250
$260–290 PF ⚒

Regency leather needlework casket, the hinged cover lined with a printed silk panel, with fitted interior, brass motif and escutcheon, on cast-brass lion's paw feet, 6¼in (16cm) wide. This attractive box could enhance a lady's writing desk or dressing table.
£150–165 / €210–230
$250–270 TMA ⚒

◀ **Porcelain box,** possibly Meissen, with engine-turned gilt-metal mounts, indistinct mark in underglaze blue, German, 19thC, 3in (7.5cm) wide.
£160–175
€220–250
$260–290 G(L) ⚒

George III mahogany tea caddy, with two internal lidded compartments flanking a mixing bowl, 12½in (32cm) wide. This is a common shape for a tea caddy but it is nevertheless a good buy.
£160–175 / €220–250
$260–290 SWO ⚒

George III mahogany caddy, with fruitwood stringing, on bracket feet, interior items missing, 10in (25.5cm) wide. This is an original box with good timber markings, colour and patination.
£200–220 / €280–310
$330–370 G(L) ⚒

Japanese export lacquered writing box, with parcel-gilt and polychromed Oriental fan decoration, the interior cover with paper compartments and a velvet writing surface, 1850–75, 18½in (47cm) wide.
£230–250 / €320–350
$380–410 NOA ⚒

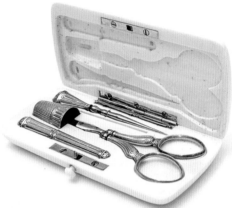

Simulated rosewood musical box, playing six airs, 19thC, 16½in (42cm) wide. These boxes were grained to simulate rosewood. This box is in a poor state of repair and requires major restoration.
£240–260 / €330–360
$390–430 SWO

Ivory-cased *étui*, with steel and gilt-silver-mounted sewing utensils, late 19thC, 4¼in (11cm) wide. This is a good example with all its original fittings, although the gilt is a little worn.
£240–260 / €330–360
$390–430 G(L)

◀ **Lacquered box and cover,** carved with fruit and foliage, restored, Chinese, Qing Dynasty, 1644–1916, 2¼in (5.5cm) diam.
£340–370 / €470–520
$560–610 G(L)

The look without the price

Regency chinoiserie work box, with hinged cover, decorated with landscapes, lined interior and lion-mask ring handles, on claw-and-ball feet, 8¾in (22cm) wide.
£500–550 / €700–770
$820–900 WW

This attractive work box is a good purchase. It is a little tired but restoration is difficult and expensive as the surface is fragile. Without scratches it could have made £700–800 / €980–1,100 / $1,150–1,300 at auction.

Lacquer

Derived from trees, lacquer is applied in numerous layers to wood or paper to render it waterproof and durable. Black and scarlet are the most common colours, and blue and green are much rarer. The process involves layering gum onto the surface, followed by colour. With time it suffers abrasion from use and fades from exposure to sunlight. It is advisable to seek professional assistance before attempting to repair damaged lacquer.

Miller's compares...

A. Tortoiseshell box,
with a hinged cover, 19thC,
4¼in (11cm) wide.
£540–600 / €750–840
$880–980 WW ⚚

**B. William IV tortoiseshell
tea caddy,** the cover inset with
a white-metal tablet, the interior
with two lidded compartments,
on bun feet, 7in (18cm) wide.
£900–1,000 / €1,250–1,400
$1,450–1,650 B ⚚

Although Items A and B are from a similar date and both
have sustained damage, Item B, with its more elaborate
design, ornamental appearance and larger size would be a
more desirable purchase than Item A. Both boxes would
need restoration by a very competent specialist.

**Regency penwork and
parquetry box-on-stand,**
the hinged cover with a
classical print of Hope,
on later tapering legs,
16in (40.5cm) high.
£600–660 / €840–920
$980–1,100 WW ⚚

▶ **Painted sewing box,** with crowned cypher
of 'J.B.', early 19thC, 10in (25.5cm) wide. The
cover of this example is warped and the front
panel appears to be split. Mauchline ware items
such as this are best bought in excellent
condition, even if they cost more to purchase.
£820–900 / €1,150–1,250
$1,350–1,450 S(O) ⚚

Elm candle box, with a
sliding cover and interior shelf,
early 18thC, 14in (35.5cm) high.
This piece has a good dark
patina which is very popular
with collectors.
£750–820 / €1,050–1,150
$1,100–1,350 S(O) ⚚

The look
without
the price

This is a good price
for a fruitwood caddy.
However, there is
discolouration to the
front of the cover
and the ivory finial
is a replacement – it
should be a carved fruit-
wood stalk. In better
condition this could be
worth £1,200–1,500 /
€1,650–2,100 /
$1,950–2,500.

Fruitwood tea caddy, the hinged
cover with a bone-knopped finial, with a
pierced metal escutcheon, Continental,
early 19thC, 7in (18cm) high.
£900–1,000 / €1,250–1,400
$1,500–1,600 B ⚚

Dolls, Teddy Bears & Toys

The look without the price

Wooden jigsaw puzzle, c1900, 9 x 11in (23 x 28cm).
£23–25 / €30–35
$32–40 J&J ⊞

This puzzle is old and has been well used, resulting in the box looking rather worn, but the farmyard scene is very appealing to collectors. If it had been in perfect condition it would be worth twice as much.

Doll's bed, the shaped scrolled metal headboard, tailboard and siderails with upholstered pads and draped lace decoration, c1890, 14in (35.5cm) long.
£28–34 / €42–48
$50–60 FHF ⚘

▶ **Curly Skittles game,**
c1900, 10 x 20in (20.5 x 51cm).
£55–60 / €75–85
$90–100 J&J ⊞

◀ **Tinplate miniature treadle sewing machine,** early 20thC, 4in (10cm) high, and a mangle.
£80–90
€110–125
$130–150 FHF ⚘

Leather doll, with painted hair and stitched, moulded face with painted features, the body with 12 holes, original lace missing, dated 1903, 12in (20.5cm) high.
£40–45 / €55–60
$65–75 FHF ⚘

Tin toys

Germany was the largest manufacturer and exporter of tinplate toys in the 19th century, producing vehicles, character toys, animal figures and novelty toys. Tin was used for making containers from the early 19th century, and many early examples were embossed. Children's themes are popular with collectors of both tins and tinplate toys. As always, condition is a major factor in assessing values, and many 'played with' examples are worth less due to damage.

Orthographical Recreations letters game, in a mahogany case, c1840, 6 x 10in (15 x 25.5cm).
£110–120 / € 155–165
$180–195 MB ⊞

Two Chad Valley toy dwarves, with moulded and painted faces, c1930, 10in (25.5cm) high.
£110–120 / € 155–165
$180–195 FHF 🔨

Miller's compares...

A. Teddy bear, with golden hair, pin eyes, stitched nose, swivel head and metal shoulder and hip joints, c1915, 5¾in (14.5cm) high.
£110–120 / € 155–165
$180–195 B(Ch) 🔨

B. Schuco mohair miniature two-face novelty bear, one side of face with black metal eyes and stitched nose, the other with metal eyes, nose and mouth and a long tongue, with swivel head and jointed shoulders and hips, German, c1930, 3½in (9cm) high.
£380–420 / € 530–590
$620–690 B(Ch) 🔨

Item A is rather plain and worn, whereas Item B is in better condition and, being a rarer item by a known maker, commands a much higher price.

Schuco

Best-known for their wind-up toys, this German company began in Nuremberg in 1912. The Yes/No bear appeared in the mid-1920s and was a huge success, not only with children but also with adults. This prompted the company to take the adult market seriously and they started producing bears that doubled as perfume bottles, compacts and purses.

Doll's pine rocking crib, the shaped head with arched canopy, both ends with pierced heart motif and finials, early 19thC, 22½in (57cm) long.
£130–145 / € 180–200
$210–240 PFK 🔨

▶ **Child's wooden fold-up pushchair,** with metal wheels and rubber tyres, late 19thC, 34½in (87.5cm) high.
£130–145 / € 180–200
$210–240 CHAC ⊞

Miller's compares...

A. Britains set of 2nd Dragoon Guards Queen's Bays, No. 44, first version, in original box, losses, paint retouched, 1897.
£130–145 / €180–200
$210–240 B(Ch) ✒

B. Britains set of Middlesex Regiment, No. 76, dated 1905, with officer dated 1909.
£360–400 / €500–560
$490–650 B(Ch) ✒

Item A is a rare first version but, due to the poor condition of both the figures and the box, the price remains low. Item B, on the other hand, is a complete set of figures and in good condition, which is reflected by the higher price.

Wooden dolls' house, painted with tiled roof, front door with moulded portico and glazed double doors, five glazed windows with stained glass, the hinged back opens to two simple rooms, c1880, 20in (51cm) wide.
£200–220 / €280–310
$330–370 B(Ch) ✒

Cast-iron pillar box money bank, dated 1892, 7in (18cm) high. This is quite a rare item.
£140–155 / €195–210
$230–250 MFB ⊞

Cast-iron money bank, 19thC, 5in (12.5cm) high. This design of money bank is fairly common in America so prices would be higher in the UK.
£200–220 / €280–310
$330–370 MFB ⊞

◄ **Travel chess set,** the veneered board backed with baize cloth, with Staunton pattern chess set, boxed, c1900, board 9¾in (25cm) square.
£230–250
€320–350
$330–370 ChC ⊞

Automaton dog, fur-covered, walks, opens mouth and yaps, moves tail, French, early 20thC, 10½in (26.5cm) high.
£240–260 / €330–360
$390–430 FHF ✒

Steiff teddy bear, with boot button eyes and stitched body, wearing hunting coat and corduroy breeches, damaged and repaired, early 20thC, 15in (38cm) high.
£260–290 / €360–400
$430–470 TMA

Steiff

Steiff began producing bears in 1880, and by 1899 were making dancing bears, polar bears and bears on rockers. The bears were originally made from plush mohair, but during the 1930s Steiff experimented with cheaper materials such as cotton, velvet and wool. The wool bears were not very well received at the time but they are now a rare commodity and, in good condition, more desirable than mohair.

Blonde mohair teddy bear,
with painted glass eyes, stitched nose, fully jointed body and cotton cloth pads, wear and repair, 1920s, 15in (38cm) high.
£260–290 / €360–400
$430–470 VEC

Mohair teddy bear, possibly Bing, with boot button eyes and jointed limbs, plush worn, c1910, 8in (20.5cm) high.
£360–400 / €500–560
$590–650 G(L)

Condition & fakes

- Condition is very important, particularly in commoner examples. Missing ears or fur cannot be restored, but new paw pads are acceptable.
- Unusual colours add to value.
- Beware of fakes – these are often suspiciously pristine. Check for thickly stitched and uneven seams, unworn noses and old labels on replaced paws. With Steiff bears, look out for fake buttons in the ear, or genuine buttons taken from less expensive Steiff dolls or worn-out bears.

Britains set of Middlesex Yeomanry, No. 83, the officer with throat plume and movable arm, one carbine butt missing, 1907.
£480–530 / €670–740
$780–870 B(Ch)

Mahogany-cased games compendium,
the fitted interior includes Solitaire board, Cribbage board, lead horses and marbles, case marked J. C. Drane, late 19thC.
£470–520 / €650–720
$770–850 FHF

▶ **Child's painted wooden wheelbarrow,** with iron mounts, c1890, 15in (38cm) high.
£490–540
€680–750
$800–880 S(O)

Kitchenware

Sycamore butter curler, c1900, 5½in (14cm) long. Treen is very collectable and this item is in particularly good condition.
£18–20 / € 25–28
$30–32 AL ⊞

◀ **Wooden butter stamp,** with a carved design, c1890, 1¼in (3cm) diam.
£20–22 / € 28–30
$32–36 WeA ⊞

Wooden bread board, with wheat and English lag carved design, c1920, 11½in (29cm) diam.
£18–20 / € 25–28
$30–32 CHAC ⊞

Butter dishes

Butter dishes, like bread boards, are becoming collectable as they are both decorative and useful. Some have sayings such as 'Manners Maketh Man' or simply 'Butter'. The liners may be glass or ceramic. Prices of butter dishes range from £10–100 / € 14–140 / $15–165.

◀ **Ceramic butter dish,** with wooden surround, dish not original, c1920, 6½in (16.5cm) diam.
£27–30 / € 38–42
$45–50 AL ⊞

Cornishware

Cornishware comes in three colours: blue, red and yellow, blue being the most common and red the rarest and most sought-after. The yellow range has a limited amount of jars and shakers. The more run-of-the-mill blue and white named jars are worth £30–50 / € 42–70 / $50–80. Those with unusual names such as Coconut or Starch can range from £100–400 / € 140–560 / $165–650. Beware as there are many reproductions around.

Cornishware tea caddy, with cover, 1930s, 6in (15cm) high. Plain Cornishware jars are ideal for labelling kitchen ingredients of your choice.
£35–40 / € 50–55
$60–65 AL ⊞

◄ **Mahogany knife tray,** c1860, 12in (30.5cm) wide. This tray has a cracked base and is therefore priced accordingly.
£35–40 / €50–55
$60–65 AL ⊞

Pine knife tray, c1900, 13in (33cm) long. Knife trays are used in the modern home for purposes other than holding cutlery, such as the storage of needlework and even make-up items. This is a good example, and to buy one in good condition with no woodworm is a sound investment.
£40–45 / €55–60
$65–75 AL ⊞

Cake mould, with painted decoration, French, Savoie, 1890, 9½in (24cm) diam.
£40–45 / €55–60
$65–75 MLL ⊞

Miller's compares...

A. Wooden butter stamp, c1900, 3¾in (9.5cm) diam.
£40–45 / €55–60
$65–75 CHAC ⊞

B. Sycamore butter stamp, with a swan decoration, c1880, 4in (10cm) high.
£130–145 / €180–200
$210–235 MFB ⊞

Butter stamps are very collectable and the more detailed the print, the more sought-after the item. Animal and bird stamps are relatively rare, so, although Item A is a good example, Item B with its swan print is of higher value.

Wooden butter stamp,
late 19thC, 1¾in (4.5cm) diam.
Butter stamps are an ideal
subject for collectors with
little space in which to
display their items.
£50–55 / €70–75
$80–90 WeA ⊞

Grimwade quick cooker, lid damaged,
c1890, 7½in (19cm) diam. The damaged
lid has lowered the price of this item.
Grimwade is very popular and this model
of bowl comes in various sizes.
£55–60 / €75–85
$90–100 CHAC ⊞

**George III painted tin spice
box,** with five wedge-shaped
compartments and a central
grater, traces of gilt, 6in (15cm)
diam. Ginger, cinnamon, cloves,
pepper, bay leaves and allspice
are some of the spices that may
have been contained in such an
item. It is unusual to find a
complete example, as the grater
is often missing.
£60–65 / €85–90
$100–105 SWO ⚒

The look without the price

Sycamore butter scoop, Welsh, c1860, 8½in (21.5cm) long.
£60–65 / €85–90
$100–105 MFB ⊞

Butter scoops were usually made in sycamore. Elm or
mahogany scoops are rarer and would double the value.

Huntley & Palmer biscuit tin,
in the form of a row of books,
c1900, 6¼in (16cm) wide. Tins
are very sought after. Although
this item is not in good condition,
it is still very desirable.
£70–80 / €95–110
$115–130 L&E ⚒

◀ **Copper aspic moulds,**
1880, fish 4½in (11.5cm) long.
£70–80 / €95–110
$115–130 each SMI ⊞

Locate the source

The source of each illustration in
Miller's can be found by checking
the code letters below each
caption with the Key to
Illustrations, pages 286–290.

Iron stand, Irish, 19thC, 14in (35.5cm) long. This is a very ornate,
rustic example. Cleaning, if required, should be undertaken very
carefully so as not to lose the original appearance.
£70–80 / €95–110
$115–130 STA ⊞

◀ **Set of iron weights,** by Kenrick & Sons, 1880, largest 5¼in (13.5cm) diam.
£85–95 / €120–130
$140–155 SMI ⊞

Tin spice rack, with original paint, c1880, 9in (23cm) high. This item would be both decorative and useful in the kitchen.
£85–95 / €120–130
$140–155 SMI ⊞

▶ **Wooden lemon squeezer,** c1870, 5½in (14cm) long. Lemon squeezers of this type have become popular again. This one has become a better colour with age.
£90–100 / €125–140
$150–165 WeA ⊞

Wood and metal grain measure, c1880, 4in (10cm) high. This measure would have been used by corn merchants when selling grain. The example here is a good, banded measure with a Victorian stamp.
£90–100 / €125–140
$150–165 WeA ⊞

Skip & Janie Smithson Antiques

Specialist dealers in Kitchen, Laundry, Dairy and related Advertising items

**Stock always available at
Hemswell Antiques Centre, Lincs
Fairs: NEC, Newark & Alexandra Place
Telephone/Fax: 01754 810265 Mobile: 07831 399180**

CONTACT BY APPOINTMENT   SINGLE ITEMS OR COLLECTIONS BOUGHT

Copper mould, c1880, 6in (15cm) diam. Copper moulds are very sought-after in the UK and the US and a collection of them makes an attractive display.
£120–135 / €165–190
$195–220 WAC ⊞

Brass and steel food chopper, mid-19thC, 6in (15cm) wide. Food choppers can be found with brass or wooden handles.
£125–140 / €175–195
$200–230 WeA ⊞

Wrought-iron game hanger, 18thC, 10in (25.5cm) high.
£130–145 / €180–200
$210–240 TOP ⊞

Steel and brass cream can, inscribed 'Run for the Cream, Tom', Scottish, late 19thC, 6in (15cm) high.
£135–150 / €190–210
$220–250 WeA ⊞

◀ **Beechwood spice erasure,** 19thC, 6in (15cm) high. Although this item appears to have woodworm, this has not affected the price greatly. It is an unusual piece for the treen collector.
£160–175 / €220–250
$260–290 SEA ⊞

Sheet-iron coffee grinder, 19thC, 12in (30.5cm) high.
£160–175 / €220–250
$260–290 SEA ⊞

Double-sided sycamore biscuit/pastry mould, c1860, 7in (18cm) wide. This is an unusual design for a mould, with writing on the reverse. It would be popular with the American market.
£160–175 / €220–250
$260–290 MFB ⊞

Copper and tin wheatsheaf jelly mould, c1880, 6in (15cm) long.
£160–175 / €220–250
$260–290 WeA ⊞

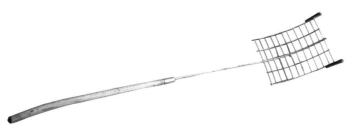

Metal curd cutter, with a wooden handle, late 19thC, 59in (150cm) long.
£180–200 / €250–280
$300–330 WeA ⊞

Brass ladle, with copper rivets, 1820, 14in (35.5cm) long.
£200–220 / €280–310
$330–370 SEA ⊞

Pewter ice-cream mould, registered date mark for 1868, 6in (15cm) high. The more decorative these items are, the more collectable they become.
£200–220 / €280–310
$330–370 MFB ⊞

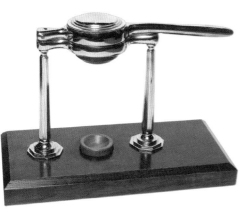

◄ **Brass lemon squeezer,** on a wooden base, 1880, 13in (33cm) wide.
£200–220
€280–310
$330–370 SMI ⊞

Danish Dairy Co butter crock, late 19thC, 5in (12.5cm) high. Butter crocks come in many sizes with many different transfers, and are very sought after.
£220–250 / €310–350
$370–410 WeA ⊞

◄ **Cast-iron grinder/mincer,** by Kenrick & Sons, modelled as the York Minster font, registered date 1895, 7in (18cm) high. Kenrick & Sons was one of the leading manufacturers of domestic appliances. This is an unusual design.
£430–480
€600–670
$700–780 MFB ⊞

Copper kettle, with an ornate brass handle, 18thC, 12in (30.5cm) high.
£310–350 / €430–490
$510–570 SEA ⊞

Lighting

Sitzendorf oil lamp, painted mark, German, 19thC, 9in (23cm) high. This is a very good price – lamps such as these are usually worth £200 / €280 / $330.
£80–90 / €110–125
$130–150 G(L) ⚘

Paris porcelain oil lamp base, with ormolu mounts, 19thC, 13in (33cm) high. This is a very good price – bases such as these are usually worth over £200 / €280 / $330.
£95–105 / €130–150
$155–170 SWO ⚘

Rewiring lights

Adapting antique lighting for electricity will generally have a detrimental effect on its value, particularly if the conversion is unsympathetic. The only exception is early to mid-20th-century lighting, whose value is unaffected by rewiring. Whether your requirements are for ceiling, wall, table or floor lights, there are plenty to be found from this period. Always consult an expert who will be able to advise on possible loss of value and the competence of a conversion. Safety is an important consideration – wiring should be checked annually and replaced when necessary.

▶ **Brass oil lamp,** with faceted glass reservoir, on a Corinthian column with step-moulded base, late 19thC, 24¾in (63cm) high.
£160–175 / €220–250
$260–290 DN ⚘

The look without the price

Victorian brass and opalescent glass oil lamp, reproduction shade, brass rubbed, 30in (76cm) high.
£190–210
€270–290
$310–350 SWO ⚘

This is a highly desirable lamp that has been made more affordable by the fact that it has a reproduction shade. In good condition and with an original shade it could be worth at least £350 / €490 / $570.

Pair of wire lanterns, Chinese, 19thC, 31in (78.5cm) high.
£175–195 / €280–310
$330–370 QM ⊞

◀ **Gauze lantern,** late 19thC, 11in (28cm) high.
£225–250 / €310–350
$370–410 WeA ⊞

Carmel glass table lamp,
American, c1900, 25in (63.5cm)
high. This type of American
table lamp is very desirable as it
has become less common and
reproduction companies have
had limited success in copying it.
**£280–320 / €390–450
$460–520 DuM** ↗

**Royal Worcester porcelain
table lamp,** with strapwork
banding in low relief within
beaded and gadrooned borders,
on a pierced gilt-metal base with
bracket feet, late 19thC, 21¾in
(55.5cm) high. This highly desirable
and rare lamp from a good
British porcelain factory would
appeal to collectors of both Royal
Worcester and oil lamps.
**£300–330 / €420–460
$490–540 AH** ↗

Stained glass lantern, with brass frame,
converted for electricity, c1890,
23½in (60cm) high.
**£320–350 / €450–490
$520–570 EAL** ⊞

Sheet-iron lantern, with
pierced heart-shaped decoration,
19thC, 5in (12.5cm) high.
**£340–380 / €470–530
$560–620 SEA** ⊞

Leaded glass hall lantern,
with oxidized finish, 1890–1900,
12in (30.5cm) high.
**£360–400 / €500–560
$590–650 JeH** ⊞

◀ **Arts and Crafts Vaseline
glass lantern,** with oxidized
finish, 10in (25.5cm) high.
**£380–430 / €500–600
$620–700 JeH** ⊞

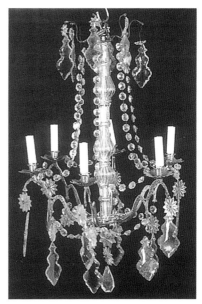

**Louis XV-style gilt-metal and cut-glass
five-branch chandelier,** converted for
electricity, 19thC, 33in (84cm) high. When
buying cut-glass chandeliers bear in mind
that exact matches for missing or damaged
drops are difficult to find, and having pieces
made to match can be expensive. Check
carefully for damage before purchase.
**£380–400 / €530–560
$620–650 B(Kn)** ↗

Brass and cut-glass hall lantern, probably Osler, wired for electricity, c1900, 19in (48.5cm) high.
£410–450 / €570–630
$670–730 B(Kn)

◄ **Ebonized parcel-gilt torchère,** in 17thC Italian style, 19thC, 58¼in (148cm) high.
£420–460
€590–640
$690–750 S(O)

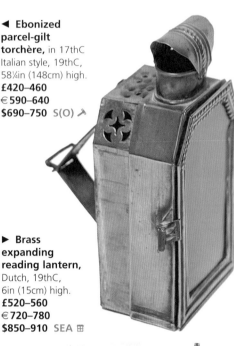

► **Brass expanding reading lantern,** Dutch, 19thC, 6in (15cm) high.
£520–560
€720–780
$850–910 SEA

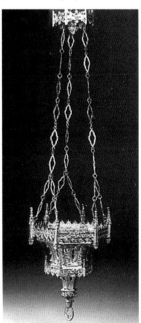

Gothic hanging lantern, the two-tier body with crocketed finials, late 19thC, 47¼in (120cm) high.
£530–580 / €740–810
$870–950 B(Kn)

Red-lacquered floor lamp, the turned standard with gilt and ebonized highlights, the moulded base with a chinoiserie landscape, on bun feet, c1900, 62½in (159cm) high.
£550–600
€770–840
$900–980 NOA

Pair of Louis XVI-style gilt-brass and cut-glass four-light candelabra, with jewel-cut-glass chains, cut spike finials, wired for electricity, 23in (58.5cm) high. Candelabra with candle cups are a better buy than ones with electric fittings only – they are worth more and offer the choice of candles or electricity.
£570–680 / €790–950
$930–1,100 NOA

Black-lacquered floor lamp, with all-over Oriental-style gilt highlights, c1900, 57in (145cm) high.
£580–640
€810–890
$950–1,050 NOA

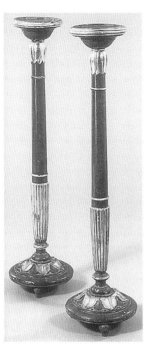

◄ **Pair of carved, lapis-painted and parcel-gilt wooden candelabrum stands,** minor losses to decoration, 1825–50, 45in (114.5cm) high. Standard lamps such as these are often subject to fashion and can rise disproportionately in price should they be featured on television or in a magazine article. At the moment they are not highly sought-after.
£580–640 / €810–890
$950–1,050 NOA ⚒

Silver-plated and cut-glass six-branch chandelier, c1890, 23in (58.5cm) wide.
£630–700 / €880–980
$1,050–1,150 EAL ⊞

Art Deco table lamp, the domed lid with a faceted final, the bronzed-metal casing fitted with satin glass panels moulded in relief with birds on flowering branches, pierced lug handles, on a pierced and moulded foot, 20½in (52cm) high.
£620–680 / €860–950
$1,000–1,100 AH ⚒

Pair of Arts and Crafts brass candelabra, American, 26in (66cm) high.
£720–800 / €1,000–1,100
$1,200–1,300 ASP ⊞

► **Wrought-metal 18thC-style three-light hall lantern,** with black-painted decoration, late 19thC, 33½in (85cm) high.
£760–840 / €1,050–1,150
$1,250–1,350 B(Kn) ⚒

◄ **Brass and *tôle-peinte* Restauration-style three-light *bouillotte* lamp,** with adjustable shade, candle arms retained, wired for electricity, c1900, 28in (71cm) high. Late 20thC copies of these lamps are available at a fraction of the price of the originals. This particular example is a copy of an early 19thC lamp, which would not have been wired for electricity.
£730–800 / €1,000–1,100
$1,200–1,300 NOA ⚒

► **Pair of Paris porcelain two-handled garniture vases,** with Italianate landscape reserves, richly gilt, drilled and mounted on giltwood pedestal bases, French, 1800–25, 24½in (62cm) high. The value of these vases has been adversely affected by drilling the bases, which can also result in damage.
£880–970
€1,250–1,350
$1,450–1,600
NOA ⚒

Metalware

Miller's compares...

A. Gilt-brass Empire-style stationery box, the cover applied with a copper relief of three classical horsemen, the sides etched with lotus leaves, c1870, 8in (20.5cm) wide.
£65–70 / €90–95
$105–115 G(L) ✗

B. Gilt-bronze casket, decorated in relief with panels of 18thC scenes, on four beaded feet, the base marked 'AB Paris', 19thC, 6in (15cm) wide.
£280–310 / €390–430
$460–510 TMA ✗

Item B is made of a much more valuable material than Item A. Also, Item B has more detailed decoration and a locking mechanism, all of which account for its higher value.

Brass bowl, damaged, 18thC, 12in (30.5cm) diam.
£80–90 / €110–125
$130–150 S(O) ✗

◀ **Brass table lighter,** in the form of Mr Punch, 19thC, 8in (20.5cm) high.
£140–155 / €195–215
$230–250 G(L) ✗

▶ **Victorian gilt-metal posy holder,** with a mother-of-pearl handle, 6in (15cm) high.
£160–175 / €220–250
$260–290 EH ✗

Pair of gilt-spelter urns and covers, on alabaster columns, beneath glass domes, 19thC, 11¾in (30cm) high. The glass dome covers on these urns have not only protected the gilt and alabaster but also added to the visual appeal of this pair.
£170–195 / €230–260
$280–320 SWO ⚲

Pair of brass candlesticks, each base inscribed 'The Friendly Brothers of St Johns Society Founded 1848', 19thC, 13in (33cm) high. The inscription has added to the value of these candlesticks, which are of a common shape.
£190–210 / €270–290
$310–350 SWO ⚲

Pair of bronze vases, with entwined branch handles, 19thC, 5¼in (13.5cm) high. The lack of rich patina on these bronze vases accounts for the very affordable price.
£200–220 / €280–310
$330–370 WW ⚲

Victorian ormolu ink stand, in the form of a recumbent dog, the hinged head forming the well cover, 6in (15cm) wide.
£210–230 / €290–320
$350–380 TMA ⚲

Brass jardinière, embossed with an armorial shield, with grotesque mask ring handles, Dutch, late 19thC, 33½in (85cm) high.
£220–240 / €310–330
$370–390 S(O) ⚲

Pair of bronze candlesticks, the socles cast with classical figurative bands, the tapering columns with deep swags, the cast and beaded bases on three cast key feet, 19thC, 12½in (32cm) high.
£250–270 / €350–380
$410–440 TMA ⚲

Novelty inkwells

Many novelty inkwells were produced in ormolu or spelter, and covered a wide range of subjects. Dogs, camels and birds, particularly owls, are all fairly common. They should be carefully checked for damage as repair can be difficult and detracts from the value if poorly done.

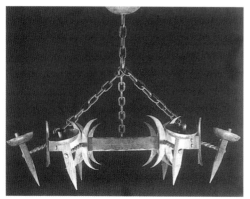

Wrought-iron rush-nip and candleholder, on a pine base, late 18thC, 8½in (21.5cm) high.
£370–410
€520–570
$610–670 S(O) 🔨

Pair of 18thC-style wrought-iron six-light chandeliers, Spanish, late 19thC, 20in (51cm) diam. This type of design tends to appeal more to the North American market rather than the European.
£320–350 / €450–490
$520–570 NOA 🔨

Pair of Louis XVI-style gilt-bronze two-light appliques, fitted for electricity, late 19thC, 13in (33cm) high.
£360–400 / €500–560
$590–650 NOA 🔨

Miller's compares...

Pair of brass table candlesticks, late 17thC, 8¼in (21cm) high. If these candlesticks bore a maker's mark they would be more desirable to collectors, and of higher value.
£380–420 / €530–590
$620–690 L 🔨

A. Wrought-iron rush-nip, with a domed fruitwood base, late 18thC, 10¼in (26cm) high.
£370–410 / €520–570
$610–670 S(O) 🔨

B. Wrought-iron rush-nip, on a yew wood base, 19thC, 8¾in (22cm) high.
£660–720 / €920–1,000
$1,100–1,200 S(O) 🔨

While both Items A and B are made of similar materials, Item B is in finer condition and is of a more elegant appearance, and therefore is of higher value.

Parcel-gilt three-piece desk set, comprising a tray, box with a brass foliate cover and an urn, with gilt-brass mounts, French, c1900, urn 3½in (9cm) high.
£470–520 / €650–720
$770–850 NOA 🔨

Bronze *jue*, cast with a *taotie* on the central band, with mushroom cap finials, 1550–1050 BC, 7in (18cm) high. A *taotie* is an animal mask. The composition of bronze items dating from the Shang and Zhou periods can vary greatly and affect the quality of the workmanship of a piece.
£480–530 / €670–740
$780–870 G(L) 🗡

Jues

These bronze vessels were used as burial gifts, many being excavated during the construction of the expansive train network throughout China in the early 20th century.

Pair of Louis XVI-style Carrara marble figural two-light candelabra, with gilt-bronze mounts, the central shaft as a putto, 1800–25, 15¼in (38.5cm) high.
£580–640 / €810–890
$950–1,050 NOA 🗡

Bronze plaque, by F. Barbedienne, French, 19thC, 12in (30.5cm) wide. The subject matter and known maker make this an interesting piece for collectors.
£500–550
€700–770
$820–900 HUM ⊞

Victorian japanned metal coal box, with gilt decoration, cast ring handles and a liner, 22in (56cm) wide.
£600–660 / €840–920
$980–1,100 WW 🗡

▶ **Cast-iron hall stand,** modelled as naturalistic branches and foliage, lozenge mark, 19thC, 35½in (90cm) high. Unless this hall stand was seriously damaged or incomplete, it is very good value. A complete example could be worth twice this amount.
£600–660 / €840–920
$980–1,100 SWO 🗡

Pair of Louis XVI-style gilt-bronze and Carrara marble five-light figural candelabra, French, late 19thC, 21in (53.5cm) high. These are desirable candlesticks at a very reasonable price.
£680–750 / €950–1,050
$1,100–1,200 NOA 🗡

Rugs & Carpets

Lori Bakhtiari bagface, west Persian, c1900, 10 x 12in (25.5 x 30.5cm).
£85–95 / €120–130
$140–155 SAM ⊞

Kashgai bagface, southwest Persian, 1875–1900, 19 x 16in (48.5 x 40.5cm). This unusual bagface would make a striking cushion or wall hanging.
£135–150 / €190–210
$220–240 SAM ⊞

Khorassan rug, the field with flowers and trailing foliage, with similar floral border and guard bands, Persian, early 20thC, 148 x 110in (376 x 279.5cm). This rug is attractive and in good condition, which makes it a good buy.
£320–350 / €450–490
$520–570 AH ✎

Rug, hand-made, with a geometric medallion design, Persian, 1920, 50 x 74in (127 x 188cm). This type of medallion rug with bright colours is not so popular today, which is reflected in the low price. However, it is a good buy for those wanting a colourful and hard-wearing Persian rug.
£105–115 / €150–160
$170–190 DuM ✎

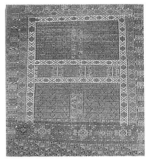

Ersari pardah, slight wear, northern Afghani, c1900, 78 x 61in (198 x 155cm). These items are used as door hangings in *yurts* and as prayer rugs. The contrast of the crimson and indigo stylized plants, with the brown and madder borders is particularly striking. This is a good buy.
£130–145 / €180–200
$210–230 WW ✎

Miller's compares...

A. Heriz runner, northwest Persian, c1910, 193 x 41¼in (483 x 105cm).
£400–440 / €560–610
$650–720 B(Ch) ✎

B. Sarab runner, northwest Persian, c1900, 167 x 40½in (424 x 103cm).
£920–1,000
€1,300–1,400
$1,500–1,650 S(O) ✎

Had Item A been in better condition and about 6in (15cm) narrower it would be of higher value. The good colours and ivory border make Item B more desirable, and it is very slightly narrower. Most people prefer runners to be under 36in (91.5cm) wide.

Afshar bagface, southeast Persian, 1875–1900, 9 x 10in (23 x 25.5cm). The chequerboard design and subtle colour mix of this piece are unusual, making it a collector's item.
£340–380 / €470–530
$560–620 SAM ⊞

The look without the price

Kashgai *kilim*, southwest Persian, c1900, 102 x 66in (259 x 167.5cm).
£420–460 / €590–640
$690–750 S(O) ⊁

This *kilim* has excellent colours but is a poor shape and does not lie flat. It also has pronounced creases at the top and bottom and would make a better throw for a sofa than a floor covering. Without these faults it would be worth in the region of £950 / €1,300 / $1,550.

◀ **Kashgai vanity bag,** southwest Persian, c1900, 10 x 9in (25.5 x 23cm).
£430–480 / €600–670
$700–780 SAM ⊞

Miller's compares...

A. Sarouk rug, west Persian, c1900, 75 x 52in (190.5 x 132cm).
£450–500 / €630–700
$730–820 S(O) ⊁

B. Sarouk rug, west Persian, c1890, 78 x 54in (198 x 137cm).
£700–770 / €980–1,050
$1,150–1,250 S(O) ⊁

The higher price of Item B reflects the fact that it is older than Item A and has a more distinctive and sophisticated design, which is popular with today's domestic market.

Pair of Kerman Ravar rugs, southeast Persian, 32 x 24in (81.5 x 61cm). These rugs have good colour and design. The cartouches in the borders have verses from the Persian poets, and the panels below the seated Prince depict a landscape with trees and a pond with geese. Their design and size would make them suitable for wall hangings.
£590–650 / €820–910
$960–1,050 S(O) ⊁

For further information on antique rugs see the full range of Miller's books at
www.millers.uk.com

The look without the price

Khamseh rug, southwest Persian, c1900, 51 x 102in (129.5 x 259cm).
£530–580 / €740–810
$870–950 S(O) ✎

This is a very attractive rug, but it is rather narrow for its length – making it less desirable for most buyers. If it had been of better proportions it could have sold for over £1,000 / €1,400 / $1,650.

Bakhtiari carpet, west Persian, c1910, 122 x 78in (310 x 198cm). This carpet would have been worth more if it were not so red and had been wider.
£590–650 / €820–910
$960–1,050 S(O) ✎

What are the popular colours?

Many reds, such as wine-red, bluey-red, orange-red, pinky-red, scarlet and pillar-box red tend to be less popular and carpets with these colours may not achieve high prices. However, soft apricots, peach, rosy-red, madder red, coral and terracotta are sought after, particularly in combination with pale and/or dark blue, ivory and gold – hence the popularity of Heriz carpets.

Kerman carpet, southeast Persian, c1900, 184 x 126in (467 x 320cm). Despite its all-over design and good size, this carpet has rather sombre colouring which is not popular with buyers.
£700–770 / €980–1,050
$1,150–1,250 S(O) ✎

Kazak rug, southwest Caucasian, c1900, 70 x 47in (178 x 119.5cm). This rug would fit into any house and greatly enhance the appearance of a room.
£700–770 / €980–1,050
$1,150–1,250 S(O) ✎

◄ **Kashgai rug,** southwest Persian, c1890, 84 x 57in (213.5 x 145cm). This is an exceptionally good price for such an attractive rug with good balance of design and colours.
£730–800 / €1,000–1,100
$1,200–1,300 S(O) ✎

Afshar rug, southwest Persian, c1900, 72 x 60in (183 x 152.5cm). This rug has an unusual and striking design and is a good size – however blue is not the most popular of colours.
£760–830 / € 1,050–1,150
$1,250–1,350 S(O) ✗

Find out more in

Miller's Antiques Price Guide,
Miller's Publications, 2004

Ways of identifying rugs

• Kashgai: wool pile on a wool foundation, banded single cord edges and low soft pile with clear cheerful colours. Generally one or more medallions, but all-over designs are not uncommon – floral devices, animals, birds, and human figures are featured.
• Kashan: finely knotted with excellent wool on a cotton foundation. The narrow single cord edges often curl under, which must be corrected. The many rich and dark colours and sophisticated curvilinear design form a pattern drawn by a master weaver. There is usually a medallion with complementary spandrels, and main and multiple subsidiary borders and scrolling patterns of tendrils, flowerheads and leaves in good clear colours on a red, madder or ivory field. The woven ends have short fringes.
• Sarouk: finely knotted with a Senneh knot, good wool pile on a cotton foundation. Often stiff to handle due to alternate warp threads being buried or doubled under. They should always be rolled, as folding can cause them to 'crack'. These have similar floral designs and colours to the Kashans, but are less desirable.
• Heriz and Gorevans: coarser than most other Persian carpets, with a wool pile on a cotton foundation. They have large geometric patterns with a medallion, stepped sides and turtle pattern in the main border. Terracotta, apricot, green, blue and ivory are common and popular colours.

Kashgai rug, southwest Persian, c1890, 84¾ x 58¼in (215 x 148cm). One would normally expect to pay more for such an unusual rug with cane fields and lattice spandrels. This is a good buy.
£800–880 / € 1,100–1,250
$1,300–1,450 S(O) ✗

Kashan runner, central Persian, c1910, 187 x 41in (475 x 104cm). These rugs are finely woven and hard wearing, and this is an unusual format for a Kashan. This example is a good size and is straight – which make it excellent value.
£880–970 / € 1,250–1,350
$1,450–1,600 S(O) ✗

Seek advice

When buying rugs and carpets take advice from an expert – seek out specialist dealers and auction houses and only buy from reputable sources.

Hamadan carpet, west Persian, c1880, 123¾ x 90¼in (314.5 x 229cm). The price of this carpet has probably been kept low by the muted pattern and the rather small size.
£900–990 / € 1,250–1,400
$1,450–1,600 B(Ch) ✗

Scientific Instruments

Miller's compares...

A. Coachmaker's boxwood folding rule, by Thomas Bradburn, Birmingham, in four sections, c1850, 48in (122cm) long.
£25–30 / €35–42
$40–50 TOM ⊞

B. Carpenter's boxwood folding rule, with brass extension arm, early 18thC, 18in (45.5cm) long.
£180–200 / €250–280
$300–330 TOM ⊞

Item A is a common type of rule. Item B, however, is rare and of more interest to a collector because it is 18in (45.5cm) long with a 6in (15cm) brass extension arm, instead of the usual 24in (61cm). It is of higher value despite the fact that it has a broken extension arm.

Boxwood Gunters scale rule, 18thC, 24in (61cm) long. This type of boxwood rule can easily be cleaned using very fine wire wool and raw linseed oil. Their value is often lowered by cracks and chips.
£40–45 / €55–60
$65–75 TOM ⊞

The look without the price

Wooden trumpet stethoscope, 1890, 5½in (14cm) long.
£85–95 / €120–130
$140–155 Cus ⊞

Mass-produced simple monaural stethoscopes such as this were used by midwives well into the 20thC. Earlier examples were hand-made in boxwood, fruitwood and ivory, and can fetch £300–500 / €420–700 / $690–1,150.

Geryk floor-standing vacuum pump, the cast-iron flywheel with a crank handle, single-valve piston, on a steel box base with four splayed legs and casters, 1930s. This would have fetched a much higher price if it had the original paint and lacquer finish.
£60–66 / €85–95
$100–110 BIG ↗

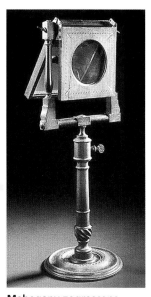

▶ **Set of cast-iron scales,**
American, 19thC, 14in (35.5cm)
wide. When buying scales
always check that the paint
finish is original as this adds to
the value – so often they have
been stripped and repainted.
£95–105 / €130–150
$155–170 DuM 🪓

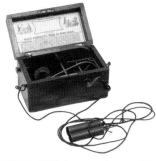

Mahogany zograscope,
with chevron-banded inlay, on a
domed base, c1800, 24in (61cm)
high. The zograscope is an optical
instrument used for viewing
reverse-printed landscapes in
the late 18thC and early 19thC.
£95–105 / €130–150
$155–170 S(O) 🪓

Nickel-plated scarificator,
French, 1890, 1¾in (4.5cm)
diam. A brass example would
be of higher value.
£100–110 / €140–155
$165–180 CuS ⊞

Magneto, 1890, in a wooden case 8in
(20.5cm) wide. These instruments often
come in attractive mahogany boxes and are
well worth buying when complete and in
good condition.
£115–125 / €160–175
$190–200 CuS ⊞

Tooth key, 1850, 5in (12.5cm) long. Horn and ivory
handles, maker's names and interchangeable keys for
tooth sizes all increase the price of these interesting
early dental instruments.
£115–125 / €160–175
$190–200 CuS ⊞

▶ **Cartwright
Halifax triple-
bladed veterinary
fleam,** the horn
handle enclosing an
additional lancet
blade, c1830,
4in (10cm) long.
£135–150
€190–210
$220–250 WAC ⊞

ANTIQUE MICROSCOPE SLIDES IN CABINETS AND BOXES

Also Quality Microscopes

WANTED

*I wish to purchase Antique
Microscope Slides*
HIGHEST PRICES PAID

Charles Tomlinson
Tel/Fax: 01244 318395
Email: charles.tomlinson@lineone.net

Urological dilator, 1900, 12½in (32cm) long.
£135–150 / €190–210
$220–250 CuS ⊞

Gaugers boxwood slide rule, by Dring & Fage, London, dated 1820, 12in (30.5cm) long. This type of slide rule was first designed by Thomas Everard in the 17thC, and was used by Customs & Excise to calculate alcohol content in beer and wine. They were made in various lengths and with different numbers of slides. Produced well into the 19thC, they make an ideal collecting subject.
£180–200 / €250–280
$300–330 TOM ⊞

Silver pocket compass, by J. H. Steward, London, modelled as a watch case with suspension ring, maker's name to interior, case marked for Birmingham 1883, 2in (5cm) diam, 2oz. The price reflects the fact that this compass is made of silver. This type of compass is more commonly found in brass or nickel, both of which sell for considerably less than silver examples.
£160–175 / €220–250
$260–290 WW ⚲

◄ **Gilt-bronze and ivory desk thermometer,** by H. Grimoldi, London, with an inscribed ivory register, 1825–50, 5¾in (14.5cm) high.
£180–200 / €250–280
$300–330 SWO ⚲

Bakelite ear trumpet, 1890, 9½in (24cm) long. Ear trumpets are sought after by collectors of both Bakelite and medical instruments. Bakelite should always be carefully checked for damage as this greatly reduces its value.
£200–220 / €280–310
$330–350 CuS ⊞

Beware the hazards of medicine chests

Some chests may still contain original medicines such as opium, arsenic or mercury. Always seek expert advice to find out how to dispose of them, as they may be poisonous.

▶ **Mahogany apothecary's cabinet,** by S. Maw, Son & Thompson, fitted with glass bottles, and a lift-out division with further bottles beneath, late 19thC, 8¾in (22cm) wide. These attractive boxes are highly sought-after collectors' items. Their prices vary greatly, depending on how much of the original contents remain.
£240–270 / €330–380
$390–440 L ⚲

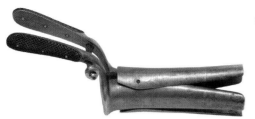

Metal speculum, 1860, 9in (23cm) long.
£310–350 / €430–490
$510–570 CuS ⊞

Metal ear trumpet, 1870, 4in (10cm) long.
£360–400 / €500–560
$590–650 CuS ⊞

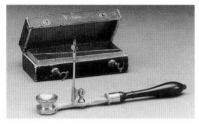

Botanical microscope, the turned wood
handle with brass mount screwing into a
brass section with combined forceps/pin on
a hinged bracket, with a simple screw lens,
possibly French, 1850–75, 5½in (14cm)
long, in a fitted case.
£500–550 / €700–770
$820–900 S(O) ⚒

Sextant, by Hayes Brothers,
Cardiff, the lattice frame with
brass and silvered scale, silvered
vernier, two sets of
interchangeable filters, mirror,
split level mirror, two telescopes
and index arm with magnifier,
late 19thC, 9in (23cm) radius.
These precision instruments are
widely collected and are sought-
after in their original, untouched
condition by collectors.
£530–580 / €740–810
$870–950 S(O) ⚒

**Leslie-style differential
thermometer,** signed
'Alvergniat Frères à Paris' on
the wooden frame carrying the
thermometer tube, the vertical
members reading against
of scale of -30 to +25, on
a turned baluster fruitwood
stand, French, late 19thC,
18in (45.5cm) high.
£700–770 / €980–1,100
$1,150–1,250 S(O) ⚒

Gilt-brass monocular microscope, by
Carpenter & Westley, London, with rack-
and-pinion focusing, the mahogany five-
drawer fitted case with a collection of eye
pieces and objective lenses with accessories,
19thC, 16in (40.5cm) high.
£750–830 / €1,050–1,150
$1,250–1,350 G(B) ⚒

Find out more in

*Miller's Collecting
Science & Technology*,
Miller's Publications,
2001

▶ **Brass botanical microscope,** with simple
magnifying lens, a spike, a pair of tweezers and a scalpel,
with a quantity of microscopical accessories including a
further simple microscope, forceps missing, nine specimen
slides, four numbered objectives and stage forceps,
late 18thC, 3¼in (8.5cm) high. These very collectable
rare microscopes are often sold incomplete, and even
so can still fetch £200–300 / €280–420 / $330–490.
£760–830 / €1,050–1,150
$1,250–1,350 S(O) ⚒

Sculpture

◀ **Parian figure of a lady,**
19thC, 14¼in (36cm) high.
£70–80 / €95–110
$115–130 SWO 🔨

Bronze

Bronze is an alloy of
90 per cent copper,
seven per cent tin and
three per cent zinc.
Individual foundries
varied in what they
added (eg mercury)
and, however hard
they tried, no two
batches of bronze
for casting could be
exactly the same.

Bronze model of a whippet, after
Pierre Jules Mêne, signed, late 19thC,
6in (15cm) high.
£90–100 / €125–140
$150–165 G(L) 🔨

Miller's compares...

**A. Parian bust of Charles
Dickens,** impressed marks,
late 19thC, 11¾in (30cm) high.
£120–130 / €165–180
$195–210 SWO 🔨

B. Parian bust of Clyte,
base inscribed 'Art Union of
London', chipped, 1853,
13½in (34.5cm) high.
£240–260 / €330–360
$390–430 SWO 🔨

**Parian group of a knight
and a maiden,** 19thC,
16in (40.5cm) high.
£160–180 / €220–250
$260–300 G(L) 🔨

There are many figures of Charles Dickens and Item A is a
common example. Although the base of Item B is damaged,
it is a rarer example than Item A, hence the higher value.

Cold-painted bronze model of a kingfisher, beak possibly damaged, stamped with the Bergman seal, Austrian, c1900, 6½in (16.5cm) wide.
£220–240 / €310–330
$370–390 G(L) ✦

Pair of Victorian spelter figures, after F. Moreau, entitled 'En Maraude' and 'Rencontre à la Fontaine', on *faux* marble bases, 17¼in (44cm) high.
£200–220 / €280–310
$330–370 SWO ✦

Cold-painted bronzes

Rather than being treated under heat with chemicals to produce a patina, cold-painted bronzes were decorated with oil paint. The colour was not treated with heat, hence the term 'cold-painted'. A great variety of cold-painted bronzes were produced in Austria, with subjects ranging from the mundane to the whimsical, and these are very popular with collectors.

Terracotta figure of a woman, German, c1810, 10½in (26.5cm) high.
£270–300 / €380–420
$440–490 MFB ⊞

Parian portrait bust of Queen Victoria, by Robinson & Leadbeater, impressed 'Jubilee 1887, R.J. Morris Sculp.', 19thC, 13½in (34.5cm) high.
£320–350 / €450–490
$520–570 G(L) ✦

Bronze bust of a boy, by Jean-Baptiste Carpeaux, on a marble plinth, signed and impressed, 19thC, 6¼in (16cm) high.
£350–390 / €490–540
$570–640 SWO ✦

Cast-iron horse group, after P. J. Mêne, entitled 'L'Accolade', base inscribed 'Falkirk', late 19thC, 13½in (34.5cm) high. This is one of the most commonly reproduced of Mêne's works.
£420–460 / €590–640
$690–750 B(Kn) ➚

◄ **Pair of Carrara marble models of lions,** late 18thC, 6in (15cm) wide. These lions have suffered losses and damage, resulting in this low value.
£480–530
€670–740
$780–870 CGC ➚

Carrara marble

Carrara marble, best known for its use for statues, has been quarried for over 2,000 years. It has been used by some of the most famous artists in the world, such as Michelangelo and Canova and is prized for its high quality and unusual transparency.

Bronze racing monkey group, by Paul Joseph Gayrard, depicting a monkey jockey taking a jump, founders' signature 'Boyer', French, 19thC, 5¾in (14.5cm) wide.
£460–510 / €640–710
$750–830 G(L) ➚

Bronze figure, by Jef Lambeaux, depicting a seated Galileo, signed, 19thC, 19¾in (50cm) high.
£580–640 / €810–890
$950–1,050 BERN ➚

Patinating & gilding

The patination on sculpture is not the natural process of ageing, as with furniture, but the application under heat of a variety of chemical 'soups'. Different chemicals give different colours. Black became more common in the mid-19th century, but Art Nouveau ushered in lighter tones such as red, brown, green and blue.

Nineteenth-century gilding was produced by the application of a very hot paste of powdered gold and mercury that ages to a greenish satin. Contemporary gilding tends to be much more garish in colour.

Bronze bust of a young lady, by Georges van der Straeten, Belgian School, with mid-brown patination, signed, c1900, 13¾in (35cm) high. Not all bronzes are signed or stamped by either the artist or the foundry, but those that are become more valuable to collectors.
£540–590 / €750–820
$880–960 S(Am) ➚

► **Bronze figure of Autumn,** with dark brown patination, French, late 19thC, 16½in (42cm) high.
£600–660 / €840–920
$980–1,100 S(O) ➚

Gilt-bronze group of two putti, French, 19thC, 6¼in (15cm) wide.
£600–660 / €840–920
$980–1,100 DN ⚒

◀ **Bronze model of a lion,** by Antoine Louis Barye, French School, entitled 'Lion assis des Tuileries', with green patination, signed, c1900, 7in (18cm) high. Barye is an artist whose work is particularly sought-after by collectors of bronzes, therefore, the signature increases the value of this piece.
£670–740 / €930–1,050
$1,100–1,200 S(Am) ⚒

Bronze model of a rabbit by a signpost, by Auguste Nicolas Cain, entitled 'Route de la Casserole', with green/brown patination, signed, French, late 19thC, 4in (10cm) high.
£720–790 / €1,000–1,100
$1,200–1,300 S(O) ⚒

Carved boxwood figure of Christ crucified, 18thC, 18in (45.5cm) high.
£780–860 / €1,100–1,200
$1,250–1,400 SWO ⚒

◀ **Bronze figure,** entitled 'The Faun with Cymbals', after the antique, 19thC, 12in (30.5cm) high. 'After the antique' sculptures tend not to be signed or stamped, which can make them difficult to date and value.
£800–880 / €1,100–1,250
$1,300–1,450 Mit ⚒

Bronze sculpture of a group of young girls, by R. Marschall, signed, Austrian, c1900, 6in (16cm) high.
£800–880 / €1,100–1,250
$1,300–1,450 MI ▦

Bronze figural group of a mounted Greek warrior, by Julius Schmidt-Felling, with dark brown patination, signed, German, late 19thC, 22½in (57cm) high. This is a pleasing bronze at a reasonable price.
£940–1,050 / €1,300–1,450
$1,500–1,700 B(Kn) ⚒

Textiles

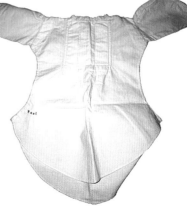

◀ **Sampler,** by H. Mitchell, worked in blue thread with the alphabet, framed, 1841, 5in (12.5cm) square. If this sampler had been in better condition it could have fetched twice the price.
£60–65 / €85–90
$100–105 TMA ➹

Late 18th & 19th century lace

Large quantities of lace were produced all over Europe during the late 18th and 19th centuries. Today the demand is for good quality pieces of a useful size and in perfect condition.

At auctions, lace is usually sold in bundles of mixed sizes of varying condition and age. Purchasers looking for specific dated examples from a particular area would be well advised to go to a specialist dealer. Carrickmacross is a good example of lace that should be bought only in pristine, unwashed, condition.

Child's miniature shirt sampler, by Jemima Post, born 1808, early 19thC, 9½in (24cm) long.
£65–70 / €90–95
$105–115 L&E ➹

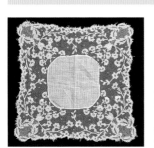

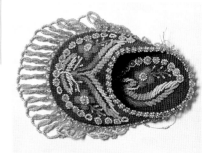

◀ **Carrickmacross handkerchief,** Irish, 12in (30.5cm) square.
£70–75 / €95–105
$115–120 HL ⊞

Pair of beaded watch tidies, c1900, 6in (15cm) long.
£85–95 / €120–130
$140–155 LGU ⊞

The look without the price

Woolwork picture, depicting a drummer boy and his friend, framed, 19thC, 12¼ x 14¼in (31 x 26cm).
£85–95 / €120–130
$140–155 SWO ➹

This woolwork picture is a desirable item but it has been badly framed. If it was in its original frame with good colour and condition, it could be worth up to £350 / €490 / $570.

Pair of beaded watch tidies, c1880, 8in (20.5cm) long.
£105–115 / €150–160
$170–190 LGU ⊞

▶ **Regency silkwork picture,** depicting St Francis, 8¼ x 6½in (22.5 x 16.5cm). The subject portrayed in a silkwork picture is important – those featuring children or animals are worth twice as much as those of a religious nature. However, any damage to the base silk fabric would make any silkwork picture worth very little.
£110–120 / €155–165
$180–195 SWO ⚘

Length of bobbin lace, Italian, late 17thC, 4 x 44in (10 x 112cm).
£115–125 / €160–175
$190–200 HL ⊞

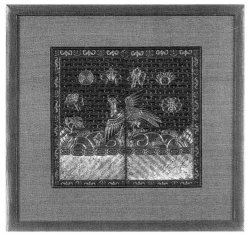

Embroidered rank badge, worked in silk and metallic threads, depicting a fly catcher and Eight Precious Buddhistic symbols, framed, Chinese, 19thC, 18¼ x 19in (46.5 x 48.5cm).
£140–155 / €195–215
$230–250 NOA ⚘

Length of Honiton lace edging, mid-19thC, 4 x 54in (10 x 137cm).
£150–165 / €210–230
$245–270 HL ⊞

▶ **Embroidered silk panel,** worked in Forbidden Stitch, the central floral medallion with a lucky bat, the corners embroidered with four more bats completing the rebus *Wu Fu*, The Five Happinesses, framed, Chinese, late 18thC, 26½ x 23½in (67.5 x 59.5cm). Subject matter is very important to collectors of these pieces. Prices are currently increasing due to a growing interest from the market in mainland China.
£195–210 / €270–300
$320–360 NOA ⚘

Beaded bag, with a silver mount and clasp, late 19thC, 8in (20.5cm) wide.
£200–220 / €280–310
$330–370 JPr ⊞

What should I know when buying beaded bags?

The price of bags has risen dramatically over the past two or three years. Bear in mind the following when purchasing beaded bags:

- repair can be very expensive and often impossible.
- smaller bags are more valuable and collectable than larger ones.
- the clasp and mounts should be checked for hallmarks and makers' stamps as these will enhance the value.
- the smaller the beads usually means the earlier the date of the bag.
- the subject matter of the design is important – flowers, animals and buildings enhance the value.

◀ **Christening robe,** late 19thC, 38in (96.5cm) long.
£210–230 / €290–320
$350–380 HL ⊞

◀ **Silk bell-pull,** worked in Florentine Stitch, 18thC, 5 x 43in (12.5 x 109cm). When purchasing a bell-pull condition is important. It should be complete with a metal handle and a bar to connect it to the chain which would have rung the bell to call the servants.
£320–350 / €450–490
$520–570 LGU ⊞

Set of four silk curtain ties, late 19thC, 32in (81.5cm) long. A set of four curtain ties is much more desirable than a pair. Fading, which tends to match the current trend in fabrics, can sometimes enhance the value. More elaborate versions from the late 19thC are worth collecting.
£360–400 / €500–560
$590–650 JPr ⊞

Christening robes

When buying a christening robe, try to find one that is hand-embroidered. Check that it has no wear and tear, and that it is of a reasonable size. Early robes were made for smaller babies than we have today – robes from the Edwardian period tend to be of a more useful size.

Beaded cloth bandolier,
Native American, 1875–1900,
38in (96.5cm) long.
£400–440 / €560–610
$650–720 NOA ⚗

Native American textiles

This is becoming an increasingly collectable subject. Much of the Native American work created in the early 1800s was specifically made for the tourist market, but generally the quality remained true to the original tribal products. It was not until the late 19th and early 20th century that there was a marked deterioration in the quality and this is easily recognizable. When purchasing, look out for moccasins, pouches, headbands and unusual items that will have extra curiosity value.

▶ **Birth sampler,** framed, dated 1882, 8in (20.5cm) square. This style of sampler has become a specific collecting category. They were more common in the first quarter of the 19thC but continued to be made up to the end of the 1880s.
£540–600 / €750–840
$880–980 HIS ⊞

The look without the price

This is a fine example of a traditional early 19thC sampler which contains many of the elements that are desirable to today's collectors – animals, birds, houses, figures, the age of the maker and the date. It has a good border, no fading and is made in silk as opposed to wool. If this example had been late 18thC, a difference of only five years, and in its original frame, it would have been worth at least 50 per cent more.

Sampler, by Emilia Simpson, framed, dated 1804, 17½ x 12½in (44.5 x 32cm).
£680–750 / €950–1,050
$1,100–1,220 HIS ⊞

Theorems painted velvet cushion,
c1840, 11 x 18in (28 x 45.5cm). Early 19thC cushions must be in good condition and with original fringing to fetch high prices. Painted cushions from the latter part of the century would be worth less than half this price. When the fabric appears to be in a delicate condition, cushion covers are frequently framed, thus extending their life and enhancing the value.
£720–800 / €1,000–1,100
$1,200–1,300 LGU ⊞

Condition of textiles

The very nature of textiles is such that from the moment they are produced they are subject to attack by moths, beetles, humans, light, damp, fungus and wear and tear. Thus the value placed on items that are in good, perfect or original condition is always going to be out of proportion to the rarity and age of the item. However, there will be exceptions. The collector who wishes to own a 17th-century stumpwork piece will be forced to compromise due to the scarcity of such pieces on the market. Look for faults, be suspicious of the perfect example and, once the item has been obtained, be sure to guard and preserve it.

Wooden Antiques

Victorian oak and mahogany gavel, 7in (18cm) long.
£16–18 / €20–25
$25–30 WiB ⊞

Apprentice carver's wooden sample board, early 19thC, 9in (23cm) wide.
£55–60 / €75–85
$90–100 TMA ↗

Inlaid mahogany card tray, c1900, 9in (23cm) wide.
£60–65 / €85–90
$100–105 TOP ⊞

Mahogany decanter coaster, by Wylie & Lockhead, the glazed top inset with a later coloured print, on three brass and leather casters, Scottish, 9in (23cm) diam. The value of this coaster is in the attribution to the cabinet makers Wylie & Lockhead of Glasgow – a Scottish provenance is always desirable.
£110–120 / €155–175
$180–195 B(W) ↗

Miller's compares...

A. Treen nutcracker, carved as a woman's head, German, Black Forest, 19thC, 7in (18cm) long.
£80–90 / €110–125
$130–150 BWL ↗

B. Treen nutcracker, in the form of a shell, German, Black Forest, 19thC, 6in (15cm) long.
£240–260 / €330–360
$390–430 BWL ↗

The shell form of Item B is more desirable than the old woman's head of Item A, and this accounts for the price difference between them. These Black Forest treen novelty nutcrackers were made in many forms. Among the most popular are dogs' heads and caricatures of old men with striking facial expressions.

◀ **Gothic-style oak and brass book slide,** c1890, 14in (35.5cm) wide.
£135–150 / €190–210
$220–250 TDG ⊞

◄ **Victorian figured-walnut watch stand,** in the form of a domed tower, with brass and ebony chequer banding and cast-brass bezel, 6½in (16.5cm) high.
£140–155
€195–210
$230–250 TMA ⚒

Burr-walnut mazer bowl, with metal lining and foot, c1900, 4¾in (12cm) diam.
£150–165 / €210–220
$250–270 CGC ⚒

Carved wood folk art life preserver, c1900, 20in (51cm) long.
£180–200 / €250–280
$300–330 HUM ⊞

Oak candle box, 18thC, 17¼in (44cm) high. This candle box is more elaborate than most country-made oak examples. The fretwork crest and heart-shaped inlay are desirable features to look for.
£260–280 / €360–390
$430–460 CGC ⚒

Pair of oak torchères, each in the form of a crowned winged lion terminating in a single paw foot, late 19thC, 28½in (72.5cm) high.
£300–330 / €420–460
$490–540 NOA ⚒

The look without the price

Beech and oak chopping block, Continental, 19thC, 24in (61cm) high.
£150–165 / €210–220
$250–270 HRQ ⊞

This modest example has a varnished finish, but a chopping block with good colour and patination could be worth several hundreds of pounds.

◄ **Fragment of an oak panel,** carved with the head of a dolphin, 16thC, 8¼in (21cm) wide. Although this panel is a fragment of a larger carving, it features a strong image that has been boldy executed.
£330–360 / €460–500
$540–590 S(O) ⚒

Lignum vitae **mallet,** carved and die-stamped with a portrait of Queen Victoria and Prince Albert to commemorate their marriage, c1840, 8in (20.5cm) long. *Lignum vitae* (wood of life) is the hardest wood known to man. The intricate carving of this mallet was probably executed on a machine lathe and is known as *holzaapel* turning.
£420–460 / €590–640
$690–750 TMA ⚲

◄ **Mahogany serving tray,** with serpentine gallery and brass handles, c1900, 23in (58.5cm) wide.
£360–400 / €500–560
$590–650 WAA ⊞

Carved oak pew finial, in the shape of a poppy head, 15th–16thC, 10¼in (26cm) high. This finial is extremely desirable as it has a rich patina.
£380–410 / €530–570
$620–670 S(O) ⚲

Locate the source

The source of each illustration in Miller's can be found by checking the code letters below each caption with the Key to Illustrations, pages 286–290.

Carved hardwood finial, in the form of a lion holding a shield, 17th–18thC, 5in (12.5cm) high.
£500–550 / €700–770
$820–900 S(O) ⚲

Elm hatchment panel, painted with an armorial, 1680–1820, 17in (43cm) square. Hatchment panels usually feature a coat-of-arms and were placed on the front of a house to denote the death of the owner. The price achieved by this example reflects the fair condition of the paintwork.
£530–580 / €740–810
$860–950 S(O) ⚲

Turned wood block, 17thC, 7in (18cm) diam. Unusual items of treen such as this well-patinated block are popular conversation pieces and can make an interesting decorative feature.
£530–580 / €740–810
$860–950 S(O) ⚲

◀ **Carved wood and glass inset specimen vase,** in the form of a bear standing by a tree trunk, German, Black Forest, c1900, 17¾in (45cm) high.
£640–700
€ **890–1,100**
$1,050–1,150
BERN ⚒

Black Forest bears

The bear was a popular subject for the Black Forest wood carvers. Furniture such as benches and hall stands were produced incorporating the figure of a bear.

Carved wood model of a standing bear, German, Black Forest, c1895, 15in (35cm) high.
£640–700
€ **890–1,100**
$1,050–1,150
BERN ⚒

▶ **Sycamore dairy bowl,** c1800, 17in (43cm) diam.
£770–850
€ **1,050–1,200**
$1,250–1,400
S(O) ⚒

Carved giltwood figure of the archangel Michael or Gabriel, Continental, 18thC, 33¼in (84.5cm) high.
£700–770 / € 980–1,050
$1,150–1,250 BERN ⚒

Tunbridge ware rosewood tea caddy, probably by Burrows, the top with stylized flower and scroll panel, the sides inlaid with alternating bands of beetles and moths within chequered stringing, the interior with mosaic lidded boxes, c1840, 12in (30.5cm) wide.
£780–860 / € 1,100–1,200
$1,250–1,400 BR ⚒

Sycamore trencher, 18thC, 9in (23cm) diam. Collectors of country treen want the items they buy to look their age, and this piece is very desirable with its exceptional colour and patina.
£800–880 / € 1,100–1,250
$1,300–1,450 S(O) ⚒

A carved wood head of Christ, 16thC, 13½in (34.5cm) high. This is a fragment of a larger carving and, for such a skilfully executed and early item, is very reasonably priced.
£820–900 / € 1,150–1,250
$1,350–1,450 BERN ⚒

Glossary

We have defined here some of the terms that you will come across in this book. If there are any terms or technicalities you would like explained or you feel should be included in future, please let us know.

abrashed: A slight shift in colour tone caused by the weaver running out of one batch of yarn and continuing with another: each batch of a natural dye will differ slightly with others.

armorial: A full coat-of-arms. Also a term used for any object decorated with the owner's coat-of-arms, especially silver or silver plate.

astragal: Moulding into which are set the glass panes of a cabinet or bookcase.

bergère: Originally any armchair with upholstered sides, now more often used to describe a chair with a square or round caned back and sides.

bevelled glass: Where a slope is cut at the edge of a flat surface. Usually associated with the plate glass used in mirrors.

boteh: The Paisley motif which may also be found in stylized form. It probably represents a leaf.

bright-cut engraving: Whereby the metal surface is cut creating facets that reflect the light.

cabriole leg: Tall curving leg subject to many designs and produced with club, pad, paw, claw-and-ball, and scroll feet.

canapé: A large settee with upholstered back and arms.

cartouche: A decorative frame, surrounded by scrollwork and foliage, often bearing an inscription, monogram or coat-of-arms.

chasing: Method of decorating using hammers and punches to push metal into a relief pattern – the metal is displaced, not removed.

corbel: Projecting moulding at the top of tall cabinet furniture.

coromandel: Yellow- and black-striped wood from South America which is used mainly for crossbanding.

credenza: Elaborately decorated Victorian side cabinet, sometimes with rounded ends, and often with glazed or solid doors.

dip circle: A dip needle with a vertical circular scale of angles used for measuring dip. Also called an inclinometer.

enamel: Coloured glass, applied to metal, ceramic or glass in paste form and then fired for decorative effect.

field: The large area of a rug or carpet usually enclosed by borders.

finial: An ornament, often carved in many forms from animal figures to obelisks, and used to finish off any vertical projection.

gesso: Composition of plaster of Paris and size which was used as a base for applying gilding and usually moulded in bas relief.

intaglio: Incised gemstone, often set in a ring, used in antiquity and during the Renaissance as a seal. Any incised decoration; the opposite of carving in relief.

kilim: A simple, pileless rug or carpet.

KPM: Königliche Porzellan Manufactur. Mark used on Berlin porcelain c1832–c1957.

lithography: Method of polychrome printing in which a design is drawn in ink on a stone surface and transferred to paper. Lithographic prints were also used to decorate ceramics.

marotte: Doll on a stick which plays a tune when spun round.

marquetry: Design formed from different coloured woods veneered onto a carcase to give a decorative effect. Many early examples are Dutch.

meiping: Chinese for cherry blossom. A term referring to a tall vase, with high shoulders, small neck and narrow mouth, used to display flowering branches.

nacreous: Made from mother-of-pearl, or having the lustre of, mother-of-pearl.

naos or cella: The inner room of a temple housing the statue of a deity.

ogee: Double curved shape which is convex at the top and becomes concave at the bottom. It is often found on the feet of Georgian furniture. Also known as cyma reversa.

papier mâché: Paper pulp usually combined with a glue and moulded into boxes, trays and ornaments, painted or japanned. Also used to make furniture building up layers of paper with pitch and oil over an iron frame.

parquetry: Decorative veneers laid in a geometric pattern.

patera: Small flat circular ornament, often in the form of an open flower or rosette, used as a ceiling or furniture ornament.

patina: Surface colour of genuinely old wood resulting from the layers of grease, dirt and polish built up over the years, and through handling. Differs from wood to wood and difficult to fake.

pilaster: Decorative flat-faced column projecting from a wall.

prie-dieu: Chair with a low seat and a tall back. They were made during the 19th century and were designed for prayer.

putti: Cupids or cherubs used as decoration.

retipping: Replacing the tips of chair legs.

salt glaze: Hard translucent glaze used on stoneware and achieved by throwing common salt into the kiln at high temperatures. Produces a silky, pitted appearance like orange peel.

scratchweight: A note made of the weight of a silver article at assay, usually inscribed on the base. It may show how many items were in a set and, by a change in weight, if a piece has been altered. The weights are expressed as troy ounces (oz), pennyweights (dwt) and grains (gr).

socle: Another name for a plinth.

spelter: Zinc treated to look like bronze. An inexpensive substitute used in Art Nouveau appliqué ornament and Art Deco figures.

spigot: A stopper or tap, usually wood, and fitted to a cask.

splat: Central upright in a chair back.

strapwork: Repeated carved decoration suggesting plaited straps. Originally used in the 16th and 17th centuries and revived in the 19th century.

tamper: An instrument for packing down tobacco in a pipe.

tine: The prong of a fork; early ones have two, later ones three.

tôle peinte: French 18th-century method of varnishing sheet iron vessels so that the surface could be painted upon. And by derivation, painted metal panels applied to furniture.

troy ounce: A measurement used to express the weight of a piece of silver. One troy ounce is comprised of 20 pennyweights.

Tunbridge ware: Objects decorated with wooden inlay made of bundles of coloured wood cut into sections; usually simple geometric designs, but sometimes whole scenes; mid-17th to late 19th century.

verdigris: Greenish or blueish patina formed on copper, bronze or brass.

wrought-iron: A pure form of iron often used for decorative purposes.

wucai: Type of five-colour Chinese porcelain decoration.

Directory of Specialists

If you wish to be included in next year's directory, or if you have a change of address or telephone number, please contact Miller's Advertising Department by July 2004. We advise readers to make contact by telephone before visiting a dealer, therefore avoiding a wasted journey.

ANTIQUITIES
Dorset
Ancient & Gothic, PO Box 5390, Bournemouth, BH7 6XR Tel: 01202 431721 *Antiquities from before 300,000 BC to about 1500 AD*

London
Ancient Art, 85 The Vale, Southgate, N14 6AT Tel: 020 8882 1509 ancient.art@btinternet.com www.ancientart.co.uk

Helios Gallery, 292 Westbourne Grove, W11 2PS Tel: 077 11 955 997 heliosgallery@btinternet.com www.heliosgallery.com

ARCHITECTURAL ANTIQUES
Cheshire
Nostalgia, Hollands Mill, 61 Shaw Heath, Stockport, SK3 8BH Tel: 0161 477 7706 www.nostalgia-uk.com

Gloucestershire
Olliff's Architectural Antiques, 19–21 Lower Redland Rd, Redland, Bristol, BS6 6TB Tel: 0117 923 9232 marcus@olliffs.com www.olliffs.com

Kent
Catchpole & Rye, Saracens Dairy, Jobbs Lane, Pluckley, Ashford, TN27 0SA Tel: 01233 840840 info@crye.co.uk www.crye.co.uk

Somerset
Walcot Reclamations, 108 Walcot St, Bath, BA1 5BG Tel: 01225 444404

ARMS & MILITARIA
Gloucestershire
Q & C Militaria, 22 Suffolk Rd, Cheltenham, GL50 2AQ Tel: 01242 519815 qcmilitaria@btconnect.com www.qcmilitaria.com

Nottinghamshire
Michael D. Long Ltd, 96–98 Derby Rd, Nottingham, NG1 5FB Tel: 0115 941 3307 sales@michaeldlong.com www.michaeldlong.com

Surrey
West Street Antiques, 63 West St, Dorking, RH4 1BS Tel: 01306 883487 weststant@aol.com www.antiquearmsandarmour.com

AUTOMATA
London
Automatomania, M13 Grays Mews, 58 Davies St, W1K 5LP Tel: 020 7495 5259 magic@automatomania.com www.automatomania.com

BAROMETERS
Berkshire
Alan Walker, Halfway Manor, Halfway, Nr Newbury, RG20 8NR Tel: 01488 657670 www.alanwalker-barometers.com

Cheshire
Derek & Tina Rayment Antiques, Orchard House, Barton Rd, Barton, Nr Farndon, SY14 7HT Tel: 01829 270429/07860 666629 and 07702 922410 raymentantiques@aol.com www.antique-barometers.com

BEDS
Wales
Seventh Heaven, Chirk Mill, Chirk, Wrexham, County Borough, LL14 5BU Tel: 01691 777622/773563 requests@seventh-heaven.co.uk www.seventh-heaven.co.uk

Worcestershire
S. W. Antiques, Newlands (Rd), Pershore, WR10 1BP Tel: 01386 555580 sw-antiques@talk21.com www.sw-antiques.co.uk

BOXES & TREEN
Berkshire
Mostly Boxes, 93 High St, Eton, Windsor, SL4 6AF Tel: 01753 858470

Somerset
Alan & Kathy Stacey, By appointment only Tel: 01963 441333 info@antiqueboxes.uk.com www.antiqueboxes.uk.com *Tortoiseshell, ivory, shagreen and mother-of-pearl tea caddies and boxes*

CAMERAS
Kent
Stuart Heggie, 14 The Borough, Northgate, Canterbury, CT1 2DR Tel: 01227 470422 heggie.cameras@virgin.net

CLOCKS
Wiltshire
P. A. Oxley Antique Clocks & Barometers, The Old Rectory, Cherhill, Calne, SN11 8UX Tel: 01249 816227 info@paoxley.com www.british-antiqueclocks.com

USA
R. O. Schmitt Fine Art, Box 1941, Salem, New Hampshire 03079 Tel: 603 893 5915 bob@roschmittfinearts.com www.antiqueclockauction.com

DECORATIVE ARTS
Dorset
Market Street Gallery Ltd t/a Delf Stream Gallery, Bournemouth Tel: 07974 926137 oastman@aol.com www.delfstreamgallery.com

Gloucestershire
Ruskin Decorative Arts, 5 Talbot Court, Stow-on-the-Wold, Cheltenham, GL54 1DP Tel: 01451 832254 william.anne@ruskindecarts.co.uk

Northamptonshire
Aspidistra Antiques, 51 High St, Finedon, Wellingborough, NN9 9JN Tel: 01933 680196 info@aspidistra-antiques.com www.aspidistra.antiques.com

Scotland
decorative arts @ doune, Stand 26, Scottish Antique and Arts Centre, By Doune, Stirling, FK16 6HD Tel: 01786 461 439 decorativearts.doune@btinternet.com www.decorative-doune.com

Republic of Ireland
Mitofsky Antiques, 8 Rathfarnham Rd, Terenure, Dublin 6 Tel: 492 0033 info@mitofskyartdeco.com www.mitofskyartdeco.com

FURNITURE
Hampshire
Millers Antiques Ltd, Netherbrook House, 86 Christchurch Rd, Ringwood, BH24 1DR Tel: 01425 472062 mail@millers-antiques.co.uk www.millers-antiques.co.uk

Kent
Pantiles Spa Antiques, 4, 5, 6 Union House, The Pantiles, Tunbridge Wells, TN4 8HE Tel: 01892 541377 psa.wells@btinternet.com www.antiques-tun-wells-kent.co.uk

Middlesex
Phelps Antiques, 133–135 St Margaret's Rd, Twickenham, TW1 1RG Tel: 020 8892 1778 antiques@phelps.co.uk www.phelps.co.uk

Oxfordshire
The Country Seat, Huntercombe Manor Barn, Henley-on-Thames, RG9 5RY Tel: 01491 641349 wclegg@thecountryseat.com www.thecountryseat.com

Rupert Hitchcox Antiques, Warpsgrove, Nr Chalgrove, Oxford, OX44 7RW Tel: 01865 890241 www.ruperthitchcoxantiques.co.uk

Otter Antiques, 20 High St, Wallingford, OX10 0BP Tel: 01491 825544 otterantiques@fsbdial.co.uk www.antique-boxes.com

Suffolk
Suffolk
Suffolk House Antiques, High St, Yoxford, IP17 3EP Tel: 01728 668122

Warwick
Warwick Antiques Warehouse, Unit 7 Cape Rd Industrial Estate, Cattell Rd, Warwick, CV34 4JN Tel: 01926 498849 aboylin1@tiscali.co.uk

West Midlands
Martin Taylor Antiques, 323 Tettenhall Rd, Wolverhampton, WV6 0JZ Tel: 01902 751166 enquiries@mtaylor-antiques.co.uk www.mtaylor-antiques.co.uk

Wiltshire
Salisbury Antiques Warehouse Ltd, 94 Wilton Rd, Salisbury, SP2 7JJ Tel: 01722 410634 kevin@salisbury-antiques.co.uk

GLASS
Gloucestershire
Grimes House Antiques, High St, Moreton-in-Marsh, GL56 0AT Tel: 01608 651029 grimes_house@cix.co.uk www.grimeshouse.co.uk www.cranberryglass.co.uk

Hampshire
Bonnons Antique Glass, Chandlers Ford Tel: 02380 273900 www.bonnonsantiqueglass.co.uk

London
20th Century Glass, Nigel Benson, Kensington Church St Antique Centre, 58–60 Kensington Church St, W8 4DB Tel: 020 7938 1137 nigelbenson@20thcentury-glass.com www.20thcentury-glass.com

Jasmin Cameron, Antiquarius, 131–141 King's Rd, SW3 4PW Tel: 020 7351 4154 or 01732 459009 jasmin.cameron@mail.com

Jeanette Hayhurst Fine Glass, 32a Kensington Church St, W8 4HA Tel: 020 7938 1539

Andrew Lineham Fine Glass, The Mall, Camden Passage, N1 8ED Tel: 020 7704 0195 or 01243 576241 andrew@andrewlineham.co.uk www.andrewlineham.co.uk

Norfolk
Brian Watson Antique Glass, By appointment only, Foxwarren Cottage, High St, Marsham, Norwich, NR10 5QA Tel: 01263 732519 brian.h.watson@talk21.com

Somerset
Lynda Brine, Assembly Antiques, 6 Saville Row, Bath, BA1 2QP Tel: 01225 448488 lyndabrine@yahoo.co.uk www.scentbottlesandsmalls.co.uk

Somervale Antiques, 6 Radstock Rd, Midsomer Norton, Bath, BA3 2AJ Tel: 01761 412686 ronthomas@somervaleantiques glass.co.uk www.somervaleantiquesglass.co.uk

Come and Visit Tombland Antiques Centre

Norfolk's Premier Antiques Centre

Ideally situated opposite Norwich Cathedral (here we are as seen through one of the Cathedral gateways). Our centre is Augustine Steward House, built by a wealthy merchant in 1549.

<u>Opening hours</u> Monday to Saturday 10.00am until 5.00pm. Plus some Sundays (phone first).

<u>HUGE SELECTION ON THREE FLOORS !!</u>

SPECIALISTS IN: Advertising, Clocks, Collectables, Cranberry glass, Ephemera, Fine and Shipping Furniture, Jewellery, Linen, Militaria, Needlework tools, Silver, Tools, Toys, Staffordshire, etc., etc.

Spaces available from £5.00 per week! For more information www.tomblandantiques.co.uk telephone Bob or Joan Gale 01603 619129 or 01603 761906.

JEWELLERY
London
Shapiro & Co, Stand 380, Gray's
Antique Market, 58 Davies St,
W1K 5LP Tel: 020 7491 2710

KITCHENWARE
Gloucestershire
Bread & Roses, Durham House
Antique Centre, Sheep St, Stow-on-
the-Wold, GL54 1AA Tel: 01451
870404 or 01926 817342

Lincolnshire
Skip & Janie Smithson Antiques.
Tel: 01754 810265 or 07831 399180

East Sussex
Ann Lingard, Ropewalk Antiques,
Rye, TN31 7NA Tel: 01797 223486
ann-lingard@ropewalkantiques.
freeserve.co.uk
*Large selection of hand-finished
English antique pine furniture, kitchen
shop and complementary antiques*

LIGHTING
Devon
The Exeter Antique Lighting Co,
Cellar 15, The Quay, Exeter,
EX2 4AP Tel: 01392 490848
www.antiquelightingcompany.com

MARKETS & CENTRES
Bedfordshire
Woburn Abbey Antiques Centre,
MK17 9WA Tel: 01525 290350
antiques@woburnabbey.co.uk

Derbyshire
Chappells Antiques Centre,
King St, Bakewell, DE45 1DZ
Tel: 01629 812496
ask@chappellsantiquescentre.com
www.chappellsantiques centre.com
*Open Monday–Saturday 10am–5pm,
Sunday 12–5pm. Antique furniture and
furnishings, decorative and collectors
items from 17th to the 20thC*

Heanor Antiques Centre, Ilkeston Rd,
Heanor, DE75 7AE Tel: 01773 531181
sales@heanorantiquescentre.co.uk
www.heanorantiquescentre.co.uk
*Open 7 days. 10.30am–4.30pm. Now
200 independent dealers in new 3
storey extension with stylish cafe*

Gloucestershire
Durham House Antiques Centre,
Sheep St, Stow-on-the-Wold,
GL54 1AA Tel: 01451 870404

The Top Banana Antiques Mall,
1 New Church St, Tetbury, GL8 4DS
Tel: 0871 288 1102
info@topbananaantiques.com
www.topbananaantiques.com

Hampshire
Dolphin Quay Antique Centre,
Queen St, Emsworth, PO10 7BU
Tel: 01243 379994/379994
www.dolphin-quay-antiques.co.uk

London
Northcote Road Antique Market,
155a Northcote Rd, Battersea,
SW11 6QB Tel: 020 7228 6850
clery@btconnect.com
www.spectrumsoft.net/nam
*Open 7 days. 30 dealers offering a
wide variety of antiques & collectables*

Norfolk
Tombland Antiques Centre,
14 Tombland, Norwich, NR3 1HF
Tel: 01603 619129 or 01603 761906
www.tomblandantiques.com

Northamptonshire
The Brackley Antique Cellar, Drayman's
Walk, Brackley, NN13 6BE Tel: 01280
841841 antiquecellar@tesco.net
*30,000 sq ft of floor space with
over 100 antique dealers
specializing in ceramics, porcelain,
clocks, glass, books, dolls, jewellery,
militaria, linen, lace, victoriana,
kitchenalia and furniture*

Nottinghamshire
Dukeries Antiques Centre, Thoresby
Park, Budby, Newark, NG22 9EX
Tel: 01623 822252

Newark Antiques Warehouse Ltd,
Old Kelham Rd, Newark, NG24 1BX
Tel: 01636 674869
enquiries@newarkantiques.co.uk
www.newarkantiques.co.uk

Oxfordshire
The Swan at Tetsworth, High St,
Tetsworth, Nr Thame, OX9 7AB
Tel: 01844 281777
antiques@theswan.co.uk
www.theswan.co.uk

East Sussex
Church Hill Antiques Centre, 6 Station
St, Lewes, BN7 2DA Tel: 01273 474
842 churchhilllewes@aol.com
www.church-hill-antiques.co.uk

Worcestershire
Worcester Antiques Centre,
Reindeer Court, Mealcheapen St,
Worcester, WR1 4DF Tel: 01905
610680 WorcsAntiques@aol.com

OAK & COUNTRY
Cambridgeshire
Mark Seabrook Antiques, PO Box
396, Huntingdon, PE28 0ZA
Tel: 01480 861935
enquiries@markseabrook.com
www.markseabrook.com

Surrey
The Refectory, 38 West St, Dorking,
RH4 1BU Tel: 01306 742111
www.therefectory.co.uk

Oxfordshire
Key Antiques of Chipping Norton,
11 Horsefair, Chipping Norton,
OX7 5AL Tel: 01608 644992
info@keyantiques.com
www.keyantiques.com

ORIENTAL
Buckinghamshire
Glade Antiques, PO Box 873, High
Wycombe, HP14 3ZQ Tel: 01494
882818 sonia@gladeantiques.com
www.gladeantiques.com

London
R & G McPherson Antiques, 40
Kensington Church St, W8 4BX
Tel: 020 7937 0812
rmcpherson@orientalceramics.com
www.orientalceramics.com

Norfolk
Roger Bradbury Antiques,
Church St, Coltishall, NR12 7DJ
Tel: 01603 737444

PAPERWEIGHTS
Cheshire
Sweetbriar Gallery Paperweights
Ltd, 3 Collinson Court, off Church
St, Frodsham, WA6 6PN Tel: 01928
730064 sales@sweetbriar.co.uk
www.sweetbriar.co.uk

Northern Ireland
Marion Langham Limited,
Claranagh, Tempo, Co Fermanagh,
BT94 3FJ Tel: 028 895 41247
marion@ladymarion.co.uk
www.ladymarion.co.uk

USA
The Dunlop Collection, PO Box
6269, Statesville, NC 28687
Tel: (704) 871 2626 or Toll Free
Tel: (800) 227 1996

PINE
Gloucestershire
Cottage Farm Antiques, Stratford Rd,
Aston Subedge, Chipping Campden,
GL55 6PZ Tel: 01386 438263
info@cottagefarmantiques.co.uk
www.cottagefarmantiques.co.uk

Hampshire
Pine Cellars, 39 Jewry St, Winchester,
SO23 8RY Tel: 01962 777546/867014

Nottinghamshire
Harlequin Antiques, 79–81 Mansfield
Rd, Daybrook, Nottingham,
NG5 6BH Tel: 0115 967 4590
sales@antiquepine.net
www.antiquepine.net

Somerset
Westville House Antiques, Westville
House, Littleton, Nr Somerton,
TA11 6NP Tel: 01458 273376
antique@westville.co.uk
www.westville.co.uk

East Sussex
Ann Lingard, Ropewalk Antiques,
Rye, TN31 7NA Tel: 01797 223486
ann-lingard@ropewalkantiques.
freeserve.co.uk
*Large selection of hand-finished
English antique pine furniture, kitchen
shop and complementary antiques*

Republic of Ireland
Bygones of Ireland Ltd, Lodge Rd,
Westport, Co Mayo Tel: 00 353 98
26132/25701 bygones@anu.ie
www.bygones-of-ireland.com

PORCELAIN
Hampshire
The Goss & Crested China Club &
Museum, incorporating Milestone
Publications, 62 Murray Rd, Horndean,

PO8 9JL Tel: (023) 9259 7440
info@gosschinaclub.demon.co.uk
www.gosscrestedchina.co.uk

Northern Ireland
Marion Langham Limited,
Claranagh, Tempo, Co Fermanagh,
BT94 3FJ Tel: 028 895 41247
marion@ladymarion.co.uk
www.ladymarion.co.uk

East Sussex
Tony Horsley, PO Box 3127,
Brighton, BN1 5SS
Tel: 01273 550770

Republic of Ireland
Delphi Antiques, Powerscourt
Townhouse Centre, South William
St, Dublin 2 Tel: 353 1 679 0331

POTTERY
Buckinghamshire
Gillian Neale Antiques, PO Box 247,
Aylesbury, HP20 1JZ Tel: 01296
423754 gillianneale@aol.com
www.gillianealeantiques.com

Derbyshire
Roger de Ville Antiques.
Tel: 01629 812496 or 07798
793857 www.rogerdeville.co.uk

Dorset
Greystoke Antiques, 4 Swan Yard,
(off Cheap St), Sherborne, DT9 3AX
Tel: 01935 812833

Gloucestershire
Peter Scott. Tel: 0117 986 8468 or
07850 639770

Kent
Serendipity, 125 High St, Deal,
CT14 6BB Tel: 01304 369165/
01304 366536
dipityantiques@aol.com

London
Jonathan Horne, 66 Kensington
Church St, W8 4BY
Tel: 020 7221 5658
JH@jonathanhorne.co.uk
www.jonathanhorne.co.uk

Rogers de Rin, 76 Royal Hospital
Rd, SW3 4HN Tel: 020 7352 9007

Oxfordshire
Key Antiques of Chipping Norton,
11 Horsefair, Chipping Norton,
OX7 5AL Tel: 01608 644992
info@keyantiques.com
www.keyantiques.com

Surrey
Judi Bland Antiques. Tel: 01276
857576 or 01536 724145

Tyne & Wear
Ian Sharp Antiques, 23 Front St,
Tynemouth, NE30 4DX
Tel: 0191 296 0656
iansharp@sharpantiques.demon.co.uk
www.sharpantiques.demon.co.uk

Wales
Islwyn Watkins, Offa's Dyke
Antique Centre, 4 High St,
Knighton, Powys, LD7 1AT
Tel: 01547 520145

Wiltshire
Andrew Dando, 34 Market St,
Bradford on Avon, BA15 1LL
Tel: 01225 865444
www.andrewdando.co.uk

Republic of Ireland
George Stacpoole, Main St, Adare,
Co Limerick Tel: 6139 6409
stacpoole@iol.ie

USA
Karen Michelle Guido, Karen
Michelle Antique Tiles, PO Box 62,
Blairsville, PA 15717 Tel: (724) 459
6669 Karen@antiquetiles.com
www.antiquetiles.com

RUGS & CARPETS
Kent
Desmond & Amanda North,
The Orchard, 186 Hale St,
East Peckham, TN12 5JB
Tel: 01622 871353

Scotland
Samarkand Galleries, 16 Howe St,
Edinburgh, EH3 6TD Tel: 0131 225
2010 howe@samarkand.co.uk
www.samarkand.co.uk

SCIENTIFIC INSTRUMENTS
Cheshire
Charles Tomlinson
Tel: 01244 318395
charles.tomlinson@lineone.net
www.lineone.net/-charles.tomlinson

London
Curious Science, 319 Lillie Rd,
Fulham, SW6 7LL
Tel: 020 7610 1175
curiousscience@medical-antiques.com

Scotland
Early Technology, Monkton House,
Old Craighall, Musselburgh, Midlothian,
EH21 8SF Tel: 0131 665 5753
michael.bennett-levy@virgin.net
www.earlytech.com

Somerset
Richard Twort Tel: 01934 641900
or 07711 939789
Science and technology

SILVER
Gloucestershire
Corner House Antiques and Ffoxe
Antiques, The Old Ironmongers
Centre, 5 Burford St, Lechlade,
GL7 3AP Tel: 01367 860078
jdhis007@btopenworld.com
www.corner-house-antiques.co.uk

London
Daniel Bexfield, 26 Burlington
Arcade, W1J 0PU Tel: 020 7491
1720 antiques@bexfield.co.uk
www.bexfield.co.uk
*Specializing in fine quality silver,
jewellery and objects of vertu
dating from the 17th to the 20thC*

West Sussex
Nicholas Shaw Antiques, Virginia
Cottage, Lombard St, Petworth,
GU28 0AG Tel: 01798 345146/
01798 345147 or 07885 643000/
07817 572746
silver@nicholas-shaw.com
www.nicholas-shaw.com

TEXTILES
Devon
Honiton Lace Shop, 44 High St,
Honiton, EX14 1PJ Tel: 01404
42416 shop@honitonlace.com
www.honitonlace.com

Lancashire
Decades, 20 Lord St West,
Blackburn, BB2 1JX
Tel: 01254 693320

London
Linda Gumb, Stand 123, Grays
Antique Market, 58 Davies St,
W1K 5LP Tel: 020 7629 2544
linda@lindagumb.com

Erna Hiscock & John Shepherd,
Chelsea Galleries, 69 Portobello Rd,
W11 Tel: 01233 661407
erna@ernahiscockantiques.com
www.ernahiscockantiques.com

Somerset
Joanna Proops Antique Textiles &
Lighting, 34 Belvedere, Lansdown
Hill, Bath, BA1 5HR Tel: 01225
310795 antiquetextiles@aol.co.uk
www.antiquetextiles.co.uk

USA
Antique European Linens,
PO Box 789, Gulf Breeze, Florida
32562–0789 Tel: 001 850 432
4777 Cell: 850 450 463
name@antiqueeuropeanlinens.com
www.antiqueeuropeanlinens.com

M. Finkel & Daughter, 936 Pine St,
Philadelphia, Pennsylvania
19107–6128 Tel: 215 627 7797
mailbox@finkelantiques.com
www.finkelantiques.com

TOYS
Isle of Wight
Ventnor Junction, 48 High St,
Ventnor, PO38 1LT
Tel: 01983 853996
shop@ventjunc.freeserve.co.uk

TRIBAL ART
Yorkshire
Gordon Reece Galleries, Finkle St,
Knaresborough, HG5 8AA
Tel: 01423 866219
www.gordonreecegalleries.com

WATCHES
Kent
Tempus, Tunbridge Wells Antique
Centre, Union Square, The Pantiles,
Tunbridge Wells Tel: 01932 828936
tempus.watches@tinyonline.co.uk
www.tempus-watches.co.uk

London
Pieces of Time, (1–7 Davies Mews),
26 South Molton Lane, W1Y 2LP
Tel: 020 7629 2422
info@antique-watch.com
www.antique-watch.com

Directory of Auctioneers

Auctioneers who hold frequent sales should contact us on 01580 766411 by July 2004 for inclusion in the next edition.

Bedfordshire
W & H Peacock, 26 Newnham Street, Bedford MK40 3JR
Tel: 01234 266366

Berkshire
Dreweatt Neate, Donnington Priory, Donnington, Newbury RG14 2JE Tel: 01635 553553
fineart@dreweatt-neate.co.uk
www.auctions.dreweatt-neate.co.uk

Law Fine Art, Firs Cottage, Church Lane, Brimpton RG7 4TJ
Tel: 0118 971 0353
info@lawfineart.co.uk
www.lawfineart.co.uk

Special Auction Services, Kennetholme, Midgham, Reading RG7 5UX Tel: 0118 971 2949 www.invaluable.com/sas/

Buckinghamshire
Amersham Auction Rooms, Station Rd, Amersham HP7 0AH
Tel: 01494 729292
info@amershamauctionrooms.co.uk
www.amershamauctionrooms.co.uk

Cambridgeshire
Cheffins, Clifton House, Clifton Rd, Cambridge CB1 7EA
Tel: 01223 213343
www.cheffins.co.uk

Channel Islands
Bonhams and Langlois, Westaway Chambers, 39 Don Street, St Helier, Jersey JE2 4TR
Tel: 01534 722441
www.bonhams.com

Cheshire
Bonhams, New House, 150 Christleton Rd, Chester CH3 5TD
Tel: 01244 313936
www.bonhams.com

Cumbria
Mitchells, Fairfield House, Station Rd, Cockermouth CA13 9PY
Tel: 01900 827800

Penrith Farmers' & Kidd's plc, Skirsgill Salerooms, Penrith CA11 0DN Tel: 01768 890781
penrith.farmers@virgin.net

Devon
Bearnes, St Edmund's Court, Okehampton Street, Exeter EX4 1DU Tel: 01392 422800
nsaintey@bearnes.co.uk
www.bearnes.co.uk

Bonhams, Dowell Street, Honiton EX14 1LX Tel: 01404 41872 www.bonhams.com

Honiton Galleries, 205 High Street, Honiton EX14 1LQ
Tel: 01404 42404
sales@honitongalleries.com
www.honitongalleries.com

Dorset
Hy Duke & Son, Dorchester Fine Art Salerooms, Dorchester DT1 1QS Tel: 01305 265080

Essex
Ambrose, Ambrose House, Old Station Rd, Loughton IG10 4PE
Tel: 020 8502 3951

Sworders, 14 Cambridge Rd, Stansted Mountfitchet CM24 8BZ Tel: 01279 817778
www.sworder.co.uk

Gloucestershire
Mallams, 26 Grosvenor Street, Cheltenham GL52 2SG
Tel: 01242 235712

Tayler & Fletcher, London House, High Street, Bourton-on-the-Water, Cheltenham GL54 2AP

Tel: 01451 821666
bourton@taylerfletcher.com
www.taylerfletcher.com

Herefordshire
Brightwells Fine Art, The Fine Art Saleroom, Ryelands Rd, Leominster HR6 8NZ Tel: 01568 611122 fineart@brightwells.co.uk
www.brightwells.com

Hertfordshire
Tring Market Auctions, Brook Street, Tring HP23 5EF
Tel: 01442 826446
sales@tringmarketauctions.co.uk
www.tringmarketauctions.co.uk

Kent
Bonhams, 49 London Rd, Sevenoaks TN13 1AR Tel: 01732 740310 www.bonhams.com

Bracketts, The Auction Hall, The Pantiles, Tunbridge Wells TN2 5QL Tel: 01892 544500
sales@bfaa.co.uk
www.bfaa.co.uk

The Canterbury Auction Galleries, 40 Station Rd West, Canterbury CT2 8AN
Tel: 01227 763337
auctions@thecanterburyauctiongalleries.com
www.thecanterburyauctiongalleries.com

Mervyn Carey, Twysden Cottage, Scullsgate, Benenden, Cranbrook TN17 4LD Tel: 01580 240283

London
Bonhams, Montpelier Street, Knightsbridge SW7 1HH Tel: 020 7393 3900 www.bonhams.com

Bonhams, 101 New Bond Street W1S 1SR Tel: 020 7629 6602
www.bonhams.com

Bonhams, 10 Salem Rd, Bayswater W2 4DL Tel: 020 7229 9090 www.bonhams.com

Bonhams, 65–69 Lots Rd, Chelsea SW10 0RN Tel: 020 7393 3900 www.bonhams.com

Cooper Owen, 10 Denmark Street WC2H 8LS Tel: 020 7240 4132 www.CooperOwen.com

Dix-Noonan-Webb, 1 Old Bond Street W1S 4PB Tel: 020 7499 5022 auctions@dnw.co.uk
www.dnw.co.uk

Sotheby's, 34–35 New Bond Street W1A 2AA Tel: 020 7293 5000 www.sothebys.com

Sotheby's Olympia, Hammersmith Rd, W14 8UX
Tel: 020 7293 5555
www.sothebys.com

Nottinghamshire
Neales, 192 Mansfield Rd, Nottingham NG1 3HU Tel: 0115 962 4141 fineart@neales.co.uk
www.neales-auctions.com

Oxfordshire
Bonhams, 39 Park End Street, Oxford OX1 1JD Tel: 01865 723524 www.bonhams.com

Holloway's, 49 Parsons Street, Banbury OX16 5PF
Tel: 01295 817777
enquiries@hollowaysauctioneers.co.uk
www.hollowaysauctioneers.co.uk

Scotland
Bonhams, 65 George Street, Edinburgh EH2 2JL Tel: 0131 225 2266 www.bonhams.com

Thomson, Roddick & Medcalf Ltd, 60 Whitesands, Dumfries DG1 2RS Tel: 01387 255366

Shropshire
Walker, Barnett & Hill, Cosford Auction Rooms, Long Lane, Cosford TF11 8PJ Tel: 01902 375555
wbhauctions@lineone.net
www.walker-barnett-hill.co.uk

Somerset
Bonhams, 1 Old King Street, Bath BA1 2JT Tel: 01225 788 988 www.bonhams.com

Lawrences Fine Art Auctioneers, South Street, Crewkerne TA18 8AB Tel: 01460 73041

Staffordshire
Wintertons Ltd, Lichfield Auction Centre, Fradley Park, Lichfield WS13 6NU Tel: 01543 263256
Photos: Courtesy of Crown Photos Tel: 01283 762813

Suffolk
Olivers, Olivers Rooms, Burkitts Lane, Sudbury CO10 1HB
Tel: 01787 880305
oliversauctions@btconnect.com

Surrey
Ewbank, Burnt Common Auction Rooms, London Rd, Send, Woking GU23 7LN
Tel: 01483 223101
antiques@ewbankauctions.co.uk
www.ewbankauctions.co.uk

Hamptons International, Baverstock House, 93 High Street, Godalming GU7 1AL
Tel: 01483 423567
fineartauctions@hamptons-int.co.uk www.hamptons-int.co.uk

East Sussex
Gorringes Auction Galleries, Terminus Rd, Bexhill-on-Sea TN39 3LR Tel: 01424 212994
bexhill@gorringes.co.uk
www.gorringes.co.uk

Gorringes inc Julian Dawson, 15 North Street, Lewes BN7 2PD
Tel: 01273 478221
auctions@gorringes.co.uk
www.gorringes.co.uk

Wallis & Wallis, West Street Auction Galleries, Lewes BN7 2NJ Tel: 01273 480208
auctions@wallisandwallis.co.uk
grb@wallisandwallis.co.uk
www.wallisandwallis.co.uk

West Sussex
Rupert Toovey & Co Ltd, Spring Gardens, Washington RH20 3BS
Tel: 01903 891955
auctions@rupert-toovey.com
www.rupert-toovey.com

Sotheby's Sussex, Summers Place, Billingshurst RH14 9AD
Tel: 01403 833500
www.sothebys.com

Warwickshire
Locke & England, 18 Guy Street, Leamington Spa CV32 4RT
Tel: 01926 889100
www.auctions-online.com/locke

West Midlands
Bonhams, The Old House, Station Rd, Knowle, Solihull B93 0HT
Tel: 01564 776151
www.bonhams.com

Fellows & Sons, Augusta House, 19 Augusta Street, Hockley, Birmingham B18 6JA Tel: 0121 212 2131 info@fellows.co.uk
www.fellows.co.uk

Wiltshire
Finan & Co, The Square, Mere BA12 6DJ Tel: 01747 861411
post@finanandco.co.uk
www.finanandco.co.uk

Woolley & Wallis, Salisbury Salerooms, 51–61 Castle Street, Salisbury SP1 3SU
Tel: 01722 424500/411854
mail@salisbury.w-w.co.uk
www.w-w.co.uk

Yorkshire
Bonhams, 17a East Parade, Leeds LS1 2BH Tel: 0113 244 8011
www.bonhams.com

Dee, Atkinson & Harrison, The Exchange Saleroom, Driffield YO25 6LD Tel: 01377 253151
exchange@dee-atkinson-harrison.co.uk
www.dahauctions.com

David Duggleby, The Vine St Salerooms, Scarborough YO11 1XN Tel: 01723 507111
auctions@davidduggleby.freeserve.co.uk
www.davidduggleby.com

Andrew Hartley, Victoria Hall Salerooms, Little Lane, Ilkley LS29 8EA Tel: 01943 816363
info@andrewhartleyfinearts.co.uk
www.andrewhartleyfinearts.co.uk

Tennants, The Auction Centre, Harmby Rd, Leyburn DL8 5SG
Tel: 01969 623780
enquiry@tennants-ltd.co.uk
www.tennants.co.uk

Australia
Leonard Joel Auctioneers, 333 Malvern Rd, South Yarra, Victoria 3141 Tel: 03 9826 4333
decarts@ljoel.com.au
jewellery@ljoel.com.au
www.ljoel.com.au

Shapiro Auctioneers, 162 Queen Street, Woollahra, Sydney NSW 2025 Tel: 612 9326 1588

Austria
Dorotheum, Palais Dorotheum, A–1010 Wien, Dorotheergasse 17, 1010 Vienna Tel: 515 60 229
client.services@dorotheum.at

Mexico
Galeria Louis C. Morton, GLC A7073L IYS, Monte Athos 179, Col. Lomas de Chapultepec CP11000 Tel: 52 5520 5005
glmorton@prodigy.net.mx
www.lmorton.com

Monaco
Bonhams, Le Beau Rivage, 9 Avenue d'Ostende, Monte Carlo MC 98000 Tel: +41 (0)22 300 3160 www.bonhams.com

Netherlands
Sotheby's Amsterdam, De Boelelaan 30, Amsterdam 1083 HJ Tel: 31 20 550 2200 www.sothebys.com

Republic of Ireland
Hamilton Osborne King, 4 Main Street, Blackrock, Co Dublin
Tel: 353 1 288 5011
blackrock@hok.ie www.hok.ie

Sweden
Bukowskis, Arsenalsgatan 4, Stockholm Tel: +46 (8) 614 08 00 info@bukowskis.se
www.bukowskis.se

USA
Jackson's Auctioneers & Appraisers, 2229 Lincoln Street, Cedar Falls IA 50613
Tel: 506 1331 9277 2256

New Orleans Auction Galleries, Inc, 801 Magazine Street, AT 510 Julia, New Orleans, Louisiana 70130 Tel: 504 566 1849

Sotheby's, 1334 York Avenue at 72nd St, New York NY 10021
Tel: 212 606 7000
www.sothebys.com

Key to Illustrations

Each illustration and descriptive caption is accompanied by a letter code. By referring to the following list of auctioneers (denoted by ⟋) and dealers (⊞), the source of any item may be immediately determined. Inclusion in this edition no way constitutes or implies a contract or binding offer on the part of any of our contributors to supply or sell the goods illustrated, or similar articles, at the prices stated. Advertisers in this year's directory are denoted by †.

If you require a valuation, it is advisable to check whether the dealer or specialist will carry out this service and if there is a charge. Please mention Miller's when making an enquiry. A valuation by telephone is not possible. Most dealers are willing to help you with your enquiry; however, they may be very busy and consideration of the above points would be welcomed.

A&O ⊞ Ancient & Oriental Ltd Tel: 01664 812044 alex@antiquities.co.uk www.antiquities.co.uk

AB ⊞ The Antique Barometer Company, 5 The Lower Mall, 359 Upper Street, Camden Passage, London N1 0PD Tel: 020 7226 4992 sales@antiquebarometer.com www.antiquebarometer.com

AG ⟋ Anderson & Garland (Auctioneers), Marlborough House, Marlborough Crescent, Newcastle-upon-Tyne, Tyne & Wear NE1 4EE Tel: 0191 232 6278

AH ⟋† Andrew Hartley, Victoria Hall Salerooms, Little Lane, Ilkley, Yorkshire LS29 8EA Tel: 01943 816363 info@andrewhartleyfinearts.co.uk www.andrewhartleyfinearts.co.uk

AL ⊞† Ann Lingard, Ropewalk Antiques, Rye, East Sussex TN31 7NA Tel: 01797 223486 ann-lingard@ropewalkantiques.freeserve.co.uk

AMB ⟋ Ambrose, Ambrose House, Old Station Road, Loughton, Essex IG10 4PE Tel: 020 8502 3951

AnAr ⊞ Ancient Art, 85 The Vale, Southgate, London N14 6AT Tel: 020 8882 1509 ancient.art@btinternet.com www.ancientart.co.uk

ANG ⊞† Ancient & Gothic, PO Box 5390, Bournemouth, Dorset BH7 6XR Tel: 01202 431721

ARB ⊞ Arbour Antiques Ltd, Poet's Arbour, Sheep Street, Stratford-on-Avon, Warwickshire CV37 6EF Tel: 01789 293453

ASP ⊞ Aspidistra Antiques, 51 High Street, Finedon, Wellingborough, Northamptonshire NN9 9JN Tel: 01933 680196 info@aspidistra-antiques.com www.aspidistra.antiques.com

B ⟋ Bonhams, 101 New Bond Street, London W1S 1SR Tel: 020 7629 6602 www.bonhams.com

B(Ba) ⟋ Bonhams, 10 Salem Road, Bayswater, London W2 4DL Tel: 020 7229 9090

B(Ch) ⟋ Bonhams, 65–69 Lots Road, Chelsea, London SW10 0RN Tel: 020 7393 3900

B(Kn) ⟋ Bonhams, Montpelier Street, Knightsbridge, London SW7 1HH Tel: 020 7393 3900

B(NW) ⟋ Bonhams, New House, 150 Christleton Road, Chester, Cheshire CH3 5TD Tel: 01244 313936

B(W) ⟋ Bonhams, Dowell Street, Honiton, Devon EX14 1LX Tel: 01404 41872

B&L ⟋ Bonhams and Langlois, Westaway Chambers, 39 Don Street, St Helier, Jersey, Channel Islands JE2 4TR Tel: 01534 722441

BAu ⟋ Bloomington Auction Gallery, 300 East Grove St, Bloomington, Illinois 61701, USA Tel: 001 309 828 5533 joyluke@aol.com www.joyluke.com

BBR ⟋ BBR, Elsecar Heritage Centre, Elsecar, Barnsley, S. Yorks S74 8HJ Tel: 01226 745156 sales@onlinebbr.com www.onlinebbr.com

Bea/ Bea(E) ⟋ Bearnes, St Edmund's Court, Okehampton Street, Exeter, Devon EX4 1DU Tel: 01392 207000 enquiries@bearnes.co.uk www.bearnes.co.uk

BERN ⟋ Bernaerts, Verlatstraat 18–22, 2000 Antwerpen/Anvers, Belgium Tel: +32 (0)3 248 19 21 edmond.bernaerts@ping.be www.auction-bernaerts.com

BEX ⊞† Daniel Bexfield, 26 Burlington Arcade, London W1J 0PU Tel: 020 7491 1720 antiques@bexfield.co.uk www.bexfield.co.uk

BIG ⟋ Bigwood Auctioneers Ltd, The Old School, Tiddington, Stratford-upon-Avon, Warwickshire CV37 7AW Tel: 01789 269415

Bns ⊞ Brittons Jewellers, 4 King Street, Clitheroe, Lancashire BB7 2EP Tel: 01200 425555 info@brittons-watches.co.uk www.brittons-watches.co.uk www.antique-jewelry.co.uk

BR ⟋ Bracketts, The Auction Hall, The Pantiles, Tunbridge Wells, Kent TN2 5QL Tel: 01892 544500 sales@bfaa.co.uk www.bfaa.co.uk

BROW ⊞ David Brower, 113 Kensington Church Street, London W8 7LN Tel: 020 7221 4155 David@davidbrower-antiques.com www.davidbrower-antiques.com

BRU ⊞ Brunel Antiques, Bartlett Street Antiques Centre, Bath, Somerset BA1 2QZ Tel: 0117 968 1734

BrW ⊞ Brian Watson Antique Glass, (by appointment only), Foxwarren Cottage, High Street, Marsham, Norwich, Norfolk NR10 5QA Tel: 01263 732519 brian.h.watson@talk21.com

BWL ⟋ Brightwells Fine Art, The Fine Art Saleroom, Ryelands Road, Leominster, Herefordshire HR6 8NZ Tel: 01568 611122 fineart@brightwells.com www.brightwells.com

Byl ⊞ Bygones of Ireland Ltd, Lodge Road, Westport, Co Mayo, Republic of Ireland Tel: 00 353 98 26132/25701 bygones@anu.ie www.bygones-of-ireland.com

C&R ⊞ Catchpole & Rye, Saracens Dairy, Jobbs Lane, Pluckley, Ashford, Kent TN27 0SA Tel: 01233 840840 info@crye.co.uk www.crye.co.uk

C&W ⊞ Carroll & Walker. Tel: 01877 385618

CGC 🔨 Cheffins, Clifton House, Clifton Road, Cambridge CB1 7EA Tel: 01223 213343 www.cheffins.co.uk

CHAC ⊞ Church Hill Antiques Centre, 6 Station Street, Lewes, East Sussex BN7 2DA Tel: 01273 474 842 churchhilllewes@aol.com www.church-hill-antiques.co.uk

ChC ⊞ Christopher Clarke (Antiques) Ltd, The Fosse Way, Stow-on-the-Wold, Gloucestershire GL54 1JS Tel: 01451 830476 cclarkeantiques@aol.com www.campaignfurniture.com

Che ⊞ Chevertons of Edenbridge Ltd, 71–73 High Street, Edenbridge, Kent TN8 5AL Tel: 01732 863196

CoCo ⊞ Country Collector, 11–12 Birdgate, Pickering, Yorkshire YO18 7AL Tel: 01751 477481

COF ⊞ Cottage Farm Antiques, Stratford Road, Aston Subedge, Chipping Campden, Gloucestershire GL55 6PZ Tel: 01386 438263 info@cottagefarmantiques.co.uk www.cottagefarmantiques.co.uk

CoS ⊞ Corrine Soffe. Tel: 01295 730317 soffe@btinternet.co.uk

CuS ⊞ Curious Science, 319 Lillie Road, Fulham, London SW6 7LL Tel: 020 7610 1175 curioussience@medical-antiques.com

DA 🔨 Dee, Atkinson & Harrison, The Exchange Saleroom, Driffield, East Yorkshire YO25 6LD Tel: 01377 253151 exchange@dee-atkinson-harrison.co.uk www.dahauctions.com

DAN ⊞ Andrew Dando, 34 Market Street, Bradford-on-Avon, Wiltshire BA15 1LL Tel: 01225 865444 www.andrewdando.co.uk

DAV ⊞ Hugh Davies, The Packing Shop, 6–12 Ponton Road, London SW8 5BA Tel: 020 7498 3255

DD 🔨 David Duggleby, The Vine St Salerooms, Scarborough, Yorkshire YO11 1XN Tel: 01723 507111 auctions@davidduggleby.freeserve.co.uk www.davidduggleby.com

DFA ⊞ Delvin Farm Antiques, Gormonston, Co Meath, Republic of Ireland Tel: 353 1 841 2285 info@delvinfarmpine.com john@delvinfarmpine.com www.delvinfarmpine.com

DIA ⊞ Mark Diamond London. Tel: 020 8508 4479 mark.diamond@dial.pipex.com

DN 🔨 Dreweatt Neate, Donnington Priory, Donnington, Newbury, Berkshire RG14 2JE Tel: 01635 553553 fineart@dreweatt-neate.co.uk www.auctions.dreweatt-neate.co.uk

DORO 🔨 Dorotheum, Palais Dorotheum, A–1010 Wien, Dorotheergasse 17, 1010 Vienna, Austria Tel: 515 60 229 client.services@dorotheum.at

DSA ⊞ David Scriven Antiques, PO Box 1962, Leigh-on-Sea, Essex SS9 2YZ Tel: 07887 716677 david@david-scriven-antiques.fsnet.co.uk

DuM 🔨 Du Mouchelles, 409 East Jefferson, Detroit, Michigan 48226, USA Tel: 313 963 6255

E 🔨 Ewbank, Burnt Common Auction Rooms, London Road, Send, Woking, Surrey GU23 7LN Tel: 01483 223101 antiques@ewbankauctions.co.uk www.ewbankauctions.co.uk

EAL ⊞ The Exeter Antique Lighting Co, Cellar 15, The Quay, Exeter, Devon EX2 4AP Tel: 01392 490848 www.antiquelightingcompany.com

EH 🔨 Edgar Horns, 46–50 South Street, Eastbourne, East Sussex BN21 4XB Tel: 01323 410419 sales@edgarhorns.com www.edgarhorns.com

F&F ⊞ Fenwick & Fenwick, 88–90 High Street, Broadway, Worcestershire WR12 7AJ Tel: 01386 853227/841724

FHF 🔨† Fellows & Sons, Augusta House, 19 Augusta Street, Hockley, Birmingham, West Midlands B18 6JA Tel: 0121 212 2131 info@fellows.co.uk www.fellows.co.uk

FU ⊞ Fu Ts'ang Lung, Rotherham, Yorkshire Tel: 01709 829805 futsanglung@hotmail.com

G(B) 🔨 Gorringes Auction Galleries, Terminus Road, Bexhill-on-Sea, East Sussex TN39 3LR Tel: 01424 212994 bexhill@gorringes.co.uk www.gorringes.co.uk

G(L) 🔨 Gorringes inc Julian Dawson, 15 North Street, Lewes, East Sussex BN7 2PD Tel: 01273 478221 auctions@gorringes.co.uk www.gorringes.co.uk

G&CC ⊞ The Goss & Crested China Club & Museum, incorporating Milestone Publications, 62 Murray Road, Horndean, Hampshire PO8 9JL Tel: 023 9259 7440 info@gosschinaclub.demon.co.uk www.gosscrestedchina.co.uk

G&G ⊞ Guest & Gray, 1–7 Davies Mews, London W1K 5AB Tel: 020 7408 1252 info@chinese-porcelain-art.com www.chinese-porcelain-art.com

GBr ⊞ Geoffrey Breeze Antiques, 6 George Street, Bath, Somerset BA1 2EH Tel: 01225 466499

GLD ⊞ Glade Antiques, PO Box 873, High Wycombe, Buckinghamshire HP14 3ZQ Tel: 01494 882818 sonia@gladeantiques.com www.gladeantiques.com

GRe ⊞ Greystoke Antiques, 4 Swan Yard, (off Cheap Street), Sherborne, Dorset DT9 3AX Tel: 01935 812833

GRG ⊞ Gordon Reece Galleries, Finkle Street, Knaresborough, Yorkshire HG5 8AA Tel: 01423 866219 www.gordonreecegalleries.com

GRI ⊞ Grimes House Antiques, High Street, Moreton-in-Marsh, Gloucestershire GL56 0AT Tel: 01608 651029 grimes_house@cix.co.uk www.grimeshouse.co.uk www.cranberryglass.co.uk

HEL ⊞ Helios Gallery, 292 Westbourne Grove, London W11 2PS Tel: 077 11 955 997 heliosgallery@btinternet.com www.heliosgallery.com

HiA ⊞ Rupert Hitchcox Antiques, Warpsgrove, Nr Chalgrove, Oxford OX44 7RW Tel: 01865 890241 www.ruperthitchcoxantiques.co.uk

HIS ⊞ Erna Hiscock & John Shepherd, Chelsea Galleries, 69 Portobello Road, London W11 Tel: 01233 661407 erna@ernahiscockantiques.com www.ernahiscockantiques.com

HL ⊞ Honiton Lace Shop, 44 High Street, Honiton, Devon EX14 1PJ Tel: 01404 42416 shop@honitonlace.com www.honitonlace.com

HOK 🔨 Hamilton Osborne King, 4 Main Street, Blackrock, Co Dublin, Republic of Ireland Tel: 353 1 288 5011 blackrock@hok.ie www.hok.ie

HOLL 🔨 Holloway's, 49 Parsons Street, Banbury, Oxfordshire OX16 5PF Tel: 01295 817777 enquiries@hollowaysauctioneers.co.uk www.hollowaysauctioneers.co.uk

HRQ ⊞ Harlequin Antiques, 79–81 Mansfield Road, Daybrook, Nottingham NG5 6BH Tel: 0115 967 4590 sales@antiquepine.net www.antiquepine.net

HUM ⊞ Humbleyard Fine Art, Unit 32 Admiral Vernon Arcade, Portobello Road, London W11 2DY Tel: 01362 637793

HYD 🔨 Hy Duke & Son, Dorchester Fine Art Salerooms, Dorchester, Dorset DT1 1QS Tel: 01305 265080

IM 🔨 Ibbett Mosely, 125 High Street, Sevenoaks, Kent TN13 1UT Tel: 01732 456731 auctions@ibbettmosely.co.uk www.ibbettmosely.co.uk

J&J ⊞ J & J's, Paragon Antiquities, Antiques & Collectors Market, 3 Bladud Buildings, The Paragon, Bath, Somerset BA1 5LS Tel: 01225 463715

JAd 🔨 James Adam & Sons, 26 St Stephen's Green, Dublin 2, Republic of Ireland Tel: 00 3531 676 0261 www.jamesadam.ie

JAS ⊞ Jasmin Cameron, Antiquarius, 131–141 King's Road, London SW3 4PW Tel: 020 7351 4154 or 01732 459009 jasmin.cameron@mail.com

JAY ⊞ Jaycee Bee Antiques

JDJ 🔨 James D. Julia, Inc, PO Box 830, Rte. 201 Skowhegan Road, Fairfield ME 04937, USA Tel: 207 453 7125 jjulia@juliaauctions.com www.juliaauctions.com

JeH ⊞ Jennie Horrocks. Tel: 07836 264896 gallery@aw18.fsnet.co.uk info@artnouveaulighting.co.uk www.artnouveaulighting.co.uk

JHa ⊞ Jeanette Hayhurst Fine Glass, 32a Kensington Church Street, London W8 4HA Tel: 020 7938 1539

JHo ⊞ Jonathan Horne, 66 Kensington Church Street, London, W8 4BY Tel: 020 7221 5658 JH@jonathanhorne.co.uk www.jonathanhorne.co.uk

JOA ⊞† Joan Gale Antiques Dealer, Tombland Antiques Centre, 14 Tombland, Norwich, Norfolk NR3 1HF Tel: 01603 619129 joan.gale@ukgateway.net

JPr ⊞ Joanna Proops Antique Textiles & Lighting, 34 Belvedere, Lansdown Hill, Bath, Somerset BA1 5HR Tel: 01225 310795 antiquetextiles@aol.co.uk www.antiquetextiles.co.uk

JRe ⊞ John Read, 29 Lark Rise, Martlesham Heath, Ipswich, Suffolk IP5 7SA Tel: 01473 624897

K&D ⊞ Kembery Antique Clocks Ltd, Bartlett Street Antiques Centre, 5 Bartlett Street, Bath, Somerset BA1 2QZ Tel: 0117 956 5281 kembery@kdclocks.co.uk www.kdclocks.co.uk

KEY ⊞ Key Antiques of Chipping Norton, 11 Horsefair, Chipping Norton, Oxfordshire OX7 5AL Tel: 01608 644992 info@keyantiques.com www.keyantiques.com

KMG ⊞ Karen Michelle Guido, Karen Michelle Antique Tiles, PO Box 62, Blairsville PA 15717, USA Tel: (724) 459 6669 Karen@antiquetiles.com www.antiquetiles.com

L 🔨 Lawrences Fine Art Auctioneers, South Street, Crewkerne, Somerset TA18 8AB Tel: 01460 73041

L&E 🔨 Locke & England, 18 Guy Street, Leamington Spa, Warwickshire CV32 4RT Tel: 01926 889100 www.auctions-online.com/locke

LBr ⊞ Lynda Brine, Assembly Antiques, 6 Saville Row, Bath, Somerset BA1 2QP Tel: 01225 448488 lyndabrine@yahoo.co.uk www.scentbottlesandsmalls.co.uk

LCM 🔨 Galeria Louis C. Morton, GLC A7073L IYS, Monte Athos 179, Col. Lomas de Chapultepec CP11000, Mexico Tel: 52 5520 5005 glmorton@prodigy.net.mx www.lmorton.com

LFA 🔨 Law Fine Art, Firs Cottage, Church Lane, Brimpton, Berkshire RG7 4TJ Tel: 0118 971 0353 info@lawfineart.co.uk www.lawfineart.co.uk

LGU ⊞ Linda Gumb, Stand 123, Grays Antique Market, 58 Davies Street, London W1K 5LP Tel: 020 7629 2544 linda@lindagumb.com

MAA ⊞ Mario's Antiques. Tel: 020 7226 2426 or 07956 580772 marwan@barazi.screaming.net www.marios_antiques.com

MB ⊞ Mostly Boxes, 93 High Street, Eton, Windsor, Berkshire SL4 6AF Tel: 01753 858470

MCC ⊞ M. C. Chapman Antiques, Bell Hill, Finedon, Northamptonshire NN9 5NB Tel: 01933 681260

McP ⊞ R & G McPherson Antiques, 40 Kensington Church Street, London W8 4BX Tel: 020 7937 0812 rmcpherson@orientalceramics.com www.orientalceramics.com

MDL ⊞ Michael D. Long Ltd, 96–98 Derby Road, Nottingham NG1 5FB Tel: 0115 941 3307 sales@michaeldlong.com www.michaeldlong.com

MFB ⊞ Manor Farm Barn Antiques. Tel: 01296 658941 or 07720 286607 mfbn@btinternet.com btwebworld.com/mfbantiques

MI ⊞ Mitofsky Antiques, 8 Rathfarnham Road, Terenure, Dublin 6, Republic of Ireland Tel: 492 0033 info@mitofskyartdeco.com www.mitofskyartdeco.com

Mit 🔨 Mitchells, Fairfield House, Station Road, Cockermouth, Cumbria CA13 9PY Tel: 01900 827800

MLa ⊞ Marion Langham Limited, Claranagh, Tempo, Co Fermanagh, Northern Ireland BT94 3FJ Tel: 028 895 41247 marion@ladymarion.co.uk www.ladymarion.co.uk

MLL ⊞ Millers Antiques Ltd, Netherbrook House, 86 Christchurch Road, Ringwood, Hampshire BH24 1DR Tel: 01425 472062 mail@millers-antiques.co.uk www.millers-antiques.co.uk

NAW ⊞ Newark Antiques Warehouse Ltd, Old Kelham Road, Newark, Nottinghamshire NG24 1BX Tel: 01636 674869 enquiries@newarkantiques.co.uk www.newarkantiques.co.uk

NES ⚒ D. M. Nesbit & Co, Fine Art and Auction Department, Southsea Salerooms, 7 Clarendon Road, Southsea, Hampshire PO5 2ED Tel: 023 9286 4321 auctions@nesbits.co.uk www.nesbits.co.uk

NOA ⚒ New Orleans Auction Galleries, Inc, 801 Magazine Street, AT 510 Julia, New Orleans, Louisiana 70130, USA Tel: 504 566 1849

OLA ⊞ Olliff's Architectural Antiques, 19–21 Lower Redland Road, Redland, Bristol, Gloucestershire BS6 6TB Tel: 0117 923 9232 marcus@olliffs.com www.olliffs.com

OLD ⊞ Oldnautibits, PO Box 67, Langport, Somerset TA10 9WJ Tel: 01458 241816 geoff.pringle@oldnautibits.com www.oldnautibits.com

OTT ⊞ Otter Antiques, 20 High Street, Wallingford, Oxfordshire OX10 0BP Tel: 01491 825544 otterantiques@fsbdial.co.uk www.antique-boxes.com

P&T ⊞ Pine & Things, Portobello Farm, Campden Road, Nr Shipston-on-Stour, Warwickshire CV36 4PY Tel: 01608 663849 www.pinethings.co.uk

PaA ⊞ Pastorale Antiques, 15 Malling Street, Lewes, East Sussex BN7 2RA Tel: 01273 473259 or 01435 863044 pastorale@btinternet.com

PAS ⊞ Tina Pasco, Waterlock House, Wingham, Nr Canterbury, Kent CT3 1BH Tel: 01227 722151 tinapasco@tinapasco.com www.tinapasco.com

Penn ⊞ Penny Fair Antiques. Tel: 07860 825456

PF ⚒ Peter Francis, Curiosity Sale Room, 19 King Street, Carmarthen SA31 1BH, Wales Tel: 01267 233456 Peterfrancis@valuers.fsnet.co.uk www.peterfrancis.co.uk

PFK ⚒ Penrith Farmers' & Kidd's plc, Skirsgill Salerooms, Penrith, Cumbria CA11 0DN Tel: 01768 890781 penrith.farmers@virgin.net www.penrithfarmers.co.uk

PGO ⊞ Pamela Goodwin, 11 The Pantiles, Royal Tunbridge Wells, Kent TN2 5TD Tel: 01892 618200 mail@goodwinantiques.co.uk www.goodwinantiques.co.uk

PICA ⊞ Piccadilly Antiques, 280 High Street, Batheaston, Bath BA1 7RA Tel: 01225 851494 piccadillyantiques@ukonline.co.uk

PSA ⊞ Pantiles Spa Antiques, 4, 5, 6 Union House, The Pantiles, Tunbridge Wells, Kent TN4 8HE Tel: 01892 541377 psa.wells@btinternet.com www.antiques-tun-wells-kent.co.uk

PT ⊞ Pieces of Time, (1–7 Davies Mews), 26 South Molton Lane, London W1Y 2LP Tel: 020 7629 2422 info@antique-watch.com www.antique-watch.com

QM ⊞ The Quiet Man, Core One, The Gas Works, 2 Michael Road, London SW6 2AN Tel: 020 7736 3384 cullis24@hotmail.com

RdV ⊞ Roger de Ville Antiques. Tel: 01629 812496 or 07798 793857 www.rogerdeville.co.uk

RGe ⊞ Rupert Gentle Antiques, The Manor House, Milton Lilbourne, Nr Pewsey, Wiltshire SN9 5LQ Tel: 01672 563344

RIT ⚒ Ritchies Inc, Auctioneers & Appraisers of Antiques & Fine Art, 288 King Street East, Toronto, Ontario M5A 1K4, Canada Tel: (416) 364 1864 auction@ritchies.com www.ritchies.com

ROSc ⚒ R. O. Schmitt Fine Art, Box 1941, Salem, New Hampshire 03079, USA Tel: 603 893 5915 bob@roschmittfinearts.com www.antiqueclockauction.com

RPh ⊞ Phelps Antiques, 133–135 St Margaret's Road, Twickenham, Middlesex TW1 1RG Tel: 020 8892 1778 antiques@phelps.co.uk www.phelps.co.uk

RTo ⚒ Rupert Toovey & Co Ltd, Spring Gardens, Washington, West Sussex RH20 3BS Tel: 01903 891955 auctions@rupert-toovey.com www.rupert-toovey.com

RUSK ⊞ Ruskin Decorative Arts, 5 Talbot Court, Stow-on-the-Wold, Cheltenham, Gloucestershire GL54 1DP Tel: 01451 832254 william.anne@ruskindecarts.co.uk

S ⚒ Sotheby's, 34–35 New Bond Street, London W1A 2AA Tel: 020 7293 5000 www.sothebys.com

S(Am) ⚒ Sotheby's Amsterdam, De Boelelaan 30, Amsterdam 1083 HJ, Netherlands Tel: 31 20 550 2200

S(NY) ⚒ Sotheby's, 1334 York Avenue at 72nd St, New York NY 10021, USA Tel: 212 606 7000

S(O) ⚒ Sotheby's Olympia, Hammersmith Road, London W14 8UX Tel: 020 7293 5555

S(S) ⚒ Sotheby's Sussex, Summers Place, Billingshurst, West Sussex RH14 9AD Tel: 01403 833500

SAM ⊞ Samarkand Galleries, 16 Howe Street, Edinburgh EH3 6TD, Scotland Tel: 0131 225 2010 howe@samarkand.co.uk www.samarkand.co.uk

Sama ⊞ Samax, Bartlett Street Antiques Centre, 5–10 Bartlett Street, Bath, Somerset BA1 2QZ Tel: 01225 466689

SAS ⚒ Special Auction Services, Kennetholme, Midgham, Reading, Berkshire RG7 5UX Tel: 0118 971 2949 www.invaluable.com/sas/

SAT ⊞ The Swan at Tetsworth, High Street, Tetsworth, Nr Thame, Oxfordshire OX9 7AB Tel: 01844 281777 antiques@theswan.co.uk www.theswan.co.uk

SAW ⊞ Salisbury Antiques Warehouse Ltd, 94 Wilton Road, Salisbury, Wiltshire SP2 7JJ Tel: 01722 410634 kevin@salisbury-antiques.co.uk

SCO ⊞ Peter Scott. Tel: 0117 986 8468 or 07850 639770

SDA ⊞ Stephanie Davison Antiques, Bakewell Antiques Centre, King Street, Bakewell, Derbyshire DE45 1DZ Tel: 01629 812496 ask@chappellsantiquescentre.com www.stephaniedavisonantiques.com/

SEA ⊞ Mark Seabrook Antiques, PO Box 396, Huntingdon, Cambridgeshire PE28 0ZA Tel: 01480 861935 enquiries@markseabrook.com www.markseabrook.com

SeH ⊞ Seventh Heaven, Chirk Mill, Chirk, Wrexham, County Borough LL14 5BU, Wales Tel: 01691 777622/773563 requests@seventh-heaven.co.uk www.seventh-heaven.co.uk

SMI ⊞† Skip & Janie Smithson Antiques. Tel: 01754 810265 or 07831 399180

Som ⊞ Somervale Antiques, 6 Radstock Road, Midsomer Norton, Bath, Somerset BA3 2AJ Tel: 01761 412686 ronthomas@somervaleantiquesglass.co.uk www.somervaleantiquesglass.co.uk

STA ⊞ George Stacpoole, Main Street, Adare, Co Limerick, Republic of Ireland Tel: 6139 6409 stacpoole@iol.ie

SWB ⊞† Sweetbriar Gallery Paperweights Ltd, 3 Collinson Court, off Church Street, Frodsham, Cheshire WA6 6PN Tel: 01928 730064 sales@sweetbriar.co.uk www.sweetbriar.co.uk

SWN ⊞ Swan Antiques, Stone Street, Cranbrook, Kent TN17 3HF Tel: 01580 712720

SWO ⚒ Sworders, 14 Cambridge Road, Stansted Mountfitchet, Essex CM24 8BZ Tel: 01279 817778 www.sworder.co.uk

TASV ⊞ Tenterden Antiques & Silver Vaults, 66 High Street, Tenterden, Kent TN30 6AU Tel: 01580 765885

TDG ⊞ The Design Gallery 1850–1950, 5 The Green, Westerham, Kent TN16 1AS Tel: 01959 561234 sales@thedesigngallery.uk.com www.thedesigngallery.uk.com

TEM ⊞ Tempus, Tunbridge Wells Antique Centre, Union Square, The Pantiles, Tunbridge Wells, Kent Tel: 01932 828936 tempus.watches@tinyonline.co.uk www.tempus-watches.co.uk

TEN ⚒ Tennants, The Auction Centre, Harmby Road, Leyburn, Yorkshire DL8 5SG Tel: 01969 623780 enquiry@tennants-ltd.co.uk www.tennants.co.uk

TMA ⚒† Tring Market Auctions, Brook Street, Tring, Hertfordshire HP23 5EF Tel: 01442 826446 sales@tringmarketauctions.co.uk www.tringmarketauctions.co.uk

TOM ⊞† Charles Tomlinson. Tel: 01244 318395 charles.tomlinson@lineone.net www.lineone.net/-charles.tomlinson

TOP ⊞† The Top Banana Antiques Mall, 1 New Church Street, Tetbury, Gloucestershire GL8 4DS Tel: 0871 288 1102 info@topbananaantiques.com www.topbananaantiques.com

TRM ⚒ Thomson, Roddick & Medcalf Ltd, 60 Whitesands, Dumfries DG1 2RS, Scotland Tel: 01387 255366

US ⊞ Ulla Stafford. Tel: 0118 934 3208 or 07944 815104

VEC ⚒ Vectis Auctions Ltd, Fleck Way, Thornaby, Stockton-on-Tees, Cleveland TS17 9JZ Tel: 01642 750616 admin@vectis.co.uk www.vectis.co.uk

WAA ⊞ Woburn Abbey Antiques Centre, Woburn, Bedfordshire MK17 9WA Tel: 01525 290350 antiques@woburnabbey.co.uk

WAC ⊞ Worcester Antiques Centre, Reindeer Court, Mealcheapen Street, Worcester WR1 4DF Tel: 01905 610680 WorcsAntiques@aol.com

WAL ⚒ Wallis & Wallis, West Street Auction Galleries, Lewes, East Sussex BN7 2NJ Tel: 01273 480208 auctions@wallisandwallis.co.uk www.wallisandwallis.co.uk

WAW ⊞ Warwick Antiques Warehouse, Unit 7 Cape Road Industrial Estate, Cattell Road, Warwick CV34 4JN Tel: 01926 498849 aboylin1@tiscali.co.uk

WeA ⊞ Wenderton Antiques (by appointment only). Tel: 01227 720295

WiB ⊞ Wish Barn Antiques, Wish Street, Rye, East Sussex TN31 7DA Tel: 01797 226797

WilP ⚒ W & H Peacock, 26 Newnham Street, Bedford MK40 3JR Tel: 01234 266366

WL ⚒ Wintertons Ltd, Lichfield Auction Centre, Fradley Park, Lichfield, Staffordshire WS13 6NU Tel: 01543 263256 (Photos: Courtesy of Crown Photos 01283 762813)

WRe ⊞ Walcot Reclamations, 108 Walcot Street, Bath, Somerset BA1 5BG Tel: 01225 444404

WW ⚒ Woolley & Wallis, Salisbury Salerooms, 51–61 Castle Street, Salisbury, Wiltshire SP1 3SU Tel: 01722 424500/ 411854 mail@salisbury.w-w.co.uk www.w-w.co.uk

Index to Advertisers

Index

Bold numbers refer to information and pointer boxes.